Confessions
of a Medium

Elibron Classics
www.elibron.com

Elibron Classics series.

© 2005 Adamant Media Corporation.

ISBN 1-4021-9396-3 (paperback)
ISBN 1-4021-1695-0 (hardcover)

This Elibron Classics Replica Edition is an unabridged facsimile of the edition published in 1882 by Griffith and Farran, London.

Elibron and Elibron Classics are trademarks of Adamant Media Corporation. All rights reserved.

This book is an accurate reproduction of the original. Any marks, names, colophons, imprints, logos or other symbols or identifiers that appear on or in this book, except for those of Adamant Media Corporation and BookSurge, LLC, are used only for historical reference and accuracy and are not meant to designate origin or imply any sponsorship by or license from any third party.

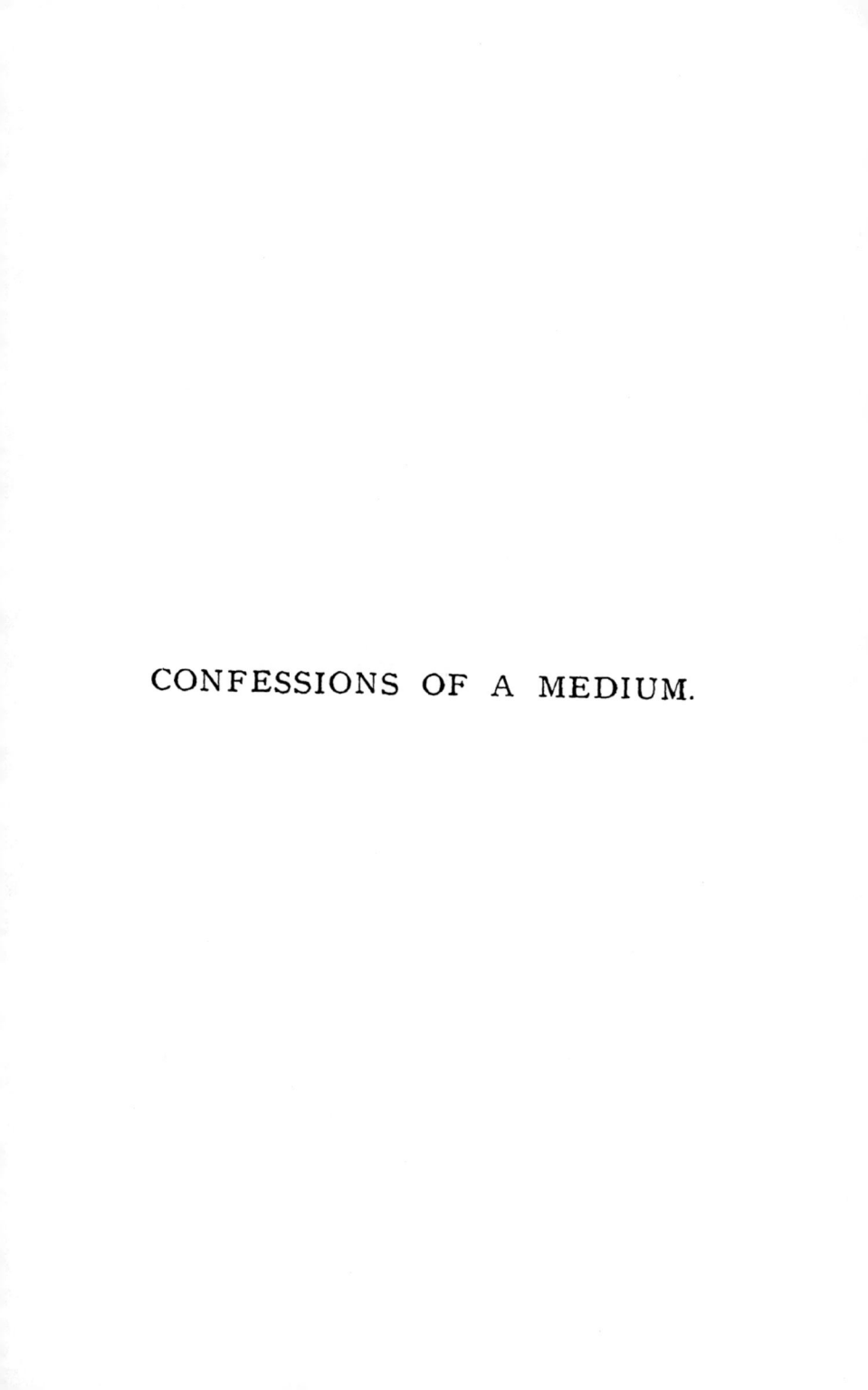

CONFESSIONS OF A MEDIUM.

In the circle. The medium at work.

CONFESSIONS OF

A MEDIUM.

WITH FIVE ILLUSTRATIONS.

GRIFFITH & FARRAN
(SUCCESSORS TO NEWBERY AND HARRIS)
WEST CORNER ST PAUL'S CHURCHYARD, LONDON
E. P. DUTTON & CO., NEW YORK.
1882.

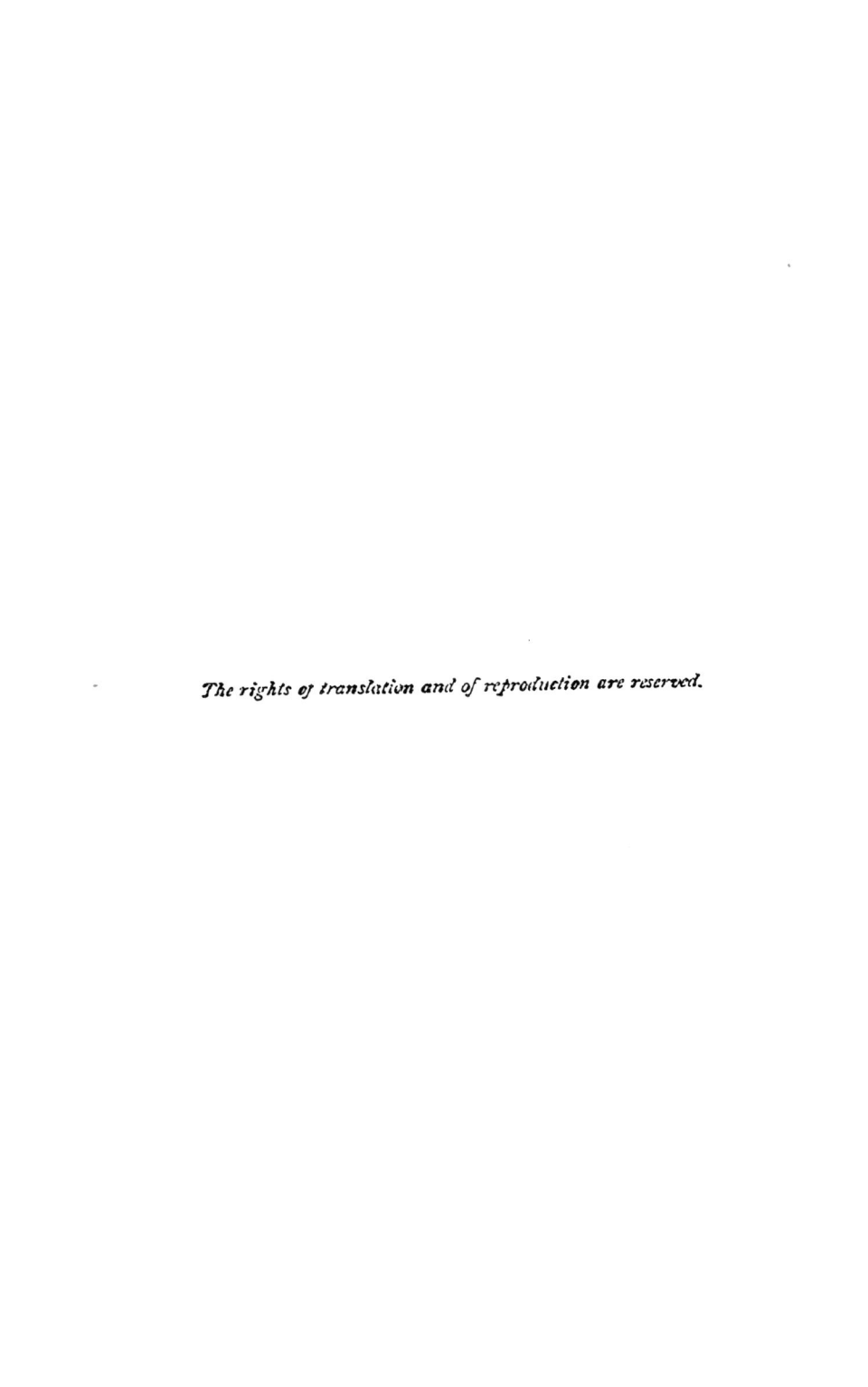

The rights of translation and of reproduction are reserved.

PREFACE.

IT is with no feelings of exultation or pride that I view the publication of this work. The pictures of fraud and faith revealed in it are not pleasing; the first indicates the depths to which a man may sink; the second that though there are more generous people in the world, of whom the world has little or no conception, it is easy for faith to degenerate to folly. I would infinitely prefer that the power to publish these records had never been given to me. I would rather that every fraud had been a fact, and every display of faith lost in a truthful sight.

I have endeavoured, assisted by my diary, to reproduce each scene in the order in which it passed before my eyes, and as faithfully as is consistent with my settled purpose of veiling from an unpleasant curiosity the names and places of abode of those at whose hands I received undisguised courtesy and unvarying hospitality. And this is the only reason why I withhold my name from the title page.

A triple reason exists for the public display of the knowledge I have gained—to give the truth to those who have been the victims of many painful deceptions, to those who are now being deceived, and to those who are in danger of falling into the hands of unscrupulous media. And I trust that my endeavour to reveal the truth may be accepted in the spirit in which it is given.

I have no acrimonious feelings against any one identified with Spiritualism. Those who abuse the generosity of their followers or clients; those who take advantage of their position, and under the veil of the strictest code of ethics delude and defraud their constituents, deserve the fullest exposure and punishment; but I refrain from assuming the position of judge or castigator, because I know from my own bitter experience that a retributive and unswerving hand will eventually deal out to them impartial justice.

If there is any truth in Spiritualism, if there is in it anything worthy of living, it will live; but in my experience of the subject I have never discovered the smallest particle of truth in its professional mediums; and furthermore, my observations force me to believe that the germs of utter ruin are contained within itself, that is, as now practised.

The very wildest doctrines, if doctrines they can be called, and in some cases the very loosest morality, are taught and practised by numbers of its adherents. Stories of the vilest immorality are freely bandied about amongst the adepts; charges of the most degrading character are openly made; and, in short, the many thousands of its honest believers in England are deluded every day of their lives, and for their sakes, as well as for the sake of others, it is high time that

Preface.

some one who knows should fearlessly speak the truth, and try, however feebly, to open their eyes to their true position.

How I myself became acquainted with them, and how I rejected a friendly warning, are fully shown. Every step of my course is told as concisely as the exigencies of the case will permit. Every phenomenon that I witnessed, and in common with others accepted, is truthfully painted, and the secret of the mode of its execution is just as truthfully revealed.

Upon returning to England from Belgium, I opened a correspondence with one of the gentlemen who had engaged our services for the purpose of holding séances; he asked me to tell him all I knew, for which he would thank me and hold me in respect.

He demanded, and with reason, that my statements should be supported by proofs, and meeting him by appointment, I unfolded the full truth, which was the least I could do in return for the true courtesy he had consistently displayed towards me.

Upon receiving the proofs which I offered, he professed himself quite convinced that he had been deceived; and then informed me, that wishing to investigate more closely when he heard that Thomson was in England, he had a few weeks previously invited him to his own house, and after staying there for some time he had left to give séances elsewhere.

Subsequently this gentleman addressed to me a letter, the tone of which may indicate that I should be guilty of ingratitude were I to do anything to reveal his name to curious eyes, and thus cause him and his amiable family pain or annoyance. I may perhaps with propriety transcribe a portion of the note itself, which runs as follows:—

"Dear Sir,—You need not have troubled to send me back the enclosed note from Thomson. It is of very little consequence *where* it was posted; the note is incoherent, and meant in any case to mislead you."

(This was in reference to a note which Thomson addressed to me.)

"Since I last wrote I have had further proofs of his dishonesty, and am amply satisfied that he is an impious impostor. His deceit upon ourselves, who have received him into our family circle with such trust and confidence, is particularly aggravating."

I have also a voluminous correspondence in my possession with another gentleman who had engaged our services, and whom I offered to meet, to answer any questions he might choose to put. I have been looking over his letters, but am unable to find anything of value from which to quote. He plainly admits his belief in a partial fraud, but still has confidence in the mediumistic qualities of Thomson. When I told him that there was no truth at all in it, he joined issue and refused to believe me. This gentleman has been for some years one of the most generous supporters that mediums and their abettors have ever deceived.

In conclusion, I would give to those wishing to investigate

Spiritualism the same advice that Punch briefly offers to those about to marry—" Don't."

If that is rejected, I will then urge upon the investigator—

Never to sit with a professional medium.

And—

Never by any chance to sit in the dark, but in the fullest light.

If the first is not received, the observance of the latter will compel more honesty, though there may not be such striking manifestations.

THE AUTHOR.

LONDON, *February* 1882.

CONTENTS.

―――o―――

CHAPTER I.

FIRST ENCOUNTER WITH SPIRITS.

My first séance. Table tilting. My second séance. The trance. High spiritual gifts promised. I am exhorted by the spirits to cultivate spiritual knowledge, . . 1-10

CHAPTER II.

A CHANGE OF VIEWS.

Religion and Spiritualism. "Let him that thinketh he standeth take heed lest he fall." Solemn warning from a Christian. Spirit identity. Evils of spirit intercourse. The warning rejected. Discussions with the spirits and the spiritualists on the divinity of Christ. Swift changes in my mind. Resign membership with the Christian Church. A removal, 11-19

CHAPTER III.

FRESH SCENES.

London. Introduction to the circles. The spirit clown. The imprisoned medium. The control who witnessed the crucifixion. Private meetings for development. Matter passing through matter. The spirit and the flower girl. I go into the cabinet for materialisation. Mesmerism. How the spirits lived under the table. The spiritual healer, 20-32

CHAPTER IV.

A Great Medium.

The great medium from Paris. Séance with him. The arm in the air. The inauguration meeting. A new test. Origin of tests. A gorgeous apparition, . . . 33-39

CHAPTER V.

A Spiritual Partnership.

I am invited to join the great medium. Cogitations. Séance for spirit face wax moulds. The double figure. The vanishing. The mould. The exhortation. I join the medium. The agreement. Materialisation of flowers. Mr Goodman. An atheist at a séance, . . . 40-48

CHAPTER VI.

A New Test.

The wire test cage. The séance at the Association. The unhappy chairman. The medium's ideas of Associations. First sitting with the test cage. A new one ordered. Séance in Harley Street. Thomson and Morton. The spirit mirror. John King. Asoka, . . . 49-59

CHAPTER VII.

Public Meetings.

The new cage at home. Developing séances. The public meetings. The spirit of light. The mesmeric sleeper. The friendly clairvoyants. Private séance with the cage. Meeting again in public. The loose lock. Private séance. Thomson is locked to the stove. Asoka comes out. All hail! 60-70

CHAPTER VIII.

A Slight Revelation.

The cage discarded. The sack test. Joey rings the changes. He asks for sugar plums. We remove to the provinces.

Contents. xiii

The first séance there. The second. Asoka speaks of the summer land. The Secret. Discussion on spirit manifestations and mediums. The exposure of the lady medium in London. Exposure of Morton in Holland. Balmain's paint. Accident on the railway. Curtain, . . 71-82

CHAPTER IX.

IN THE COUNTRY.

Preparation for an extensive campaign. Arrange with Mr Gordon for a series of séances. I am to be formally introduced as a medium. Thomson's views of Spiritualism. Story of the lost drapery. First séance with Mr Gordon. Searching of Thomson. I assist the power. Story of the lost medium. Story of the flaming medium. Story of a man burned to death with phosphorus. Arrange with Mr Ashton for a series of séances. Tests, . . . 83-92

CHAPTER X.

DEVELOPING.

Lessons. How the hands are liberated at the table. How the copper wire test was overcome. Physical manifestations. The spirit puts the musical-box right. Lily cannot come for want of a dress. The Sceptic. The elevated chair. The tambourine ring. The sack again. Thomson gets out of a difficulty. The Sceptic and the girdle. I am a medium for the physical. Thomson's advice to me, . 93-101

CHAPTER XI.

STRANGE MANIFESTATIONS.

Mr Wilson. He wishes to bring us into contact with the press. Three séances in one day. The Sceptic's séance. The over-crowded room with the press. We arrange for a week of public meetings. Spirit guides. The musical-box leaves the room. The floating table. Promises from Asoka and Joey. A clairvoyant test. The sneers of the press. Joey asks for flowers. He goes out to dinner. A genuine séance expected. Also the Sceptic, . . 102-115 xiv　　　　　　*Contents.*

CHAPTER XII.

THE POWER INCREASES.

The Sceptic again. Luminous hands and faces. Disappearance of the chairs. "Good gracious! what's that?" The sideboard. We are developing. How the weighing machine test was overcome. The two gimlets. Scientific men and gentlemen. How Thomson escaped from the cage. Mr Wilson and the press. Lessons. The floating sofa. How the spirits are at home, ... 116-124

CHAPTER XIII.

MORE PUBLIC MEETINGS.

Lessons. The needle and cotton. Public meetings. The "phenomenon" and his subject. Muscular mesmerism. The knowing tailor. He requires referees to watch the referees. Physical manifestations. The puzzled tailor. He takes home the sack. A chattering chairman. The tailor again. Puzzled again. Thomson is disgusted. His remarks. Resolve to keep to private séances. They pay better, and with less danger, ... 125-135

CHAPTER XIV.

EXPLANATIONS.

The sack mystery explained. Mr Wilson again. His tidings. His friend the rich man. The post-card. Life and light combined. Thomson's opinions of Spiritual Associations. Mr Ashton's lumbago is cured by the spirits. His spirit son. Stories of high controls at séances. When is the genuine coming? 136-147

CHAPTER XV.

THOMSON FURTHER UNBOSOMS HIMSELF.

The advertisement. Thomson refuses to sit with the press. The bouquet. The clairvoyant test. "Where's Olaf?" The materialisation of flowers. Thomson cuts his way out of the sack. How he escaped from the stove. The séance in Harley Street. "Is he in the swim?" The three jealous mediums. The battle of the mediums. Louey. The mysterious lady. She arranges for a séance to take place, but not at her own house, ... 148-157

CHAPTER XVI.

THE DOUBLE FORM.

The double-form. Practical sympathy of Mrs Gordon. The mysterious lady and her mysterious friends. The séance of agony. Preparations for the double-form. Story of the man knocked down by the spirits. The tambourine paints a pair of moustachios. "Olaf." Mr Wilson and his séance. He engages us for his wealthy friend. Five séances in one day. The clergyman and the hand. Our mysterious lady is a friend after all. She doesn't forget the fees. Thomson doesn't like the church. The double-form. Success. Farewell from Mr Ashton, ... 158-172

CHAPTER XVII.

LOOK INSIDE.

Arrival at another town to meet Mr Wilson's wealthy friend. Heralded by the bellman. Find ourselves mistaken. Toothache cured by spirits. Thomson advises me to give lectures under control. His remarks on trance speeches. The manly Christian friend. Mr Lilley. He takes us home. Séances at house for moulds. "Look inside." I offend Mr Lilley. Lessons. The medium Long. His bribes. The new era. The Logos. The two aspirants for that dignity. They quarrel. Preparations completed for the moulds, 173-184

CHAPTER XVIII.

JOHN KING AND HIS FOLLOWERS.

Spirit souvenirs. John King. Spirit titles. Telegram from high quarters. Thomson's experiences with monarchy. The learned company of "correspondences." The mystery of the wax moulds revealed. Akosa and Lilly. Their faces. Attempts to repeat the moulds. Rescinding of the order to go abroad. Invitation to Brussels, . . . 185-192

CHAPTER XIX.

PHOTOGRAPHS OF AKOSA AND LILLY.

"Extraordinary manifestations in London. The production of spirit face wax moulds by materialised spirit forms. Unity, duplication, and re-absorption of duplicated forms into one. Transfiguration and vanishing of materialised spirit forms. All witnessed in a good light." Phrenological delineations. Editorial remarks. Two years after. The revelation, 193-212

CHAPTER XX.

ON THE CONTINENT.

Brussels. Our first séance there. John King. Delegates from Charleroi. Fresh tests. The suspicious characters. Carnival Sunday. Spirit photographs. The disguise prepared. The missing table. A new test cage. Photographing a numerous hand. John King. He can't get out. The cage unfastened for him. All hail! Philosophy of spirit. Napoleon III. We leave Brussels, . . . 213-221

CHAPTER XXI.

A FULL REVELATION.

Liege. I am the medium for materialisations. In the Ardennes. The secret fully revealed. Thomson admits that all manifestations are the results of trickery. A short sketch of Thomson's mediumistic career as told by himself. The wonderful spirit photograph in London. We agree to renounce Spiritualism. Deserted. M. de Chênée. The crisis. Day and night in the Ardennes forest. Lost— Found—Freedom. End, ... 222-232

CONFESSIONS OF A MEDIUM.

CHAPTER I.

FIRST ENCOUNTER WITH SPIRITS.

"THAT may all be possible, but still it does not prove the wisdom of meddling with such things. The Bible, which I take for my guide, tells me that in the latter times many shall be led away by 'seducing spirits.' And, judging by what I hear of Spiritualism, it is exactly what is meant by the Apostle. Besides I have heard that people who 'investigate,' as you call it, soon lose all reverence for holy things; and quite forego all that which makes life not only endurable, but glorious."

"Oh, nonsense! I fail to see why Spiritualism is not capable of being demonstrated, just like any other subject, scientific or otherwise. You can go once, and if you see anything that offends, you need not go again. Besides, which, if it is really true, you must admit that it entirely overthrows Materialism; and then think what a weapon it would be, to assist you in your preaching and teaching."

"I desire no better weapon than the one I have. If people will not believe the pure teachings of the Redeemer they would not believe even if the dead arose. I consider it is far nobler to exercise faith, than knowledge, in matters pertaining to the Kingdom of Heaven; I have no desire to know, because I believe, and that is more than sufficient for me."

"Well, think over it, and let me know to-morrow; I don't believe it can hurt you much, just to see what it is like."

"To *see* what it is like! If I understand aright, that is just what one does not do amongst these spiritualists, simply because they hold their meetings in perfect darkness."

"Why trouble about the means used? I dare say the making of clay to cure the blind man by Jesus seemed silly to the Jews."

"What ridiculous nonsense to compare them with Jesus! When He performed His mighty work, He did it in the broad light of day. He did not call for dark rooms, and the paraphernalia that these people employ, when He restored the dead to life, and flung open the doors of his Creation to the blind. He did not require all this mystery when He quelled the angry sea, or bade the lame to walk. Disease, Demons, and Death alike fled at his approach, but it was all done in the light."

"I wish you could engage in ordinary conversation without preaching; but to-morrow I'll see you, and when you have thought over it you may consent. I hope you will, because I want to go very much, and I should like you with me."

"If you want me with you very much, I will promise that I will do just as I always do when I require Divine assistance. I will seek the Lord in prayer, and then I shall do right."

The above conversation took place in the summer of 1878, at the town of ——. A gentleman with whom I was very intimate, had received an invitation to attend a spiritualist meeting, and had gained permission to extend that invitation to a friend. I must confess to a little curiosity to know something of the doings of people, about whom at that time some excitement prevailed. I had seen a record published by the Dialectical Society, detailing their investigation of the subject. The "Christian World," too, had thrown open its columns to allow it to be discussed, and the opportunity had not been neglected by the spiritualists, numbers of whom had invaded each weekly issue of the paper.

There had also been accounts of meetings, held in the

town adjacent to my house, published in the local journals, which, to say the least, were startling.

All this had caused me to think upon the subject, but I firmly believed that the emissaries of Satan had been let loose for a time, and permitted by a Divine Providence to test the faith of the followers of Christ. And I wondered at the stupidity of people, who could allow themselves to be so easily led astray. In my mind I likened them to the Israelites, who were so often running after false gods, and enduring the consequent and righteous punishment of their faithlessness. Nevertheless I resolved to abide by the verdict evoked by prayer to God, and that night I implored the Almighty to grant me a sign, by which I might know if it were wicked to attend such places.

It is probable that the curiosity lurking in my mind influenced the decision at which I arrived. Whether or no, I gave my consent to be present, at the same time scarcely feeling easy at the step I had taken, but I comforted myself with the determination never to go again.

Sunday evening was the time appointed, and with many misgivings I, with my friend, entered the house of spirits. We were courteously and kindly welcomed. After a little genial conversation about nothing in particular, the latest expected sitters arrived, and we were—about a dozen in all —placed round a circular table. Curiosity now took firm hold of me, to the exclusion of every other feeling. I looked about, half expecting to see mysterious forms issue from various parts of the room. I did not like to show my ignorance regarding the procedure, so I narrowly watched the others, to see what they would do. We were sitting in a subdued light, but quite sufficient to discern each other plainly. And now, all our hands being laid on the table, close to the edge, we patiently sat for about fifteen minutes, but nothing occurred, and I began to feel a contempt for such stupid conduct; and the cutting sarcasms of Elijah uttered on the memorable occasion of his contest with the priests of Baal occurred to me, and with the prophet I thought, "Perhaps they are asleep, or on a visit, or they may be deaf!"

Really it was too ridiculous, a dozen intelligent people sitting round a table, watching it in solemn silence, and with their hands on it like prisoners. And an almost uncontrollable desire to laugh seized me, but my fear of wounding the feelings of the courteous host and his wife fortunately prevented the explosion; and as if to assist the repression of such unseasonable merriment, just trembling on the verge of open manifestation, somebody, much to my relief, proposed that we should sing a hymn, and, while joining in the strains of "Over there," the hidden volcano of mirth harmlessly expended itself.

Nobody could think of more than the first verse, and that not very perfectly, so we sang it over and over again until —hush!—a rap! no—a tilt! yes, the table slightly oscillated.

"Are you there, kind friends?" inquired one of the sitters.

A slight undulatory movement of the table, repeated three times, was given by way of response.

"If you are here, please give three raps or tilts for 'yes,' two for 'doubtful' or 'dont know,' and one for 'no.'"

This simple code of signals was to be our mode of communication.

"Are the conditions right?" was now asked.

One tilt of the table.

"Is there too much light?"

Three tilts.

The room being darkened a little more, much to my relief, for I was afraid the unpreventable expression of amusement on my face might be noticed, and give umbrage to the circle.

"Are we all right now?"

One tilt.

"Are we sitting right?"

One tilt.

"Will you kindly indicate those who are to change places, dear friends?"

Three tilts.

After a good deal of shifting about we got fixed right, and then commenced a series of questions, all being more or less satisfactorily answered, until eventually the mistress of the house, ever alive to the proprieties of the occasion, inquired if I wished to put any questions to the spirits?

Considering myself a novice, as indeed I was, and fearful of transgressing some rule of spirit etiquette, I declined, suggesting that somebody else might have matters of importance to inquire about.

"Oh, no, we observe a rule, that everyone shall have a like opportunity of conversing with the spirits," declared the lady.

"I really don't know what to ask?"

"Perhaps you would like to know if you have any spirit friends present?" she suggested.

My mind instantly reverted to two of my little sisters, whom I had lost, one very recently, and, although I was becoming interested in the proceedings, I did not like to try to imagine them, as moving a table about, when I felt confident they were in the brightest and most peaceful of heavens.

At this moment, the thought struck me that now would be a good opportunity to try the spirits, with questions relating to their condition.

"If you really are spirits, will you kindly tell me if you love God?" I asked.

Three violent tilts of the table, meaning "yes" in the most emphatic manner they were capable of expressing.

"Is it right to pray to God?"

Three still more violent movements.

"Are you happy?"

The table fairly bounced off the floor, and seemed as if seized with convulsions, an affirmative about which there could be no mistake, and I began to feel comfortable.

"Have you any message for me?" I next enquired.

By means of tilting at various letters of the alphabet

which they required, and which we repeated many times, they slowly arrived at, "You have friends near you, and they are saying, 'Ever progressing unto perfection.' They desire us to tell you that they love you, and that you will be a medium of the first order."

"What is a medium?"

"A medium is a vehicle for the transmission of God's best gifts to mankind."

"Do you wish me to come again?"

Three lively tilts.

A gentleman, whom I afterwards learned was an adept, proposed to me to look under the table, and see if somebody might not be slyly moving it. But I felt unwilling to commit such a breach of good manners, being there in the character of a guest; besides, I began to feel interested, and did not wish to show that any unworthy suspicion dwelt in my mind, and I hastily declined.

"But it would be more satisfactory to you," persisted he.

"I am satisfied," I declared. "It is not probable that a dozen persons would come from various distances, simply with the view of deceiving each other."

"But I wish you would look under the table whilst it is moving."

"If it will give you any gratification, I have no objection," I rejoined, and forthwith I crept under the table. Of course I saw no one touch or assist the table in its movements, and I came up again, and took my place in the circle. A pause now ensued, during which the table began slowly gyrating; and then, as if deliberately calculating something, it tilted three times, then rested, another triple tilt, and another rest, and so on until each member of the circle had in this fashion received a "good night." Before leaving the house, we engaged in a little conversation on the subject, and I being a stranger, some little trouble was taken to enlighten me. They talked of the wonders daily occurring among spiritualists, which raised my curiosity to its extreme point. They spoke of materialisations and physical manifestations, of duplication and levitation, and many other things equally foreign to my experience, and I wondered if such things could be. One of the company undertook to impart to me some of the knowledge he had gained; and remembering that the spirits had told me I should be a medium, I inquired after the manner of obtaining that extraordinary gift.

"Oh, they mean that you have certain peculiar powers, which, if properly developed, will enable you to transmit spiritual information to others less endowed. You will thus become a fountain of living knowledge."

"What do you mean by being 'properly developed'?"

"I mean that you must sit regularly in circles, and in a short time the spirits will be able to tell you what sort of medium you are."

"What sort? Are there several orders of media?"

"Yes; you may be a medium for trance, or writing, or materialisations, or physical manifestations—in short, there are too many classes to enumerate; but you will soon learn, if you wish."

"Don't you think that we are transgressing the divine injunction regarding 'familiar spirits'?" I queried.

"Does it not strike you that it may be as beneficial to cultivate the assistance of pure spirits, as it is dangerous and sinful to evoke the presence of evil? Are we not enjoined by Jesus to 'try the spirits'? You could not quote a better book than the Bible, for that is in reality a book of spiritualism; from beginning to end it is full of stories of spiritual manifestations."

Puzzled, and in a state of mental confusion, I knew not what to make of all this. I was aware that wicked men could wrest the Scripture to their own inclinations; but surely this man was not wicked. His conversation was pure, and his reverence for sacred things was manifest. I had been unceasing in my supplications to God to grant me His spirit, and this might be His manner of answering my prayer. Envy had perhaps maligned these people, who were so different from those I had expected to find.

"We shall be very pleased to see you when we meet again next Sunday evening. I think you are a good medium, the spirits seldom make mistakes," said the hostess. Then, bidding us a cordial "good-night," we separated, and thus ended my first séance.

"Well, what do you think of it now?" inquired my friend on our way home.

"I prefer not to utter a hasty judgment. I am not clear but that I have been too premature already."

During the following week I felt a little uneasy in my mind. It seemed as if folly had guided my feet, and vanity my head. Did I unconsciously possess abnormal virtues, which, if developed, might render me all-powerful in the service of God? And was it possible that these people knew the secrets of spirit culture?

I was fearful, yet I was enchanted, fascinated, and allured by the spell of gaining that power to which I have alluded, I found myself the following Sunday once more sitting in the spirit circle.

Again the table seemed as if imbued with conscious life; and by means of the established code of signals, as used on the previous occasion, we received messages which fastened still more strongly the alluring chains that bound me to the prosecution of spirit cultivation.

A new phase also presented itself on this occasion, after premonitory symptoms, which appeared alarming to me in my state of inchoation—one of the circle went off into a sleep; but this was the least astonishing part of the phenomenon. With eyes closed, and rigid form, he sat apparently lost to all sense of surrounding conditions, but that some intelligence moved him was plainly visible when he began to speak to us.

I was informed that this was common enough among spiritualists, and afforded an exact illustration of the descent of the Spirit of God upon man, as in the times of the seers of old, and that the frequently recurring phrase, "And the Spirit of the Lord came upon, &c.," was nothing more than being entranced or sent to sleep, and compelled to serve as the mouthpiece of the controlling spirit-messengers of Heaven.

This free rendering of the Bible did not please me, and I was disposed to combat such an extortionate demand upon my credulity, for I was brought up at the feet of an orthodox Gamaliel, and I asserted in answer that Christ had removed the necessity for that mode of Divine interposition.

"And does not the Bible say that God is the same always?" inquired the circle.

Curiosity to see more of this new aspect of Spiritualism ended the discussion, and I awaited the denouement, with mingled feelings of excitement and expectation. Nor did those feelings suffer any diminution, when the spirit by the mouth of the sleeper addressed me, substantially as follows :—

"If you seek advancement in spiritual science, you must use the privileges offered. If you desire an enlargement of spiritual life, you must strive to attain perfection, which can only be gained by knowledge and purity ; these, in turn, come only as a reward for victory over self, and when the noblest aspirations of the soul are ever seeking further development, and more exquisite fulness, this height can only be attained by close and constant communion with God, who sends His spirits as ministering angels to all who will listen. There are powers lying dormant in your soul, undreamt of in your most extravagant desires. There are hidden faculties of your intelligence, only fettered by ignorance of the laws, that should give them a world-purifying freedom, which, if liberated, would change your whole being, and dazzle you by their magnificent grandeur. These heights, and depths, and lengths, and breadths of spiritual life and light may be reached and enjoyed by you. There are laws that govern this, which you must learn, there are paths that lead to this, which you must tread. But you must be faithful and unswerving, turning neither to the right hand nor to the left. To gain the indicated goal, the summit of happiness, each spiritual law must be unhesitatingly obeyed. 'Seek ye the Lord while He may be found,' is no idle exhortation; hitherto you have sought Him, but in a darkened light. Now the way is open, the path pointed out, follow on; so shall ye go upwards, and in after times you shall look back to this meeting as to a spiritual marriage. Remember, and farewell."

Nothing could be better, no suspicion of collusion or seducing spirits now entered my mind. I determined that this could be nothing less than the completion of Christianity, and the proper field for the full display of the spiritual gifts promised by the Master and His appointed ministers—the Apostles. There was nothing to offend the most rigid disciple of Evangelism, and my fears, regarding the upsetting of my religious views, swiftly fled.

This was the opening of my spiritualistic career.

CHAPTER II.

A CHANGE OF VIEWS.

RELIGION and Spiritualism were now the opposing forces at work in my mind, and I struggled long to harmonise them. I thought that the two might be united, and thus form one grand whole, before which the powers of evil must flee in terror.

I threw my whole soul into the investigation of the all absorbing question of Spiritualism. I attended many séances, and obeyed, as far as in me lay, the rules given by the spirits. I listened with the utmost sincerity to their exhortations, until at last I was entirely captivated; and, under the delirium of the enchantment, I thought that Spiritualism was a new gospel, and the unfoldment of a better dispensation.

Entertaining this view, I devoutly consecrated my life to it, as the supreme cause of God and humanity. The spirits recognised my enthusiasm and self-sacrifice, and reiterated their pledges that I should become a powerful medium, and an Evangelist in the predicted new Era. I naturally coveted the best gifts, and my highest ambition was to devote myself to a movement so sublime as that which essayed to bring heaven and earth into close and constant communion.

My attendance at the place where I had formerly worshipped God with true devotion grew more and more irregular, and complaints were addressed to the chief minister, for I held a responsible position, besides conducting the musical worship of God, and the neglect of the latter sometimes caused a serious hindrance to the service, the blame naturally resting upon me.

No actual falling off from a single article of my faith had as yet ensued, and if any violence had been offered at that period, it would have been stoutly resisted. I grew to believe that Spiritualism and Religion were in reality synonymous terms, though the professors of each were not well pleased with one another. I observed the rancour with which Spiritualists—especially those who had been members of any one of the different churches—attacked the Christians, who retorted, that they—the Spiritualists—were given over to the Devil.

I thought these differences were not so serious but that they might be happily reconciled; and I believed that this desired consummation might fall upon me to achieve. I assured myself, over and over again, that I was doing the will of the Saviour, and so strong was the faith in my own impregnability, that I was sure nothing could overturn my reverence for sacred observances.

Had I been less confident, I should doubtless have been more secure. Had I reflected upon the words, "Let him that thinketh he standeth, take heed lest he fall," the after consequences might not have been so serious. But the transition was so unconscious and swift that I was afterwards astonished at the revolution in the map of my belief. Before, however, any of the moorings that held me to the Christian faith had parted, I met a gentleman from London who had been conversant with the subject for several years, and being as yet but on the threshold of the inquiry, I was anxious to gather the result of his analysis.

"I believe that spirits can communicate with us," he said, "but I consider it dangerous to evoke powers which cannot be allayed. If positive and negative forces, such, for instance, as acids and minerals, are placed in proper order, an electric battery is the result. And if a certain number of people, whose converse dispositions represent positives and negatives are arranged according to given conditions, then a human battery is the effect, and this the spirits are able to employ for their own purpose."

"But are there not ministering ——"

"Yes, but what proof have you that they are ministering spirits? That is just one of the chief things in Spiritualism which should deter us from its investigation. I once met the spirit, John King, at a séance, and afterwards when I met him again, he declared that it could not have been he. In vain I asserted that the spirit had all his distinctive peculiarities.

"'That proved nothing,' he answered, 'for spirits have the power to assume any shape at will.'

"That incident taught me a lesson, and I have since been careful not to give spirits the power to deceive me. This one thing, 'spirit identity' has never been conclusively proved, and until it is, I maintain that we had better avoid them altogether."

"Does not the Bible, which is full of accounts of spirit manifestations, tell us to 'try the spirits'?"

"I believe in the Bible, from Genesis to Revelations, and without pressing my point further, I will take this opportunity to give you a friendly warning. I have for several years carefully investigated the subject, and my advice now to you is to have nothing to do with it. For it will ruin your health and wreck your faith."

"Apparently it has neither weakened your faith nor injured your health," I retorted, for his physical health was as robust as his faith.

"The terrible ordeal through which I have passed has had the effect of strengthening my faith, which, though strong, was within a hair's breadth of being scattered like chaff before the wind. And I assure you my health suffered considerably. I was nearly driven mad with pain and anguish, and if God had not signally helped me, I should have been a wreck."

"In what manner were you injured?" I asked, interested.

"The spirits, in some mysterious way, brought strange powers to bear upon me, and attacked me in every vulnerable point which they could discover. They affrighted me when asleep, and astounded me when awake, until seeing my danger, I fled from them and took refuge in the omnipotent arms of the Saviour. A Saviour indeed to me! It was not for nothing that the Israelites were so strictly commanded to avoid dealing with familiar spirits."

"My experience so far has been quite different to that. I have seen nothing to offend the most sensitive, or affright the most timid."

"Neither did I at first; and the more you say only convinces me that you are in great danger, and I am anxious to give you timely and earnest warning."

"I thank you for your kindness, but you admit there are many orders of spirits; and that admission induces me to imagine that you must have got into the company of evil spirits."

"But unfortunately you cannot tell until too late that they are evil. If you open the door for one class you are under the danger of being invaded by the other."

"The spirits with whom I have come in contact must surely be pure. They strongly and consistently advise us to open all our meetings with singing and prayer."

"The Devil can quote Scripture," he quietly remarked.

"True, but I apprehend he won't advise others to do so."

"When he has put on you his spectacles, so that you shall read his way, he won't object."

"I think my faith is so strong that I may safely venture upon the prosecution of the subject, and I feel confident the people with whom I sit are good, and desirous of promoting good in others. Regarding the spirits, I am quite happy in their presence. I feared, when first I went there, they could only be imps of mischief, but I have had good reasons to change my views."

"Listen to me," he earnestly replied. "I have gone through just such an experience as you are contemplating, and if the few words I now utter may save you, then my trouble and pain will not be for nought. Ten years ago I heard of Spiritualism, and I went to a great number of séances. At first nothing occurred to alarm me on account of my religion, but as time passed on I found that my whole faith was being undermined. The spirits made me believe that the

Book of Genesis was a fabrication; that the account of the Creation and the fall of Adam and Eve was but the remains of some old Phallic legend; that the Pentateuch was a jumble of history and poetry loosely strung together by various writers at different times, and in order to invest it with sacred authority, they ascribed it all to Moses. They shook my belief in the existence of a personal Devil, and declared that he was only a scarecrow, put up by an interested priesthood to frighten an ignorant and credulous people; and that hell itself was nothing more than an apocryphal bundle of fireworks, manufactured for the purpose of bolstering up an intolerant priestly hierarchy. They next tried to divest my mind of all reverence for Christ himself, and asserted that He was a man like unto ourselves. This latter is the chief thing they aim at; and when they have once overturned your belief in the divinity of Christ, then all the rest is easy. But, fortunately, I saw my danger, and fled from such intercourse; and then the veil was torn asunder, and I trembled to think of my narrow escape, but rejoiced to think that their machinations had failed. I pressed closer than ever to the " Rock of Ages," and I was sheltered by Him who has all power given into His hands. Ah! many, many good and earnest Christians have I known to be led astray, and all their faith and love flung to the four winds of Heaven. It is for the purpose of preserving you that I give my experience, and I trust you will consider well the step you are taking, otherwise I predict that it will be your ruin."

"I have no fear on that head, because I feel so strongly grounded in the faith that nothing will uproot it. But I will bear in mind your warning, and make a point of questioning the spirits, and if they say aught against the dignity of Christ, then I will have nothing more to do with them."

.   .   .   .

Again I am seated at the table among the spiritualists, and with the words of warning uttered by my friend still ringing in my ears.

When at last I had an opportunity of addressing the spirits, who expressed their willingness, through the table,

to answer any questions I saw fit to ask, I began the catechism :
"Do you believe in Jesus Christ?"
"Yes."
"Do you believe that He is the Son of God?"
"Yes."
"Do you believe He came to save the world?"
"Yes."
"Some have lately warned me that I am incurring great danger by seeking your society; also, that you deny the divinity of Christ. Will you kindly inform me on these points?"
"Read 1 Cor. 12 ch. We do not deny the divinity of Christ."
"You say that every man, from his birth, is attended by two spirits—one pulling him downwards, while the other endeavours to draw him up?"
"Yes."
"Are those beings or powers extrinsic?"
"Yes."
"Can they manifest their existence to our physical senses?"
"Given proper conditions, Yes."
"What is your object in coming back to earth?"
"To do good."
"Do you believe in eternal punishment?"
"No!" emphatically. "For what are you stopping?"
"In Matt. xxv. 46, Christ says, 'The wicked shall go into everlasting punishment.'"
"God is love."
"But you contradict the words of Christ."
"No. Confer with Mr A. We will control him to tell you the full truth regarding these matters."

I did confer with Mr A. many a time and oft; but without introducing those conversations here, it is sufficient to say that the vaticinations of my friend were completely verified.

The Biblical account of the Creation was discarded, and I began to think it a pitiable piece of credulity to accept the record dealing with the overruling of the orbs of

Heaven by Joshua. I refused any longer to believe that the Devil had any other than a legendary existence, or that hell fire was aught else than a probationary state of remorse for the conscience-stricken, who might, when the penalty of disobedience was exacted, take their places in a sphere according with their purified souls.

I diligently sought for chronological and other accounts in the Bible which bore any appearance of discrepancy. I read monotheistic books, and learned disquisitions on the eternal and inseparable oneness of the Creator, and at last arrived at the conclusion that Christ was none other than a great moral and social reformer; and that although the spirits could ascribe to Him "divinity," yet they were right to refuse to "deify" Him.

I compared His life and works with those of Buddha, Confucius, Mahomet, and others, and thought I could find equal beauties in all. I pored over the early existence of the Christian Church, and conceived a hearty dislike, almost amounting to a personal hatred, to Athanasius, whilst my admiration for Arius knew no bounds. And last, but not least, I read Tom Paine, and voted the Bible a collection of falsehoods, tending only to fetter the mind, and degrade the Almighty.

I began to consider myself a pioneer, and determined that no church, or section of a church, offered sufficient scope for the full exercise of my powers. I elevated reason and intellect, and subverted feeling and faith. I decided that faith was synonymous with credulity, and that Goethe's "Gefühl ist alles" was the secret of religious life, and a fair representation of the result of an ephemeral emotion, the outcome of a dwarfed and enfeebled intellect.

I perused Pantheistic works, until my mind was almost in a state of chaos, and if at that time I had been questioned regarding my belief, I should have been a little embarrassed for an intelligible reply. Natural science combined with atheistic philosophy successfully proved, as I considered, that everything in the Universe was the result of chemical action. The rainbow which formerly called forth my love for the mercy of the Almighty was now only decomposed sunshine. The sun, moon, and stars lighted up my soul, not with simple love for their "Great Original," but created only a strong analytical desire, and appeared as ponderous engines, moving in mighty cycles, full of animal life.

The law of reason enchained me, and nature, instead of showing forth the works of a loving Father, was but a panorama, working in obedience to specific laws laid down by an unchangeable God, whose mandates were obeyed without an actual presence. And Man—but the glorious consummation of an eternal and evolutionary process.

The simple faith of my childhood was engulphed in the seas of Spiritualism, Deism, and Rationalism. Religion, except the religion of intellect, had lost all charm for me. I sought knowledge, but failed to distinguish between that and wisdom. The pleasant little Bethel, which had erstwhile been to me as the very gates of Heaven, now seemed a fit place in which, for Ignorance, to shout folly.

My position in the church, of which I had been for several years a member, was, as a matter of course, incompatible, holding such views, and I took steps to sever that connection. But, let it not be imagined that this was done thoughtlessly or contemptuously. I often looked back to the seasons of joy I had passed there, before the fierce heat of controversialism had scorched up the unquestioning faith of my childhood, and I thought it best to withdraw quietly, and not give pain to the friends with whom I had enjoyed sweet fellowship, and whom, spite of present different views, I thoroughly respected. For they were faithful, and worked according to the light which was within them.

It was like the breaking of a holy betrothal, and with the customary sophistry of the faithless one, I imagined that I had found a better bride, and that it would be wicked, as well as irksome, to continue an alliance when mutual unhappiness would reign.

The disjunction was effected, and I was launched out on the trackless surges of Spiritualism, Scepticism, and Specula-

Questions to the Spirits.

tion, a trinity which has landed me in regions from which it is impossible to return.

And I was happy amongst my new friends; they were courteous, and generous. The master of the house where we held our meetings was one of the most kindly men living; he has since gone to verify the truth regarding his belief.

I sat in the circle regularly, and never missed an opportunity to gain information bearing on the subject. I studied its various aspects as far as it was possible with the limited means at my disposal. I questioned the spirits as to the conditions of the next life, and their replies shattered all my former ideas.

We had progressed from table tilting and rapping to a higher phase. The spirits could now control our media, and through them, talk to us, face to face.

"Is the change that we call 'death' painful?" I inquired one evening of Manāva, our principal guide.

"No; it is a breathing away, except to those who have led immoral lives."

"What becomes of them?"

"They have to work out their own redemption."

"What is death?"

"A change from one life to another. You are as much in eternity now as you ever will be," returned he, and his answers gave to me food for thought for a long time; but I was wishing for higher manifestations than those we had ever obtained, and I was not sorry when the affairs of my daily life rendered it necessary for me to go away from that town.

I prepared for my departure, and the spirits promised me a great and noble future. They gave me counsel for my guidance, and bade me consult them whenever I wished or needed.

And now the swift and magic transformation effected, and with fresh hopes, and expectations, thoughts, and feelings, —in short, so thoroughly changed that I could scarcely recognise myself—I left for that great centre of life and death—London.

CHAPTER III.

FRESH SCENES.

LONDON—where the noblest and the basest alike dwell side by side, and where are to be found representatives of almost every creed and faith on earth. Where, in the streets, one jostles against Christian and Infidel, and passes on all unconscious of the fact. Into this maelström of surging humanity I entered in the spring of 1879.

In accordance with my directions, I sought out the leading spiritualists, and asked for introductions to the circles. One gentleman, upon whom I called, said—

"Now, you must be careful with whom you sit; because you are of a nervous type and sensitive disposition, and if you go and sit with rough and raw people, they will draw all the power from you, and leave you soulless as an old rag. Now I know exactly the place where you will do good and get good; their meetings are held once a week, and I will give you their address and the hour of meeting."

Everything now seemed to smile upon me; I had a chance of sitting with properly developed mediums. In the town I had just left, we had never been able to get beyond a certain point. True, we had been promised great things, but the conditions had invariably been broken; either somebody was absent or somebody else came, either being more than enough to disturb the influence. But here, in London, they managed everything much better. Now, I felt sure of gaining the promised powers.

Sunday at last came, and in the evening I found my way to the indicated place. Yes, this was just the station for spirits—a long room, capable of comfortably holding the thirty people present. The windows were carefully blocked, and everybody decorous and expectant.

By way of opening the proceedings, we were asked to sing a hymn, and while so doing, the several mediums amongst us were being controlled; tiny sparkles of light too were seen flashing about over our heads, and strange sounds came from different parts of the room. Yes, surely this was the place in which to get my powers developed.

Everybody seemed to be in real earnest; sometimes when for a moment, perfect silence prevailed I fancied I could see faces peering at me through the gloom and whispering to me, and I steadily returned the gaze whilst mentally beseeching them to assist me.

"Good evening; God bless you all," came from one of the controlled mediums.

"Good evening," we answered. "Have you anything to tell us?"

"Nothing particular. I have just looked in to see how you are getting on. But I must be off, for I have to go to another meeting, and I see a lot of spirits around who want to speak to you. Good night."

"Hulloh! Here we are again. How are you, old cock!" rang out on our startled ears from another medium.

"You be quiet, and conduct yourself properly, or you shan't come again," remonstrated the spirit leader of the band, and who forthwith gave us a long discourse on the beauty of the spheres. "That spirit, who but just now addressed you in slang, is one who is still in the lower degrees. He was a clown on earth, and his old habits cling to him still; he is not wicked, because he spoke in that manner, he is simply what you would call a 'rough gem.' But you must not speak harshly to such spirits; on the contrary, help them upwards by prayer. Of course, you know that we have all sorts of spirits here, just as you have all sorts of men with you. Good night, and God bless you."

"Stay one moment, please; is Sira coming to-night?"

"No, I think you had better break up now. It is not good to sit too long at one time. Next Sunday he is coming, and many others whom you know. Good night."

"Hulloh! Good-night, all," shouted the clown spirit.

"I thought you had been gone ever so long ago."

"I left my hat behind, so I came back to fetch it."

"I didn't think spirits wore hats," said his questioner.

"Oh, yes, they do old boy, but another thing made me come back. You heard old 'stick-in-the-mud' (the spirit leader) blow me up because I spoke? Well, I pulled off one of my shoes and flung it at his head, and then I had to bolt pretty quick I can tell you. The next time I'll hit him over the head with my fiddle; but I am off now. Good-night all."

After this we sang the doxology, and departed to our homes, fresh food for thought being given to me by these new spirit encounters.

The following Sunday I again went to the same place, the company this time being increased by several others, who came from all parts of the town; some from the suburbs, and some from nearer home. I was gratified now to meet with a medium of some renown. I was informed that he had suffered for the cause; that is to say, he had been charged by the enemies of Spiritualism with fraud, and the result had been six months hard labour.

We believed him to be a martyr, and treated him with the respect due to such people. I sat down beside him; but from motives of delicacy did not like to refer to the sad occurrence. But he introduced the subject himself without hesitation, and I was pleased to listen to the recital of his wrongs.

"It ever was, and, I suppose, it ever will be," I answered, "that the pioneers of every great cause have been stoned and imprisoned. You have not been exempted from the usual cruel persecution, and Paul did not consider it a disgrace because he had been in prison; on the contrary, he boasted of the fact. To suffer for a principle is no degradation. I would not be afraid of imprisonment in defence of Spiritualism, and I am pleased to see that you look upon it in the same way."

"Yes, I have been there once, and I am ready to go again. I was not alone there, for my guides were always with me; and one day I offered the chaplain a seance, but he refused to listen to me. Ah, the dear spirits did not forget me. Little Lily, one of my guides, one day brought me an orange, and another time she gave me some flowers, and they disappeared every time the gaolors came round, so that I was not discovered."

"How grand all this is, and yet if we told it to outsiders they would not believe us," I responded.

Suddenly he began to shiver and I knew that he was about to be controlled. In a few minutes he stood up and said, "I am 'Busiris,' and I am come to tell you of the glories that await those who are faithful. I stood on Calvary when He died, whom your theologians call God. I witnessed His agony and I wondered at His patience. He died, not for man, but for a principle. He died for nobody, but He lived for everybody."

My feelings at this time were beyond description. In the presence of one who had seen the death of Him of whom, spite of the change that had so swiftly come over me, I still, in my inmost heart, could not think but with reverence. And I was constrained to ask myself if, after all, I was not throwing away the crown for the bauble. The promises of the spirits had not yet been fulfilled, and I began to hear things of some of the principal people in the spiritualist ranks that did not please me. But away with such cowardice; there are black sheep in most flocks. I must work faithfully and not be discouraged. I turned again to the spirit and questioned him concerning the wonders he had witnessed.

"Is it true that darkness covered the face of the earth for three hours, that the veil of the temple was rent, and that the graves gave forth their dead when Jesus was crucified?"

"No, that is all legend."

"Have you seen Jesus in spirit life?"

"Yes, and His mission ended not with His earth life. In

conjunction with other Christs, Buddha, Mahomet, and Luther, and many more, He is still the teacher and exemplar of purity. But as I have spoken for a long time to-night, and the power is exhausted, I must depart; but I will come again and satisfy you. Farewell."

This meeting exercised a considerable influence over my mind. Ah, if I could gain those promised powers I would be content to sacrifice anything. I did not consider it arduous work to run about to various places in search of spiritual knowledge.

I remember, too, that a few of our large company suggested to me the necessity of closely following the spirits in every particular, and in order to do this we must sit oftener than once a week; in accordance with the resolutions we adopted we kept our counsel, and fixing upon one certain evening we determined to maintain the circle intact.

At the time appointed we met and passed some definite rules which were not in any case to be broken. And now began our developing course. We were careful to exclude every ray of light, and we secured a darkness sufficient to satisfy the most exigent of mediums.

At our first séance, when we had been sitting some few minutes, one of our members suddenly exclaimed—

"What a sweet odour! I can now smell it, as if passing backwards and forwards before my face."

"I can smell it too, quite well," declared another.

"I did not like to mention it, when first it came to me, because I thought it might be imagination," returned the first speaker, and then he added, "Why, it is smelling wood! Have you brought us some herbs and flowers, dear spirits?"

Three tilts of the table.

I could now plainly distinguish the pungent odour of the herb, it was as if being passed slowly before my face. I was confident that nobody was able to enter the room, except ourselves, without our knowledge; every aperture had been carefully secured, and yet this sweet plant was going round to each member of the circle in turn; this we knew, for the odour came and went several times.

We thought that the materialisation of flowers was being manifested, and we began to expect great things, not forgetting to congratulate ourselves that we had organised these private meetings. I wondered if it were possible for spirits to bring any substance into the almost hermetically sealed room; the manifestation was familiar to the older adepts, and known as "matter passing through matter." I asked if I might find a piece in my button-hole when the meeting was over, for I was anxious to see whether it was materialised, or only an ordinary object conveyed through a dead wall. I was informed that my wish was granted, and immediately I again experienced the pleasant neighbourhood of the plant; and I knew that it was in the desired place, for I felt hands placing it there, but I was told not to break the circle, and then even more wonderful things would occur.

Gratefully our thoughts arose to the spirit spheres, and earnestly we besought them to assist us in our upward efforts, and, in answer, we obtained, to me, a new manifestation.

"Let this be a sign that we will support you," said the spirits, through one of our number, who had passed under spirit control, and at the moment a bunch of roses was put into my hands. And then we were permitted to get a light to see our gifts, and change the circle. I saw now the smelling wood in my button-hole, and the roses, dripping with wet, in my hand, but I noticed they were not fresh cut.

"Whence came these roses?" I asked, when we had rearranged ourselves before a little cabinet, which we had made for the medium. We were now sitting in a semicircle in front of this, instead of round the table.

"I have just come in from the streets, and I took them from the basket of a flower-girl at Broad Street Station. It is raining now, and that accounts for their being wet."

"But is it right to take goods from people and not pay for them?" I asked in a respectful tone.

"We did pay for them; we impressed a gentleman to give double price for a bunch, so that the girl lost nothing."

"I should like a basket full of strawberries," said one of our circle.

"But I would prefer not to have them unless you can materialise money to pay for them," I rejoined.

"Oh, we can do that, just as easily as we can make anything else. Don't be alarmed, we always know how to remunerate those from whom we take goods."

"Am I developing as a medium?" I anxiously inquired.

"Yes. Go on, and God will bless your efforts. You have a great work to do, and you must not be discouraged by difficulties; the future will unfold the mighty enterprises in which you are selected to take a leading part."

"Shall I develope as a trance or a physical medium?"

"Both; we want you now to come into the cabinet, and take the place of this medium, and we will try and show ourselves through your mediumship. You are rapidly developing, and we want to show your powers."

I took my seat inside the cabinet, the other medium coming out to the circle. It must be confessed I felt rather nervous, for I knew not what might happen. I had heard strange stories of mediums being suddenly exposed when in the cabinet, and to the horror of the audience nothing but a thin shadow was seen to indicate his presence while his substance was being used to clothe a spirit. I did not wish to be reduced any nearer to a shadow than I was already, and I felt it would be very awkward if any accident occurred to prevent an equitable restitution of my corporeality.

The minutes slowly dragged past, I did not dare to move; the heavy breathing of the silent circle outside reassured me a little, at last one of them exclaimed—

"Look at that light! Can you not see it?"

"No," responded the others.

"Well then, it must be a clairvoyant light, but it is to me quite discernible; I am sure he must be a good medium."

I felt encouraged at this, and earnestly hoped that better things might follow, but nothing more occurred at the present meeting, and we soon after sang the doxology and separated.

Those were not the only meetings which I frequented, I found that there were circles in every part of the Metropolis, and for some months I was busily engaged in trying to gather all the knowledge I could; I did not begrudge the energy expended in its pursuit, nor did I wish to keep my spiritual accomplishments for my own pleasure. I felt that I was going through a course of education, and while learning these things, I thought that others might benefit by my experience.

London was a large place, and doubtless there were vast numbers thirsting for knowledge of the "Summer-Land," and to these I resolved to give my services. I had been educated in a church which always, and wisely, finds ample work for its young men and maidens, and the wholesome discipline I had undergone whilst with them, well fitted me for such an enterprise. I felt that I must work for the cause, and here, in mighty London, full scope existed for the free display of my ardour and experience.

This resolve brought me into contact with many circles, who were desirous of profiting by my greater erudition, and in order to qualify myself for teaching others, I worked hard to obtain the necessary power. I became familiar with Spiritualism, or, as some love to call it, Psychology, in its various expressions. I read mesmerism and magnetism, also Phrenology and Physiology, and when armed with these, I was eager for the conflict.

At one of these developing circles a lady said—"You are a mesmerist, I understand?"

"Yes Madam, I have that power, gained by practice."

"Can you mesmerise my son?"

"Yes," I replied.

There were only five present at this sitting, and the son in question looked like anything but a promising subject. But I managed to influence him, and his head fell forward on the table, and he began to groan and snort in a very uncomfortable manner.

"I hope he is in no danger. Can you wake him?" asked the lady, concerned for her son.

"Oh, he is in no danger. I can wake him when I wish." And I made him get up and walk to the window, which I opened to allow the cool air of the summer evening to blow upon him, and under the effects of which he soon showed signs of consciousness.

"Do you think he is a medium?" queried the lady.

"Yes, and under proper training he will develop very quickly," I answered.

"What is your fee?"

"Oh nothing, I regard this as much too grand to make of it a matter of trade."

This was rather an extraordinary meeting, for before I left, all the circle, with the exception of myself, were, or pretended to be, sent to sleep, and saw strange things. Soon afterwards I found that the demand upon my powers was much in excess of the supply, and in consequence I was compelled, although unwillingly, to confine my visits to a few select circles, and amid these experiences, sometimes my mind occasionally reverted to my christian friends; and if I thought of them with respect, it was at the same time mingled with a slight tinge of pity, that they were still in the bondage of spiritual darkness; so completely was I metamorphosed, that I even charged myself with gross credulity for ever having believed in anything regarding the spirit-world short of actual knowledge. I thought of the ever changing but never ceasing glories of the "Summerland" that awaited those who were faithful to their great calling; I encouraged myself with frequent reference to the constantly repeated promise of the spirits regarding my own particular endowments and their ultimate end.

I had served under the colours of Christianity, but now I was fighting under the banner of "Progress," and I greedily listened to the spirits' description of the wonderful and gorgeous wealth that would shortly be opened up to the world.

One day I received an invitation from a gentleman well known in spiritualistic circles to visit him at his rooms, when I would meet a few earnest inquirers who considered my work likely to be successful, seeing that with it was associated no thoughts of filthy lucre, by way of fees.

We arranged ourselves in the room of our host according to given rules, and sat down to the table for spirit intercourse.

"Are you there, dear friends?" at length inquired the host.

No answer.

"Please give us some indication of your presence," he implored.

No answer.

"Are we sitting right?"

Still no response.

"This is most extraordinary—most marvellous!" declared the host. "I wonder what is the matter? Will you speak to them?" he continued, turning to me.

I essayed my powers of persuasion, but still no result.

"Oh, they are coming!" suddenly cried one of the sitters. "I can feel the cool wind passing over my hands, and I fancy, too, that I can hear voices whispering."

That, however, was confined to the senses of the speaker, for none of us could distinguish anything, and accordingly we agreed that he must be a good medium.

"I am inclined to think," said our host, "that the magnetism must have escaped from the table, although, I am very careful, and always have sheets of brown paper pinned round the edge, and falling down to the floor; so that a little dark cave is formed, in which the spirits may dwell in safety, and preserve their power. I am afraid, however, that the light has dispersed the aura. But really, to tell you the truth, I am afraid to continue these séances."

"Indeed; for what reason, pray?" we all exclaimed.

"Because I find the spirits are developing me more than is pleasant. I can feel them by my side, both when asleep and awake. And one of my guides, little Cissy, comes to me at all times."

"Does she come materialised so that you can see her?" we inquired.

"No; but I can feel her. She comes at night, and strokes and pats me on my face and hands so softly, so gently; but it makes me nervous. I really cannot stand it. I have been told by fools who know nothing of Spiritualism that it is rheumatism and imagination; but I know better. Still it is better that you have these meetings at some other place."

"You can all come to my rooms, if you like," said Campbell, a gentleman who had but recently learned anything about Spiritualism, and whose ardent temperament became so full of it that he almost went crazy. "Ah," continued he, "I think Spiritualism opens up such a grand field of inquiry, and is calculated to dispose of many of the great questions affecting life and death, that I am astonished our great scientific men do not resort to it, in order to gain a solution of the many problems now vexing them. Look, for instance, at the incalculable benefits one may gain by developing the wonderful healing powers lying dormant in many of our natures. I am studying that special phase, and I mean to use my powers whenever a chance occurs.

And the opportunity that he so earnestly desired soon came, and he was not slow to improve the occasion. True, he had had no experience; but the perusal of a book dealing with the subject had so exercised his mind, and elevated his faith, that if only his power had been commensurate with his desires, disease would speedily have been banished from the world. We were both invited by an inquirer to assist at a séance in his house; and on our way thither Campbell talked

The Spiritual Healer. 31

so wildly of his healing attributes, and proposed to use them in such a reckless manner, that I felt constrained to try to moderate his enthusiasm. I suggested that he should gain more knowledge of the theory and practice of the spiritual healing art, in order to qualify himself to successfully cope with bodily infirmities. But he would not view it at all in that light. He maintained, with great warmth, that mutual faith was the only element requisite. I endeavoured to convince him of his mistake, but it was of no use; and we quarrelled three parts of the way to our destination.

But our wrangling was not so serious as to prevent us appearing to our friends in tolerable good temper. Though, much to my disgust, he would not keep quiet during the séance, he persisted in airing his new found treasure, until he almost deafened us by his clangour. But I could not be seriously angry with him, for I knew it proceeded from a kindly disposition, although I earnestly wished his tongue shorter.

"Now, Mr Campbell," said our entertainer, "if you really can heal diseases, I have a relative living abroad who has been afflicted for many years. He is so very ill that, although but a young man, he has almost lost the use of his limbs, and our gratitude would know no bounds if you could restore him to his wonted health and strength."

"Yes, yes," said he, gladly seizing the opportunity. "I only require faith and I'll do it. Remember the faith of the Centurion, which called forth the praise of Jesus, and He said we should do greater things if we only had faith."

And Campbell grew so excited, that a portion of his intense earnestness was communicated to us. He bade one of the gentlemen go to the piano and play some sacred melody, while he arranged us in a circle on our knees, all joined hand in hand, then he lowered the lights, and took his place also in the ring.

"Now music, sweet and soft, if you please, and all fix your thoughts on the sick man, and pray earnestly for his recovery."

And while the sweet cadence of the music softly stole over us, we reverently bowed down, and implored the Almighty to show forth His power and raise the sick man to his wonted health. We remained in this position for some little time, and then Campbell commanded us to rise, and assured us that we had touched a divine chord, which should reach and beat responsive in the heart of the object of our prayers, and that it could not fail to restore him. He then ordered the relatives to enclose a prescription to their friend, which he would write, and also inform him that he must, at a given and corresponding time, with his doctor, pray to God for help. I forget whether allowance was made for the difference of latitude.

The prescription itself consisted of some verses from the Bible, with a command that the recipient should perform a charitable action every day.

If Campbell did not succeed in his praiseworthy endeavours, he certainly deserved the reward of success, but I am afraid it ended in failure. And not many weeks afterwards, he grew so disgusted with the subject, that he refused to listen to it with patience ; and vehemently declared that he had found out enough to convince him that it was all delusion. These and similar occurrences fell under my notice in the enlarged sphere of my operations ; but I grew more and more intensely devoted to the cause, and worked hard to qualify myself to take a part in the drama that was unfolding itself before my expectant eyes; the first act of which I had played so earnestly and so faithfully.

CHAPTER IV.

A GREAT MEDIUM.

JOYOUSLY I wended my way along the streets to the house of my friend Campbell, who, like myself, was full of Spiritualism. We had projected schemes of importance, which were to thoroughly revolutionize the present spiritual economy, and we were sanguine as to the beneficial results likely to arise from such excellent combinations.

"Guess who is here!" shouted Campbell, when I had arrived.

"Nay, I never waste time in such reckless pursuits; I will throw myself on your charity."

"Well, I am afraid you wouldn't easily guess. You have heard of the great medium through whom such stupendous manifestations have been obtained on the Continent?"

"Oh, yes, every spiritualist knows him. You mean Thomson?"

"Yes, he is one of the mediums about whose honesty I think there can be no doubt. He is coming here to-night, in fact we expect him every minute. Ah, here he comes."

Campbell was right, it was the great medium Thomson who now entered, and we were soon engaged in a lively conversation on the theme nearest our hearts. I looked upon him as a very fortunate person, and I wondered if ever I should reach such an eminence. I listened to him with undivided respect, which was increased to admiration, when he gave us both an invitation to attend his meetings in London.

We also learned that he was engaged to give a séance at the house of one of our friends the following evening, and as we too had appointments at the same place, we did not doubt but that a surprise was intended for us. After spending a pleasant time together, we separated, with mutual assurances of fraternal good will.

"Punctuality is the essence of politeness," I believed, the next night, when some of the guests were rather slow in bringing themselves to the meeting, and I think I would then have subscribed a law to make unpunctuality a penal offence; but while waiting for the laggards the mixed company of sceptics and believers could not argue upon anything more appropriate than Spiritualism.

"I don't care what you say," shouted one enthusiastic believer to a gentleman who had ventured to doubt the genuineness of spirit manifestations. "I tell you I have seen all this with my own eyes. I have been a spiritualist for many years, and—what! you never believe hearsay evidence! Pray, have you ever been to America or Australia?"

"No."

"Do you then believe in their existence?"

"Of course I do."

"Then believe in Spiritualism," demanded our friend.

"No, I cannot see the force of that reasoning."

"Then, you go home to your mother," retorted the believer, and his opponent submitted to this rough style of address with perfect good humour. Consequently, it did not disturb the general harmony.

The latest guest having now arrived we were soon arranged in a circle, when the spirits quickly made their appearance and performed their work. They rang the bells and played the music, they swung the guitar about over our heads, and knocked the ceiling itself, besides many other little things.

The gentleman who had been so unceremoniously relegated to his mother's tuition, to learn the force and beauty of analogy, received a proof far more convincing than argument. He had been placed in a line with the medium and the window, through which, spite of everything, a little ray of light streamed, just sufficient to show a hand and part of an arm swiftly moving about in the air, and apparently quite detached from a body.

At the conclusion of the séance, he mentioned the circumstance, and confessed he was quite unable to account for it by any published hypothesis.

"I shall be very pleased to see you at my séances," said the medium cordially.

"Many thanks, I shall be very pleased to come; I am quite interested, and shall be glad to learn more of this."

I had myself spent an agreeable time, and my attention had become even more intensely rivetted to the subject, and I thought that nothing could be grander than to devote one's whole energy to the exposition of such a theme. I almost envied the medium, but I concluded he had had to work hard to gain such powers.

An inauguration meeting was held by a number of friends at Thomson's house to give him a welcome back to England, and wish him God speed in his work, for he had been away for a few years, but several of the company had known him personally in former times. Many congratulatory speeches were uttered by some of the leading spiritualists on this memorable occasion, neither did they forget to proffer an abundance of advice, to all of which Thomson listened with great respect. The evening was spent in happy conversation, and everybody was pleased to know that he intended to hold "At Home" séances twice a week, and all anticipated that a glorious work would be done.

Meanwhile, my intimacy with Thomson grew, until we became very familiar; he said he wished me to go to all his séances at home, the first of which would take place the following Friday evening.

True to the appointed time, I presented myself, and was pleased to see a goodly company already assembled. One gentleman then got up and said—

"I have to propose that we apply a very rigid test which I have elaborated, and, as the medium does not object, I will now submit the idea for your approval. I think it is the most conclusive ever used, because it is one that answers not only for the honesty of the medium, but also for the circle. You are all aware of the fact that mediums are charged with fraud and deception, and although our medium has been tested times innumerable, and his *bona fides* placed almost beyond suspicion; yet, in order to remove any and every cause of possible complaint, I will invite your co-operation in the employment of this test to which I allude."

We all professed our willingness to adopt the idea, and the originator then informed us that he had caused little eyelets to be let into a round board, and near the edge. The board itself would be laid upon the table and completely cover it. We found, when it was brought forward, that the eyelets were carefully arranged at measured distances, and in such a manner, that there were two opposite each person, whether lady or gentleman, one for the right hand, and one for the left. Beginning at any point in the circle, a piece of copper wire was passed through the wristband of the first sitter, through the eyelet in the board, through the other wristband again, and then onward to the next sitter.

In this manner the wire was threaded through and through, fastening each person to the board, and to his neighbour on either side, and in fact to the entire circle.

The company—including Thomson—being thus interlaced, the ends of the wire were tied together, the joint was covered first with paper, then with wax, and a seal was set on it, and then the lights were extinguished. I did not much relish all this intricate preparation, because it seemed to evince too much suspicion, and that element, I considered, would retard the manifestations; but I knew also, that argument was almost as detrimental as suspicion, and I made no remark, but cheerfully submitted to the temporary imprisonment, and the result convinced us that nothing could be more perfect, and we acknowledged it to be such.

"Now those people who go about trying to injure

mediums may come here if they choose; if so, they will have to give their hands as hostages for good behaviour," said the originator of the test.

"Yes, I think mediums ought to be protected," rejoined another. "Those men who go about 'exposing,' as they call it, themselves take false beards and other things into a séance room and drop them about, and then declare that they have caught the medium using them."

"I am sure our mediums have much to contend against," remarked a lady; "but surely with this test, even the most sceptical will be satisfied. Just think of the manifestations we have now witnessed, and with such severe conditions; to talk of trickery, is an insult to our common sense."

"I wish we could dispense with all this testing," added another lady, "for I am sure it weakens the power. I wonder who was wicked enough to think of it first? He must have been a man who would use deceit himself, to have had such unjust suspicions regarding others."

"The reason why tests were first employed," informed a gentleman, "was because jealous people denied that spirits performed the things which we so often witness. You know this is a suspicious age, and people will accept nothing on trust; so they asked that mediums should be safely secured in order to hinder them from simulating or personating a spirit: hence the tests."

"I have no objection to use some kind of test, but I have a strong objection to assist at this copper-wiring again," broke in another.

"Oh, indeed; pray what is your objection?" tartly rejoined the originator.

"I have only to say that it might be very inconvenient to be wired up like this if a fire should break out on the premises."

This horrible picture disturbed even our equanimity. We felt the force of the objection, and although we were in constant communion with the spirits, we did not wish to be dismissed to join them in this summary and disagreeable fashion. And we knew that in the event of a fire this awful consummation was not only possible, but very probable; so after the test had received a few more trials, we respectfully but firmly discontinued its use. The manifestations had been granted with it, although, perhaps, with not quite so much force.

But this was only the first part of the sitting. We had had a rare success, but now the materialisation was to follow, and we did not doubt but it would be very grand.

I distinctly remember that night. Thomson arranged us in a semi-circle before the curtains of the cabinet, into which he afterwards retired.

While patiently waiting for the appearance, the conversation in low tones turned upon the apparel of the angels, who we are taught are "clothed with light as with a garment." Somebody started the idea that, according to a fixed law of the higher life, the purer the spirit the whiter and more dazzling his garments. It was remarked that by a somewhat rough and ready correspondence that law is reflected in this material sphere; where the richer the man the more costly his apparel. That is to say, dress is the reflex of man's condition—here of his social, there of his spiritual—and, for aught I know, it is in the abstract strictly true. But our metaphysical conference was here interrupted by the appearance, which assumed a form, and stood before the cabinet. Devout and awe-stricken we sat gazing on the illustrious but condescending personage, even as Abraham sat in the tent door when the Lord appeared to him on the plains of Mamre.

Joy thrilled through every bosom, for faith was now lost in sight. The spectacle we had reverently come to see was graciously given to us. With one accord the company broke forth—

> "See then he comes, all majesty and grace;
> How bright his garments, and how fair.
> Thus do we judge how pure the soul,
> How great, how good, how wise."

Closely he folded his garments of light around him, and stood solemn, erect, and motionless. Not a word escaped his lips to break the mighty spell. The loftier spirits are reticent, though gracious. We did not fall at his feet, for we remembered the apocalyptic story of a gorgeous apparition, and we feared to incur the familiar reproof on that occasion administered against an apostle's incipient idolatry. But in our heart of hearts we worshipped him. He would not permit us to touch his transfigured flesh, or resurrection body, but with a prohibitory gesture, and an angry frown, he rebuked one or two of the more adventurous of the company, who had rashly essayed the experiment. At length his majestic austerity melted into the sweetest tenderness, and, three times, he bowed with exquisite grace. He looked on us with a rare beneficence, and filled us full of joy unspeakable, and now, amid the solemn stillness that prevailed—as if Time himself had stayed his course to watch us—he bowed himself almost to the ground. Recovering soon his perpendicular attitude, he slowly raised his right hand, and pointed to the skies. We read in that sign, "Heaven is my home." He breathed "farewell" into our spirit ear, and quickly vanished out of sight.

CHAPTER V.

A SPIRITUAL PARTNERSHIP.

ONE day, when conversing with Thomson about the great work to be done in England, he proposed to me to join him, so that we might labour together in public.

"I think," said he, "that wonderful manifestations would follow. This is my plan: We will take a hall, and hold public meetings. You must begin with a lecture, and after a little singing I will sit for materialisations. I know it will be successful, for my guides have often urged me to take this step. In short, that is the reason I am in England. Private séances are all very well in their way, but only a limited number of people can sit at them. On the other hand, if they were public, great numbers could be convinced. I have had such meetings before, and they have been successful. I have waited to find a competent coadjutor, and the spirits tell me that you are the man."

"I have no objection to give lectures," I answered, "but you know that we cannot always depend upon the manifestations occurring; and if a mixed audience were gathered together, I don't think the sceptics would understand paying for admission, and get nothing in return; besides, you must not overlook the fact that very nice conditions are required, which, in public, are not likely to be gained."

"Don't be alarmed at that, the spirits have never yet deceived me. They say that the time has come for bold action, and the only question is, Will you assist me? You have been to several of my séances, and you see what the spirits can do, but let me tell you, that that is nothing like what they can do."

"I will think about it, and let you know in a few days,"

A Spiritual Conflict. 41

I answered, for the proposal startled me, and I was unable to come to an abrupt decision.

I took counsel with some of my spiritualist friends, who seemed to think that although it was daring, yet it was feasible. I had not thought of the profit likely to arise, for I was willing to give my services, which would only be required at night, leaving the days for the pursuit of my ordinary avocation. I viewed Spiritualism in much too serious a light to make it a question of business. I pondered over the scheme, but could arrive at no decision. Sometimes I thought this was the golden opportunity for which I had long waited to conduct me to the fulness of light and knowledge. Never again might I receive such a brilliant offer.

But, anon, it occurred to me that I was unfit for so responsible a position, and, like Moses, I was disposed to shift the burden upon the more capable shoulders of somebody better qualified; but I, who had so longed for a desirable field in which to work, and with my whole soul burning with a holy ardour to hold aloft the insignia of my principles, surely now the star had dawned I would not be guilty of cowardice.

The question haunted me; I could not decide, and in a rage at my own pusillanimity, I determined to call upon Thomson. But I had chosen an unfavourable time, for I learned that he was engaged in giving a séance. I knew it was not desirable to disturb him, and I went away, but left a message saying that I would return again shortly.

I walked up and down the streets, a prey to contending emotions, recollections of heroes who had dared all crowding thickly upon me, and I wondered if such men had ever been tormented by the like cowardly fears and doubts. What a destiny! Far too grand and noble for me. I would be content with much less than copartnership with such a man as Thomson, who had stood before kings and princes, and had come triumphantly through many an ordeal, which had increased the lustre of his name and his high calling.

I had allowed fully half an hour to pass before venturing to call again, but now I thought his séance will have been finished.

"It isn't over yet," said the attendant; "but I think it will be very shortly. Perhaps you had better wait. Please go upstairs."

I softly made my way to the door of the séance room and listened. I waited on the landing, as no other room was vacant. All within was silent, and I stood for a moment to consider whether I should wait, but an involuntary cough betrayed me, and I was startled to hear from within the broken voice of the spirit Joey calling out in shrill tones—

"Is that Mr Parker?"

"Yes," I softly answered, for I was fearful of disturbing them.

"Open the door at once and let him in," he called to some one inside.

"But I shall disharmonise the conditions," I returned, through the door.

"Oh no, you won't. Your influence is good, and helps us very much. You must come in."

This reply almost answered the questions troubling my wavering mind, and when the door was opened I softly entered. All within was gloomy. A small spirit lamp, carefully shaded, and turned very low, served to show me, though very slowly and indistinctly, the occupants of the room— only a gentleman seated at the piano, playing some simple little melody, and a young girl sitting beside the table.

I was informed that this was a very important meeting, and held for the purpose of obtaining wax moulds of spirit faces, such as a few days previously had been given to another gentleman through Thomson's mediumship, and that just now the manifestation was on the point of being repeated.

"All hail! all hail!" now came in stentorian tones from the cabinet, and addressed to myself.

"I am supremely happy to meet you again," I responded

"but I trust the fresh influence I bring will not hinder the work now in progress."

"Have we not said that your influence is favourable? We shall now be able to complete the moulds which a short time since we were in some doubt, because of the waning power. You have brought the necessary reinforcement."

"Will you be able to show yourself to-day?"

"Yes, we have been sufficiently materialised to come out several times already, but I am now coming again. Music please."

Soon a slight rustling sound came from the curtains which seemed to be gently agitated, and in the aperture created I observed part of a dazzling white garment; this was a foretaste of better things. A moment afterwards the curtains were thrown open and the spirit form stood before us, and with upraised hand advanced into the room.

Slowly and majestically came the colossal figure, and when quite close to us, it suddenly raised its soft gauze covering, and threw it completely over my head.

And in the gloom of the chamber, now hushed to silence, I discovered a second and smaller form under the raiment, which now covered three. I took the little proffered hand and raised it reverently to my lips; the larger form then placed his own right hand on my head, and bending low, softly whispered a blessing upon me, which thrilled my whole being, and to which my soul responded. The gauze was then withdrawn from my head, and the two spirits slowly moved to the other side of the room, where I now discovered two small vessels placed on trestles, one filled with hot liquid wax, and the other with cold water.

The two forms, which looked like one, manipulated the wax and water for some little time, and then returned to us, when the larger pointed to his face, which action we interpreted, "Take off the mould."

After removing it, the spirit retreated a short distance, and separated himself entirely from his smaller companion, and while we sat gazing on the disjoined figures, the little one suddenly vanished.

This startling manifestation almost stupified us. I rubbed my eyes and pinched my arms to satisfy myself that I was not dreaming. I stared hard at the spot whereon, but a moment before, the form had stood, and then my gaze fell upon the other, who stood as if enjoying our surprise, and he too slowly retired to his cabinet.

"Well? Does that satisfy you as to our capacity to do great things?" asked the heavy voice of the spirit.

"I am really too much astonished to say anything," I replied.

"Now you must be guided by our medium, who is asleep at the present moment, and knows nothing of what is passing, but we will impress him to follow the right direction."

"Who was the little spirit?"

"Tanto."

"How was it that she so suddenly disappeared?"

"Materialised spirits can vanish like a flash of lightning. We just dissolve the atoms of which they are formed, and the physical senses can no longer discern them, although they are still present. We were able to do that because you came, just to convince you of our power, and to satisfy you that you must aid the medium in his work. Your influence will enable us to perform that which will startle the world. So you must no longer hesitate; the way is open, follow on, and God bless you; for the present I must say farewell."

We then examined the wax mould, which was pronounced to be perfect, and from the same face as that given but a few days previously.

The owner triumphantly bore it away, leaving me to further conversation with the medium, who asked—

"Well, have you thought any more of my proposal?"

"Yes, indeed, I have thought a great deal about it."

"So have I, and the spirits have been telling me that with your aid they can do wonders. And they say that you must join me altogether! We will have an agreement, and as you give up your present occupation, you must live, so you shall have an equal share of everything."

This was another phase, and, I thought, required fresh consideration, but Thomson said that I must give an immediate answer, as the spirits were preparing themselves for a great campaign, and they were only stopping for me; and I answered—

"Very well, then, I will be guided by the spirits, and come with you."

"That is right, and now we will settle all preliminaries, and have an agreement, so that everything may be quite *en regle.*"

I was fairly in the work now, and I thankfully acknowledged that the spirits had more than kept their word. They had promised me great things, and at last they were on the point of being realised. I had implicitly obeyed them all the way through, and they had brought me into communication with one of the greatest, if not the greatest medium in the world, and he, their chosen instrument, was but obeying the mysterious impulses called forth by his guide, when he so earnestly besought me to join him.

Now that the die was cast, I likened myself to the disciples, who had given up all to follow the Master. But still there was one feature I did not view with favour: I wished that we could dispense with fees; I did not like being paid, and how earnestly I wished that we could do as the great ones of the world had done in times long gone by, when they went out, fighting against evil, without money and without price. But Thomson argued that we must live, and the rich ones would not do the work; so there was no way out of the dilemma, although every guinea I received robbed my work of some of its lustre, and lowered me in my own estimation.

A Mr Goodman had taken great interest in us, and he witnessed the signing of the agreement, the terms of which seemed a little too favourable for me. I could not rightly understand how this renowned medium should propose for me to have half the fees, but this too I placed to the credit of the spirits, and I resolved to work hard to win my share of the proceeds.

One day, shortly after this, when Mr Goodman was present at a séance, three beautiful bunches of artificial flowers were either materialised or levitated—one for Mr Goodman, one for Thomson's cousin, Lou, and the other for me.

When the séance was ended, I accompanied Mr Goodman for a walk, and he very much astonished me by quietly saying—

"Don't encourage that bringing of flowers."

"Why? I thought that was such a beautiful manifestation."

"Well, you observe that these flowers are artificial, and must have been brought from some shop. It looks too much like conjuring, and I hope you won't lend yourself to anything of that kind."

"Indeed, no," I earnestly replied, "I look upon this as far too grand to be prostituted to that level."

Mr Goodman looked at me searchingly for a few moments, and seemed to say, "Well, you are either a precious fool, or else remarkably 'cute;" but he did not say anything. He had been a spiritualist for several years, and his faith was tempered with a little discretion.

In accordance with my enthusiasm, I never neglected an opportunity of snatching a victory from the enemy—all were enemies who were not spiritualists—more especially the atheists, one of whom I knew intimately, and had frequently spoken to him regarding the folly of his negation when he had proofs at his hand to prove the contrary.

"Show me these wonderful things," he demanded one day, when I had been more than usually pressing.

"I shall be happy to do so if you will come to our séances."

"When do they take place, and what am I to do?"

"You will have to do nothing but sit still and observe. We hold them twice a week."

We agreed that he should come up the next evening, and when he came, being a fresh sitter, he was placed in the circle round the table, but as far from the medium as possible.

It is sometimes considered injurious to the power for a new comer to be too close to the medium during the course of the manifestations, as it induces an opposing influence which disturbs the even flow of the aura.

This circle like all others was under test conditions, that is to say, we all sat round the table with joined hands, Thomson and myself being opposite to each other. The table itself was covered with various objects—a guitar, a tambourine, a bell, and a few other little things.

My friend the atheist had looked on our preparations with some degree of curiosity; and then the lights were extinguished. All our séances were held in perfect darkness.

Very soon the guitar was touched, then moved, and at last it was taken up by invisible hands and swiftly borne aloft and about the room, apparently even to the furthermost corners, the strings being violently thrummed the while, the bell also ringing out a noisy accompaniment; and then the tambourine, as if not willing to be outdone, began waltzing about over our heads, and occasionally giving a sitter a thump, which, coming from such a source, was gratefully received.

There were one or two clairvoyant friends present, and they began to describe the forms of many spirits which they could see floating overhead and silently moving about amongst us, although they, the spirits, were sufficiently objective to the clairvoyants, who, being also clairaudient, could hear them talking to each other about ourselves. Several of the sitters now called out that they could feel hands touching them, and forthwith each person began to express a violent wish to feel the dear spirit hands. One old lady solemnly declared that she could see her husband standing before and lovingly smiling upon her.

Many other manifestations equally astonishing were given to us; and after the lapse of a few minutes, when everybody had been satisfied, we changed the form of the circle for the materialisations.

In this part we were permitted by the spirits to have a

little light, but not more than enough to see each other indistinctly, and having been placed in the usual semicircular fashion before the curtains of the cabinet, wherein Thomson had retired.

While waiting for the appearance I asked my atheist friend for an opinion regarding the physical manifestations, and I was gratified to hear a favourable verdict. He declared that he was very much astonished, and almost admitted his belief in spirit agency. He said he could not understand how any one, even if he had been at liberty, could manage to perform that which he had witnessed, as he had seen the door locked, and had noticed how careful everyone had been to maintain the circle unbroken.

"What will you say to your unbelieving friends?" I queried.

"I shall merely relate what I have seen, and leave them to draw their own conclusions."

"Then you admit your inability to explain the mystery?"

"I will admit that I am very much puzzled."

"Why don't you discard your unwise prejudices and assent to our declaration that it was all the work of the disembodied?"

"No, no, I cannot do that, I don't put everything down to the Devil that I cannot understand. I'll wait a little."

"What a long time the spirits are, to be sure," suddenly ejaculated an impatient sitter. "Are you here, dear friends?"

"Yes, we are all here," shouted Joey.

"What is the reason you don't show yourselves then?"

"Because the power is very scant; we used it nearly all at the table, and the two fresh people have upset the conditions."

"Oh, Joey," I implored, "do try and come; this is the first materialising séance that my friend has ever attended, and I should so much like for him to see a spirit."

"Can't help it, really; your friend must come again. We will see what can be done next time. Good night, and God bless you all."

CHAPTER VI.

A NEW TEST.

ONE morning Mr Goodman called and found me alone. Thomson had gone to the country to give a séance and had taken his little cousin Louey with him. I thought at the time it was very unwise to take her, as she had not been invited; but he said she wanted a run out to the country as she was not in good health.

"How are you getting on with Thomson?" enquired Mr Goodman as soon as he had taken his seat.

"Very well, indeed," I answered; "but we are thinking of having a test cabinet made for our seances."

"I shall be happy to make you a present of one. How do you want it made, and of what material?"

"You are very kind, Mr Goodman; we want simply an upright iron-wire cage, capable of being folded up like a screen, and it must be made in such a manner that everybody will be convinced there is no trickery in it."

"Come along then at once. I am a practical man and like to do a thing straight off without any idling."

Accordingly we went off at once, and having given a sketch of the required article, and receiving an assurance from the maker that it should be delivered in a few days, we went off on some other business. On our way Mr Goodman suddenly said,

"Now, Mr Parker, you are engaged in this work, you will require a good deal of money. Thomson tells me that you are short of cash. How much do you want?"

"I really do not want any, I thank you," I replied.

"Well if you do let me know at once. But there is one other thing—I want you to give a séance to the Spiritual Association."

"Yes, of course. We shall be pleased to come and give it any time most convenient to you."

I was pleased at the opportunity to gratify our friend, and all the more readily promised, because I thought Thomson would wish to repay him in some way for the great trouble and money expended on his behalf; but my surprise was almost unbounded when, upon his return to town, I told him what I had done. He answered,

"I wish you had not promised a séance. To tell you the truth, I have very small respect for these Associations. They are a parcel of meddling, muddling busybodies, who consume a vast amount of time in quarrelling with each other, but never do any real good to spiritualism."

"Mr Goodman says it will be very beneficial to us if we get their favour."

"Do those noodles think they are going to keep on testing me? Why, for several years they have had things obtained through my mediumship exhibited in their rooms. But since you have promised, I will go; though I vow it shall be the last, and I don't believe anything will take place this time, for my guides like these people as little as I do. They give themselves great names and airs, and think that makes them great. Any fellow can hire a couple of rooms or a house and christen it 'Institution,' or anything he likes."

"But surely there can be no doubt about the respectability of these people," I replied.

"I say nothing against their respectability; but as I have had a great experience with them I haven't much respect for their ability, and I don't mean to fetter myself with them in any way. If they imagine they are going to bind me down just as long as it suits them and then throw me over when I am no longer needed, they are greatly mistaken. I haven't been a medium for ten years to be tutored by such people now. I expect they will want us to give them a séance once a week for the benefit of the Society! Oh, I know them of old."

Unpunctuality.

"I am sorry to hear you have such a bad opinion of them."

"Well, if they choose to come here they are welcome; but I won't run after them. My reputation is too firmly established for me to be at their beck and call. You will find that we had better avoid these institutions and associations, for if we go to one we shall inevitably offend all the others."

This unhappy disunion amongst the leading spiritualists had already attracted my notice, indeed it could not be otherwise, but I hoped that they would yet sink their differences, and work together for the general good of the cause; but I never saw those hopes realised. I regarded it as a lamentable and pitiable exhibition of rancour displayed towards each other, and the only one thing, it seemed, in which we were all at one was the unanimity with which non-spiritualists were attacked, particularly the Christian, "intolerant and dogmatic."

A few days afterwards we went to give the promised séance, but through an unfortunate misunderstanding we were exactly one hour late.

The chairman of the meeting evidently considered I was the culprit, and he glared at me furiously and savagely. I offered the sincerest apologies, but he deigned not to answer, except by a curious sort of grunt about "Waste of time," &c. I hastened to atone for my ill-behaviour, and hurried forward the proceedings, but I saw clearly that forgiveness would be a matter of time. I was disposed at first to regard his conduct as ungrateful, seeing that but for me the séance would never have been given, but better feelings soon prevailed, and I endeavoured to find excuses for him in my own heart. I told myself that he was in a position where every minute was of value, and consequently he did well to be angry.

When we entered the séance room we observed a queer sort of machine, a cross between a sentry-box and a coffin, stuck upright in a corner, and which we were informed was the cabinet for the medium.

"Come along, I have no time to lose, I have wasted enough already," snapped the chairman; and leading Thomson to the box he bundled him in, and quickly shot home several bolts and screws, and with such an air of grim revenge as almost to make me think he never meant to let me have him out again. And then he swung the curtains along enclosing the cabinet, with an appearance of "Now I've got him."

Contrary to my expectations, Thomson bore all this with perfect good humour, but I saw a smile flit over his face which seemed to augur ill for the success of the meeting. The thought, too, struck me, that this was not the proper spirit to show, when about to evoke the powers of Heaven; more likely, I thought, powers of a different altitude.

We, of the audience, now took our seats outside, and soon were listening to the dulcet tones of the musical-box, which I was deputed to control.

Ten minutes slowly passed and then another ten, and at last I saw that patience had entirely deserted the circle.

"Are they never coming?" snorted the chairman. His anger and impatience were truly comical, and being organist I seized the opportunity to bend forward to screw up the box; in reality to conceal the almost uncontrollable smile which pressed to my face. There was enough light to have exposed any sign of levity, and I did not dare to offend further for fear of worse consequences.

Altogether an hour passed, and at the end of that time I asked the spirits if they could do anything, and received a single rap in reply, indicating a peremptory "No!"

My fears of Thomson's prolonged incarceration were quite groundless, for the chairman went forward as soon as we had procured more light, and unscrewed the "coffin," in order to let out the prisoner, who to our great alarm fell forward in a deep mesmeric sleep at our feet. I employed the method usually adopted in similar cases, but for a short time it was of no avail. Soon, however, he showed signs of returning consciousness and opened his eyes, sighed, looked wildly around, and then with assistance he rose to his feet.

"What is the matter?" said he, dreamily.

" Nothing," growled the chairman, meaning that either in the fullest or the least sense of the word, whichever we choose; and then, having given us a curt "good night," he disappeared, and, after a pleasant chat over a cup of coffee with the kind-hearted Mrs Meldon, we too departed.

"You see now how it is," said Thomson to me when we were once more alone. "I told you I thought nothing would happen, because my guides don't like them. Don't let us have anything more to do with such people. And then think of the ill-humour of that chairman; that wasn't the way to go to a séance."

"Well, but his time may be very valuable, and it was my fault," I returned, apologising for the chairman.

"What's his time more than other people's? besides he ought to have accepted your apology. These important people always think creation going to smash, if they lose a train. But don't worry about them, let us talk of something better. The cabinet is coming home to-morrow and then you'll see something wonderful."

The next day found a critical group of friends assembled to view the cabinet, which came home all complete and true to the plan, and it was determined to test its powers at once, so a séance was projected for the same day.

The circle met according to appointment, and consisted of an eminent German professor, the editor of a Spiritualist paper, our friend Mr Goodman and a few more well-disposed and earnest inquirers. The cabinet was simply an upright wire cage about six feet high, and could be folded up like a screen, the door, merely one of the four sides, could be shut closely, and was fastened by three spring padlocks outside, one at the top, one in the middle and the other at the bottom, and were considered to be quite out of the reach of the person inside. It was deemed next to impossible for anyone to climb over, as it would then collapse, nor could it be lifted up to allow of anyone to crawl out, not to speak of the difficulty of getting back again. But we resolved to make it even yet more complete, and we tied pieces of tape to the cage and nailed them to the floor outside, and with wax we imprinted on them a crest. We then tied a piece of cloth over the top and sealed the strings of that likewise. Everything being pronounced perfect, we locked in the medium and took our seats in the adjoining room separated from the other by a curtain, and in utter darkness we anxiously awaited the result.

We had consumed nearly half-an-hour in elaborating the preparations, but we did not consider the time ill-spent. I was as much interested as any one, for I felt if we witnessed a materialisation under such conditions, it would be a test case of the most conclusive sort; the like of which had never before been seen.

Every minute seemed an age, and my suspense was almost beyond endurance; but in the midst of my reflections, and when I had almost begun to despair of success, lo! there appeared before us, in the opened curtains, a lofty form in dazzling white. Silent and motionless it stood while we sat gazing on it with wonder and admiration, and then it slowly raised its arm, covered with white garments, and pointed upwards; after which it melted from view, and the curtains soon hid it from our sight.

A few more minutes passed in hushed silence and we heard the voice of Joey calling out from the cage that all was over, and that nothing more could be done that day, for the new cabinet required much spiritual magnetism, to enable them to work with ease. When we examined the cage and fastenings we found everything exactly as it should be; not a seal or a lock had been touched, and the medium himself was in a deep sleep from which it was difficult to awaken him.

Several suggestions were next made by some of the company who were test-mad, to make the cage even yet more stringent; but it remained for the editor to outstrip all the others in the extravagance, I had almost written stupidity, of his demands. He privately proposed that the joint-screws should be placed outside instead of as now inside; but not much notice was taken of him, as the insinuation pointed to the necessity of removing at least twelve very small screws and their replacement in the dark, and his absurd proposal met with well merited silence. It was agreed though that some useful improvements might with propriety be effected, and the next day, when I returned from a visit, Thomson informed me that he had sent away the cage, and had given orders for an entirely new one which, though structurally the same, would satisfy every demand; a new movable and closely fitting top and bottom fastened by outside padlocks and the addition of a continuous wire-joint for each corner would make it nearly perfect.

"In the meantime," added Thomson, "I have just received a letter from Harley Street, W., inviting us to give a séance there to-morrow evening. And they also ask if we have any objection to the presence of Morton? They think with two such mediums the power will be immeasurably increased. What do you say?"

"I haven't the least objection, on the contrary I am very pleased; I think it would be infinitely better if mediums would for ever renounce their little jealousies and work harmoniously together."

The next evening found us at a house in Harley Street in company with Morton, who had been invited to act with us. This medium had attracted a large amount of sympathy, because he had been cruelly used and taxed with fraud, by mischievous people with whom he had sat on the Continent. But the exposé had served to increase his popularity amongst the friends at home, who upheld him and showered fresh favours upon him; in short he was in our eyes a martyr.

After some time spent in conversation we all descended to the library, which was to be used as the séance room, and there we found everything excellently prepared for us, but as our entertainers had had some experience in these matters, there is nothing at which to wonder.

On a large table in the middle of the room were placed all the paraphernalia used at the physical manifestations; and in a corner stood a large handsome screen for the materialisations.

"Do you find everything you require?" asked the mistress of the house.

"Yes, everything is just as it should be," I replied.

"That is right. You see we are so anxious to have a good séance, and with two such powerful mediums, I think the conditions are good enough to warrant our belief in a success."

More complete darkness could not very well be secured,

as was discovered when we had taken our seats round the table and had extinguished the lights.

"Dear me! what is that?" suddenly exclaimed a lady at the end of about ten minutes.

The object which had called forth this question was an illuminated something that nobody seemed to understand. It was up in the air over the table and slowly moving about, sometimes stopping for a moment opposite one of the circle. It was of the size and form of an envelope, and transparently bright and beautiful.

"Perhaps it is a letter from the spirit world," suggested somebody.

"No, it can't be that, because the surface is quite clear. Oh, it is quite close to my face. Thank you, dear spirits. Why, it is bright enough to show up the spirit hand holding it! There! it is gone."

"No it isn't, it is before me now," called out a lady.

"Oh really it is quite too beautiful. Why, it is a spirit-mirror!"

Three times it moved up in token of assent before the lady who had made such an accurate guess, and then, after going round the circle, it disappeared as suddenly and mysteriously as it had come. The physical manifestations that were given at the same time passed off almost unheeded, the mirror was the chief attraction, and was the basis of many speculative remarks.

"I hope John King will come to-night," said a lady, when the two mediums had entered the cabinet for the materialisations.

"So do I, and Irresistible too," said another, and then quietly added, "Oh, what a magnificent appearance! Is that John?"

"No, it is Asoka with his crown and girdle of light, look at the big A on the front of his turban," answered 'Peter' from the screen.

"How do you manage to make such nice things?"

"Quite easily," replied Joey, when Asoka had returned to the cabinet. "But when our wire cage is finished, we are going to have public séances, and then you will see the spirits come out all clothed in dazzling light. We are now developing it and you must support our medium. But John King is now coming."

"Good evening, John," said we as soon as we heard the familiar voice of John.

"Good evening, God bless you all," roared he in return.

"The power is very strong to-night, is it not, John, dear?"

"Not so strong as we should like. Our two mediums must give you some more sittings, so that in a short time we shall all be strictly *en rapport.*"

"John, dear," said a young gentleman, "Will you tell me if I am a medium?"

"I cannot say the first time, you must come to me again."

Everybody was anxious to propose questions relating either to past events or the future, and often to the terms of mediumship, and all received answers more or less satisfactory.

When the séance was finished and the two mediums had come from behind the screen the hospitable hostess kindly inquired how they felt after such arduous work.

"I am sure," said she, "you must have lost a great deal of power and are very tired. Supper is laid, come along."

Thereupon we all followed into another room, and amid the good things prepared for us we enjoyed ourselves like honest labourers; and during which, what more natural than that the conversation should hinge upon the wonders we had just witnessed?

"I always enjoy seeing dear John King, he is so kind, and what a grand voice he has," remarked the hostess, and added, "Are you really going to give séances in a public hall, Mr Thomson?"

"Yes, that is what the spirits tell us we must do, and we have an iron wire cabinet being made for that purpose. It will come home to-morrow and we shall begin in a few days."

"Don't you think it is dangerous to admit a miscellaneous

audience, many of whom wont understand the conditions required, and then you may have a lot of rough people present?"

"These meetings are projected under the direction and by the express command of my guides, Madam, and then we shall exclude the rough element by high prices and thus be sure of a polite audience."

"But how will the poorer spiritualists be able to come?"

"We will issue free tickets for them."

"That is very kind, and I am sure you ought to succeed. Please to book me six seats."

Thomson glanced across the table to me as if to say, "You see I was right; we shall be highly successful."

At the end of this very pleasant evening we three spirit exponents, Morton, Thomson, and I, departed.

"I wouldn't be surprised," said Morton, when we had left the house and were walking along the streets, "if you make a pot of money over those public meetings, and if you want a third man, here's one; but," glancing at me, "remember, no conjuring."

"Indeed you may rely upon it we shall have nothing to do with any trickery," I quickly responded.

"Excuse me one minute, Parker, I want to speak to Thomson," said Morton, and the two fell back and I walked on alone until they had finished their private conference, when they soon again joined me, and a little further on, our roads being different, Morton bade us "goodnight," and Thomson and I went on well pleased with the promising aspect of affairs.

CHAPTER VII.

PUBLIC MEETINGS.

"IT is perfection itself; nothing could be more satisfactory," exclaimed a friend when he saw the cage which had been brought home remodelled according to Thomson's order.

"Yes, it is perfect, and I am quite confident that nobody could get out if once fairly locked in," said the maker, who was present, and who had been informed of the future destiny of his handiwork.

Several friends came in during the day to see the latest development for medium testing, and they all expressed their entire belief in its power to prevent the escape of any would-be erring medium.

Thomson and I had made every arrangement with the proprietor of the hall, and others, whose services we needed to carry on our meetings. We had still a day at our disposal before the opening night, and this interval Thomson considered, might be well utilized to develope the power, and one night, when our visitors had all gone, we began the course.

Thomson went into the cage and Louey and I sat in the outer room, where we observed precisely the same order as if strangers were present.

"There are many things I want to tell you," said Asoka when he had come out from the cabinet, "and as we are now alone I can teach you a few useful lessons. First, you are much too anxious to please everybody. You must be sterner. There is too much time spent in inventing tests; and as the medium can't speak, being asleep in the cabinet, you must act, and forbid such folly. Suspicion and Spiritualism cannot co-exist. And again, there is Mr Goodman who doesn't like the idea of these public meetings, and he is trying to dissuade you from them. He is a very good man, but does not understand us. You must take no notice of his sermons, but be guided wholly by us. The meetings will be grand successes if you are wise; we will do our share and you must do yours. When the medium is in the cabinet you must allow no one to approach him. After the meeting the cage may be examined by anybody."

"Don't you think, Asoka, that it would be a wise step to ask the Editor of the *Magazine* to be chairman."

"No, certainly not! Have nothing to do with any party. If you invite his assistance you will offend better people who belong to other parties. And then he will be fussy and important and spoil everything. I repeat that you must be guided by our instructions; but for the present I must say farewell—and remember."

We had several of these developing meetings, at all of which I was strongly enjoined to obey none but the guides. One of these séances and the last, was held late one night at the hall by way of rehearsal, in order to see if the place were properly darkened, but the measures we had taken to exclude every ray of light, particularly those from a troublesome full moon, were complete, and we found that our labour left nothing to be desired.

At last arrived the momentous night, and we opened the proceedings to a tolerably good and extremely friendly audience, with a bright and sparkling little concert, under the leadership of one of our devoted friends who, for the artistic skill he displayed, was rewarded with a well deserved notice of approval from the leading fashionable journal.

At the end of a short lecture which I delivered, and to which the audience respectfully listened, Thomson himself came forward, and it was easy to see that the concert and lecture were only listened to under a sort of mental protest. The whole interest was centred in the medium, and amid breathless silence, I locked him in the cage, and then, having taken a seat in the front row in the audience before the platform, I gave the signal and the lights were, lowered almost to extinction.

The strong suspense under which I now laboured was almost unendurable. I hoped and prayed for success, but spite of all the assurances of the spirit I was horribly afraid of a failure.

I knew that the greater portion of the audience would condone a lack of power, but those who were not spiritualists, would not care to understand, much less excuse it; I had firmly resolved to return the money in case of non-success, but it was not that which troubled me. I did not care to contemplate the many jeers and gibes of those over-wiseacres, who prophesied all sorts of mischief from our daring attempt to show forth the power of spirit in public.

Our musical conductor, like everybody else, had to vacate the platform at this period, and as the piano was there and music was an absolute necessity, he tried to evoke melody from the bowels of a wheezy old organ, which stood in a corner. He contrived to extract many unearthly groans from the crazy machine which, for lack of better, did duty for music.

"Turn out the lights," said Joey from the cabinet. Our eyes had become almost sufficiently used to the gloom to see everything in the place, but when, in obedience to that mandate, utter darkness prevailed, and we were, of course, unable to see, and our ears too being assailed by the yells and moans of the organ our sense of hearing was as useless as our optics.

Presently, during a lull in the storm produced by the organ, we heard a rustling, and soon a tall weird form was dimly visible, glowing with a faint light.

Curiosity to see the form was as powerful in the mind of our excellent organist as in our own; I was thankful that he too was not a machine, and, curiosity assisting, we were permitted to view the wonder in silence.

The appearance advanced to the front of the platform, and waved aloft a bright streak of light, and also allowed us who were near him to handle the object.

The Spirit of Light. 63

There was not, as some thought, the least sign of phosphorus, nor indeed of any other chemical with which we were acquainted. Close examination proved it to be as we had decided, a long strip of cloth material brilliantly illuminated. I had been promised, as a reward for obedience, that the spirits would materialise a whole garment of the like gorgeous appearance, and seeing this so freely displayed, I felt confidence in those promises. For about ten minutes, during the deepest silence, the form moved about solemnly waving the shining length, and then it slowly and mysteriously disappeared behind the curtains where the cage was fixed in a recess of the wall at the back of the platform.

"Music, please," again said Joey. It was unavoidable, we must endure the affliction, and off again started the organ on its horrifying mission until, happy release, Joey informed me that the séance was ended.

Our organist was truly glad to escape from his post, and now that the spirit's command no longer operated to fasten him to the stool, no inducement would compel him to play out the audience; and with a firm resolve I rushed to his vacated position and after many labours extracted, a little at a time, the notes of the old hundredth which frightened the audience out of the building.

When everybody had solemnly filed out of the place, Thomson, who during my unorpheus-like performance on the unruly instrument, had been round to the front of the house to speak to several friends, now came back and said—

"I have seen Colonel Fairfield, and he wishes us to go and give a séance with the cage at his house to a party of friends."

"He is satisfied then? When are we to go?"

"To-morrow night. He is quite delighted, and so were several other friends I have seen. I told you we should do well. It's all right; but we must manage to dismiss the audience a little better the next time, that organ is enough to give them the nightmare."

"I don't know what to do because you know the piano is moved away after the first part, and it is almost impossible to get at it."

"You must make a speech. What did that man want round at the dressing-room? I thought he was a detective."

"Oh he was in a mesmeric sleep, and said I had sent for him; which I never did," I vowed.

This referred to a man who had been controlled during the evening in the hall, and which had necessitated his removal, as the spirit which moved him became very violent. Some malicious people said he was under the control of spirits from the neighbouring tavern. Neither was he the only one upon whose organism the spirits acted; several clairvoyant and clairaudient mediums were present, and they saw many forms moving about amongst us speaking of our great enterprise, and encouraging us by words of wisdom and actions of grace, which they repeated for our edifications. One person declared to six spirits out upon the platform at one time, and also saw a mighty spirit by my side when I was delivering the lecture. But as those phenomena are only objective to the medium himself, they were not precisely the kind of manifestation we required. As for myself, I was consoled with the reflection that if we had not achieved a high victory, neither had we suffered a defeat; and this was sufficient to save us from the derision of the enemy.

The next evening we drove with our cage to Colonel Fairfield, who had a party of his friends to meet us. Some of them were dreadfully sceptical, and insisted upon the cage being secured by tapes and seals in such a way that left no possible loophole for escape, even if the medium wished to do so. I was not at all displeased with the rigidity of these tests, and I offered no objection. Thomson had instructed me never to oppose tests at a private house, for those people paid high and had a right to demand anything short of that which might entail physical suffering or degradation; and any objection would be almost an equivalent to an admission of guilt; besides it mattered not the least to us, for if the application of tests should by chance generate suspicion, and so hinder or destroy the power, the blame of failure would rest, not with us, but with those who engaged our services.

Before using the cage, we sat down to the table for physical manifestations, but nothing occurred beyond a slight touch of one of the strings of the guitar, which was lying on the table, and a few raps, which gave us to understand that the power was being reserved for the materialisations, and we soon fastened the medium in the cage, which stood in a room adjoining to, and separated only by a curtain from that in which we sat.

"I do not like to sit with suspicious people," said Lady Ellin, "for they always spoil the séances with their tests, which after all are only meant to show off a little cleverness."

If everybody were as pure and ingenuous as this lady, tests would certainly be unknown, but she was assuming that nobody would condescend to wrong another.

"I think tests may be used with advantage, and without evincing any particularly abnormal amount of suspicion," rejoined a gentleman.

"Quite right, quite right!" called out Joey from the other room. "We don't object to tests, but unfortunately the time you wasted to-night over the tests has weakened the power, and I am afraid nothing can be done, but we are trying hard, very, very hard."

"Are the conditions all right, Joey?"

"No; there is too much light coming in through the window, but don't trouble about it now. You must be more careful another time."

I was sorry to hear this, for a personal reason: the colonel blamed me for the omission; he considered that it was my business to look after those things, and I don't believe he has forgiven me to this day for that oversight. I really blamed myself more than he did, and determined to take a lesson from this occurrence.

E

"Why is the presence of light so injurious?" asked a lady.

"Because the atoms that we have to collect, with which to build up the form, are dispersed by its decomposing action."

"Do try and come, dear spirits," implored another of the company.

"I am afraid we cannot do anything to-night. Have you any questions to ask?"

"No; it would please us better if you were to come out to us, but as you say you cannot, it is of no use to ask."

"Not a bit; you must have another séance, and I will come then. Good-night."

Our gallant host consoled himself with the remark that these miscarriages were sure signs of the truth of Spiritualism, because, if it were trickery, there would be no such thing as failure, for no one ever heard of a prestidigitateur failing to perform his programme.

As it was quite clear we should get nothing, there was no further necessity to prolong the sitting, and we went and let loose the prisoner, who came smiling from his place of confinement, and apparently quite oblivious of the failure.

A few nights afterwards again found us at the hall for the second meeting, but as it was very cold and snowing hard, our audience was of the scantiest description, and unfortunately they were nearly all visitors with free tickets.

The proceedings were merely repetitions of the first, with the exception of an accident which seriously alarmed me. At the end of the meeting, when I went upon the platform to release Thomson, I saw the bottom lock was hanging down unfastened! I felt confident that it was not so at the beginning, and I could not in any manner account for it. But I did not then stop long to consider; I quickly hid up the offending object from inquisitive and unfriendly eyes, and no one else saw it.

I did not, in my own mind, blame Thomson, but thought

that the power was weak, and that the spirits, to obviate the disgrace of a failure, had unlocked the cage and brought him out in a magnetic sleep to personate a spirit, and had, unfortunately, neglected to secure the last lock. This view of the case was strengthened, when I remembered that during the course of the materialisations, my ears, which were preternaturally quick, had heard, ominous as a death-knell, a sharp click!

I told Thomson of this later on, when we were alone, but he shifted the blame upon me, and declared that it was my carelessness or nervousness. I proposed that it might perhaps be prudent to invite two gentlemen from the audience to act as referees. But this met with a decided opposition, for he averred that such a thing would immediately reduce us to the level of conjurors, and that the rest of the audience would promptly declare that the referees were in league with us, and it would infallibly induce disorder.

He asserted that an audience is always more orderly if kept at a respectful distance, but he severely censured my culpable negligence anent the lock, for if I had not been quick to cover up my own folly, we should have been branded as cheats and nearly ruined.

This did not at all satisfy me, but I exonerated him, and thought that he was anxious to screen the spirits, and lay the blame upon me.

We did not hold any more public meetings for some time, and for this I was pleased, as our friend Mr Goodman had been offended at our "making a show of Spiritualism," independently of the extreme danger of the proceeding and the consequent disgrace of a possible *exposé*, through the inability of the public to understand the higher phases of Spiritualism; but I had disregarded his earnest warning, and considered that I must at all hazard obey my spiritual guides.

It would occupy too much space, and require too much of the reader's patience, were I to record every séance which we gave at this time. I must confine myself to a description of those of principal note.

One morning we received a telegram, with a prepaid answer, from a gentleman living near Grosvenor Square, inquiring if it would be convenient for us to give a séance to himself and a party of his friends the same evening.

As the time was convenient, and did not interfere with our other arrangements, we sent back an affirmative reply, and a few hours later we ourselves followed, and were very kindly received by our telegraphic correspondents.

"Now, Mr Thomson," said our client, "I want to know if you will allow me to use a certain test, which I have specially invented for this séance? Not that I doubt your honesty, but I wish to be able to speak confidently of this to my sceptical friends."

"I will submit with pleasure to any test you may choose to employ, providing it does not entail personal suffering, or place me in a degrading position."

"Oh! this test won't do anything of the kind; see here, I have had strong leathern belts made, one to be locked tightly round the body, and the others to be fixed to that, and locked, and then carried to the bars of the stove, and then also locked. We all consider this is stringent enough to satisfy any reasonable mind, and we are convinced if, with this test, we see the form, it won't be you."

Thomson was quickly fastened in this eccentric manner, and we seated ourselves in the next room; every light was of course extinguished, and the usual harmony from the musical box was soon given off to assist the power.

Presently Joey commenced speaking on the other side of the curtain, and we asked him what he wanted.

"Nothing. Asoka says he is afraid to come out, as the power is not good. Go out! go out! you have plenty of strength."

This latter was addressed to a fellow-spirit, who answered in heavy tones—

"Yes! I can go now, but watch carefully that the power current is maintained, and that the medium does not fall over."

"Good evening, Asoka," we called out.

"All hail, all hail!" and the curtains were lifted, and we saw the colossal image, which addressed us so freely when invisible, but never speaking a word when before us, and only stood with weird and solemn gesture, waving his right arm, and pointing upwards.

We had no difficulty in discerning all this, for the illuminated band was placed around and descending from the shoulders, and in the front of the turban was fixed a shining glowing light, while in his hand he carried the bright mirror, which, when he held near to his own face, enabled us to see his features—apparently those of an Oriental, as such he claimed to be.

"May I shake you by the hand?" respectfully implored one of the circle.

In answer the form stepped forward, raised its arm, and flung back the gauzy material enveloping it, and with a stern grace which almost appalled us, stretched forth its right hand, which the questioner tremblingly took.

"Why, it feels as warm and natural as human flesh! but the hand is much larger than that of the medium," exclaimed he, and then the hand was withdrawn, and the form itself slowly retreated until it stood in the opening of the curtain, when it again solemnly raised its hand, and holding the mirror aloft waved it thrice, and then that disappeared from view, while the dazzling white form seemed as if dissolving before our eyes, until only a speck remained, and that also quickly vanished.

"Are you satisfied?" cried Joey from inside.

"Yes, perfectly," replied our host, "and many, many thanks."

"I will try and come now if you will wait a little longer," returned Joey.

"Yes, do please, we shall be delighted to see you."

"All right, keep the music going, and I will try."

We waited for several minutes to see the little black spirit boy, and then he mournfully announced! "Ah, the power is too much used up by Asoka, and there is none left for me. I cannot come now, but you must have another séance, and I will try then. Good night, and God bless you."

"Good-night, Joey! good-night!"

Everybody expressed their entire satisfaction with the result of the test; there was not the least appearance of dishonesty, and the unhesitating manner which had been exhibited in submitting to the restriction, increased its moral effect and greatly strengthened our reputation.

CHAPTER VIII.

A SLIGHT REVELATION.

"WHAT shall we substitute in its place? You know our clients will demand some sort of test," I asked of Thomson one day when we had arranged to give a séance to a party of our aristocratic supporters. We had discarded the cage, and must have something to allay the suspicions of hostile critics.

"There will be no difficulty about that. I have a sack which can be used, and give just as much satisfaction, and for a cabinet we can utilize the big screen. But you must not allow the people to waste so much time in preparations, because as you well know it destroys the power."

I had known the sack to be used on previous occasions, but I was anxious to see it again, and was rather pleased at the opportunity which soon occurred. When our friends arrived the sack was submitted to them for their approval, and as they were quite willing to employ it there was no further difficulty; but before using it we sat round the table for the physical manifestations. It is scarcely necessary to refer to these at much length; a description of one generally covers all, sometimes they slightly differ a little in detail, but their uniformity is general. As soon as we had finished at the table we prepared to put Thomson in the sack. Tapes and seals and other necessaries were all ready, and we quickly tied a piece of the tape round each of the medium's wrists, sealing the knots and leaving two long ends with which to tie the hands to the chair.

One of the ladies with a bodkin then ran a piece of the tape through the seam at the top of the bag, which, when Thomson was inside, enabled us to pull up tightly round his neck, fastening and sealing it at the back of the neck. The two ends on the wrists were then passed through two little holes of the bag by the medium, and tied and sealed in like manner as had been the others.

Everything being adjusted to our entire satisfaction, the medium went behind the screen, and very soon we heard Joey shouting—

"Good evening!"

"Good evening; who are you?" returned one of the gentlemen.

"I'm Joey!"

"And who is Joey?"

"Me!"

"And who is 'Me'?"

"Joey!"

"Well, who is 'Joey' and 'Me' put together?"

"I!"

"Oh, if you are going to ring the changes like that, I am afraid we sha'n't obtain much satisfaction," drily replied the questioner.

"Keep cool," responded Joey in mocking tones.

"But Joey dear, won't you come out to-night? Now, don't be offended," put in one of the ladies.

"Oh, I'm not offended, but people sometimes ask such stupid questions, and they never give me anything."

"Why, what can you want?"

"Major Johnson used to bring me sugar plums."

"Sugar plums! surely such things are of no use to you?"

"Aren't they! you just try me?"

"But they are for little children."

"Well, ain't I a little child'en; I'm Joey, and Me, and I, put together. Oh, I can eat them, and enjoy them too; you ask Major Johnson, I sat on his knee once."

"Do try and materialise yourself; I should so much like to see you standing by my side."

"I did stand by your side when you were all round the table, and I carried the guitar about the room and made all those lights, and did all the other physical manifestations."

"Was that really you?"

"Yes, but you didn't see me because I wasn't dressed."

"Wasn't dressed! What do you mean?"

"I hadn't got a body on."

"Well, put on a body, and come out now, will you, dear?'

"I don't think I can this time; you see if the weather isn't nice it spoils my dress, but don't you forget next time to bring me some sugar plums, then I'll come out and kiss you. I like ladies, they are always good."

"How is your medium?"

"Oh he's all right—fast asleep and snoring in this sack thing, where you've put him, he *does* look funny."

"How is Asoka; is he here?"

"Yes, he's here, and getting his shiny girdle ready. Ah, you ought to have been with us the other night; it was grand, the power was so strong, and he looked like fire."

"I do hope we shall see him to-night, and then, Joey dear, I'll bring you some sweeties."

"We'll try, but you know you can't expect everything at once; you are sure to get what you want if you come again."

"Where did you live when on earth, Joey?"

"I was a little black slave boy; I used to live in a place where there were great big caves with 'stick-'em-tights' hanging from the roofs, and we used to have such games with them, but my master whipped me to death, and I died and came here."

"Poor thing; I shall be so pleased to see you."

"Yes, I know you will. I do like you, and I am going to try and do something special for you, because you are so good; look there, what do you think of that?"

And then we could see a form, seeming to stand on the top of the screen, and holding up the shining mirror, reaching nearly to the ceiling.

"Oh, thank you, Joey; that is beautiful."

"Wait a bit; I'll borrow Asoka's coat, if he will lend it. No, he says he dare not expose it to the air to-night. Never mind, I'll come next time, I must go now. Good-night, General;

good-night, piccaninny girl; good-night, Henri; and oh, good-night, you sweet lady, who *is* so beautiful; and good-night everybody, and God bless you all."

We had of late received a few invitations from the provinces, but we did not deem it prudent to leave London, until there came one from a lady living near to one of our largest manufacturing towns, and inquiring when it would be convenient for us to visit them, also the terms required?

This induced us to remove our quarters, and we soon left London for fresh and even more promising pastures.

The same day we arrived, we were informed that a large and influential company were to meet us for a séance in the evening, and that in the meantime we were to consider ourselves "at home." We passed a pleasant time until the company came, and then adjourned to the séance room.

The physical manifestations were not of a high order, but this was attributed to the light, which came in from one or two of the windows that had been very badly "darkened up." To secure the entire absence of light in this place would have almost necessitated changing the room, for the windows occupied nearly the whole space of one or two sides; seeing the uselessness of prolonging the first part, we soon prepared for the second, and as the sack test was used, precisely the same care was taken to thoroughly secure the medium as on previous occasions.

It was in my department to place the circle in proper order, and in accordance with their various dispositions, and although, on this occasion, I apprehended no danger from fractious or treacherous members, I was careful to remove temptation from the path of any of an unfriendly type. Thomson had frequently charged me to be watchful, and not allow any one to seize the form, as such an undesirable interference might seriously endanger his health, if not even his life. Instances were on record of a medium suffering extreme tortures by seizure, and I could never be too guarded.

I was intensely anxious for a successful materialisation. I hoped that our courteous and hospitable hostess would be rewarded for all the trouble she took to insure our comfort, and I had also learned that she had incurred some ill-deserved opprobrium for admitting her belief in Spiritualism.

It seemed, however, that we were doomed to disappointment, for a long time passed and nothing occurred.

"Can't you do something, Joey?" I implored.

"I am afraid not."

"I am so disappointed."

"Can't help it," he answered curtly.

"What is the reason?"

"There are several reasons. The medium is tired with his long journey. And there is the spirit of a woman here who so much wanted to come, and we let her try, but she has not only failed, but has used up all the power."

"Who is the spirit?"

"She says her husband is present, and that she has only been in the spirit world for a short time."

"It must be my wife," said the gardener, "whom the lady had, at his earnest request, allowed to sit with us."

"Yes, yes! and she gives you her love, and she says, 'Tell him I am so happy, and would so much like to come.' She is standing by your side now."

"We are very sorry because we cannot see you, but I suppose it can't be helped," said the hostess.

"I am sorry too," replied Joey, "but as we are going to stay in the neighbourhood for some time, you will have further opportunities of seeing us; and then you can also improve the conditions, which are not favourable for our manifestations. Good-night all, and God bless you."

This failure was a terrible blow to me, yea, so keenly did I feel it, that I am not certain if a portion of that mortification does not still cling to me; and yet somehow it increased my faith in Thomson's mediumship, for I argued, "if this were trickery it is strange, on such an occasion when a success would have materially benefited us, that he should not have given them their desires; and at many previous séances he had been secured with far greater stringency, and yet a success had been registered."

But the failure most surely robbed me of all enjoyment in the pleasant company and surroundings, when we retired to finish the evening with music and other diversions in the drawing-room; and I was not sorry when everybody had departed, and the candles coming signalled bed-time.

The morning broke bright and beautiful, and we quickly got up and went out into the grounds to enjoy the crisp, fresh air, and the early sparkling sunshine, so different from the terrible fogs which we had just left behind us.

At breakfast-time Thomson proposed a séance all to ourselves, and as there were only about half-a-dozen including everybody, perhaps the diversity of the antagonistic aura would be easily overcome by the superior and concentrated power of the spirits, who could control and direct it at their will and pleasure, although there was no cause for fear on the present occasion, as all were thoroughly friendly.

It may be imagined the proposal met with no opposition, and we soon afterwards adjourned to a smaller and more appropriate séance room than that of the previous evening, and we tried our hardest to secure the most favourable conditions for a success.

"Good-morning, all. We shall be able to materialise ourselves, and come out this time," came the welcome tidings from the cabinet, when we had been sitting for a few minutes.

"Good-morning, Joey, dear, we shall be delighted to see you."

"Well, I don't know that I shall materialise myself; because Asoka wants to come, and there won't be enough power for two, I'm afraid."

"Is your medium quite rested this morning?" asked our ever solicitous hostess.

"Oh, yes. Never again make a medium sit the same day he travels."

"Why?"

"Because he is fatigued, and we can't collect the power."

"Good-morning, friends! All hail, all hail!" at this moment broke in the deep voice of Asoka.

"Good-morning, Asoka. We are pleased to give you our best welcome," we returned, and immediately, there appeared the figure of the bright and shining Asoka. He stayed but for a few minutes, and then returned to his cabinet, when he again spoke.

"Many thanks. I come from the splendours of the summer land, to tell you of its joys. I too have passed through the bitter tribulations of life's heaviest burdens; but its fiercest trials are as nothing in comparison to the very smallest of our pleasures, which more than compensates for everything."

"We were terribly disappointed last night, because we were not permitted to see you."

"Yes; but in a strange circle sometimes we fail to materialise; however, as we intend to work here for a time we may meet again."

And immediately afterwards he again stood before us, waving his bright girdle, which he allowed us to handle, though not permitting it to go out of his possession, but the mirror he gave up to us, holding me responsible for its safe return.

The conversation and the appearance, as may probably be understood, were not simultaneous, because the power was not sufficient to allow him to speak except from behind the screen; but both he and Joey kept up an interesting dialogue, the contrast between Asoka's heavy voice and Joey's small broken tongue being rather curious, Asoka uttering philosophical teachings, and Joey firing off sharp repartee, thus forming a lively and beguiling entertainment; and we were rather surprised when Joey informed us that their time was expired, and go they must. The regretful farewells were exchanged, and the séance came to an end.

The same morning we left that place, to go to the large

town within a short distance, in order to seek out the spiritualists, and arrange for a lengthened sojourn.

The journey was not long, and we sat quite alone in the compartment of the train, when Thomson began to speak of the exposure of a lady medium, which had lately occurred in London. It appears that two gentlemen had been invited to sit in the company with her, and their suspicions being aroused, when the form came out they seized it, and found it to be none other than the medium herself.

The *exposé* they had published to the world by letters written to the London daily papers, which had been reprinted in almost every journal of note in the kingdom.

"It is a very unfortunate affair for the cause, and will injure the medium very much," I remarked.

"Not a bit of it, she will be looked upon as a martyr, and her fame will increase through this immense advertisement. You note my words; the spiritualists will rush to her assistance with every mark of sympathy, and they will say that those two men broke the conditions, or that they attracted with them evil spirits, which controlled her, and brought her out while in a mesmeric sleep, or a thousand other excuses. She won't suffer, you see if she does."

"If her appearance was due to the promiscuous introduction of strangers, greater care should be shown, and if she is intentionally guilty, then the sooner such mediums are exposed the better will it be for all concerned."

"What nonsense you talk; in that case every medium would be shut up forthwith."

"What do you mean?" I exclaimed in astonishment.

"I'll tell you something now which I intended to tell you some time since. Every medium must help out occasionally!"

"The question is, how far is that 'helping out' carried?"

"About one séance in four is genuine."

"Was that séance with my friend (the atheist) genuine?"

"Yes, that was all right."

"Were those face wax-moulds of the two spirits all right?"

"Yes."

"H'm, about one in four you say? Which was the last genuine séance?"

"The one we gave this morning."

"Could you have got out of that sack last night?"

"I could have done so, but I didn't choose; I expected the spirits, and they didn't come, so we had a failure, which you will find will do us good."

"I am very glad to hear this revelation."

"I shouldn't tell you anything, only I have thought several times of late that you suspected something, and young Lou used to say, "Depend upon it, he knows more than you think," and I expect that that is the reason why you have been so silent of late."

"I did suspect something certainly ever since the time I found that lock undone at the hall."

"Oh, well, the first of those public meetings was really genuine, but at the second, when I found the spirits didn't come, I was compelled to act, for all that, a medium must be prepared; occasionally it happens that the spirits don't come near for eight, and even ten séances; and who do you think would support a medium with whom sometimes nothing happened for so long a time? Why, nobody would believe in him, and he wouldn't be able to live."

"Do the principal leaders of Spiritualism know of this?"

"Of course they do, but those who have no pecuniary interest in the movement are ashamed to withdraw from a position they took up when they were more unsophisticated. But the majority of those who make a living out of it will naturally stand by the mediums through thick and thin."

"I cannot think that of the editor of the *Magazine*."

"Very well then, I ask you what could be clearer than that *exposé* in Belgium with Morton? And yet look how he stood by the medium."

"In that case I thought he was justified."

"Bosh!"

"Thank you."

"Well, I hate to hear people talk such nonsense; that was a case clear as daylight; seven or eight well known gentlemen of repute, on the spot, sign their names to a statement setting forth what actually occurred; and here is a man two or three hundred miles away, who practically calls them liars! I don't blame him, of course, for sticking up for the medium."

"Then do you think in this last case (of the lady medium) she is really guilty?"

"I don't think anything about it."

"You mean that you *know?*"

"Yes, and I also *know* something else; that she was a great fool for not having somebody with her to prevent a seizure. This case is even clearer than was Morton's, and the men who seized her are in too high a position to be called liars by anybody."

"At that second public meeting of ours at the hall, if anybody had seized the form, they would have seized you?"

"Yes."

"But at the first?"

"They would have seized the spirit."

"How was it that the appearance in both instances was precisely the same?"

"I suppose you mean those bright things; they were prepared by me, under the direction of my guides, and when they can't materialise any light they use these, and if they can't come and use them or any, I must. But you can always tell when the spirits themselves are present; there is sure to be something to betray the difference, like that unfastened lock at the second meeting, for instance; and that is why it is safer for two to work together, for then one can cover up the deficiencies of the other; if you had not then been sensible and sharp I must have been exposed."

Revelations.

"Have you those illuminated things with you?"

"Yes, here they are;" and Thomson pulled from his pocket the long girdle and the mirror, which he handed over to me. I found that the sudden disappearance of the latter, which I had often noticed at séances, was due to the fact that only one side was illuminated, consequently either side could be shown at will.

"Of what stuff are these made?" I inquired.

"The spirits told me when and how I could get and use it. Very few people know anything about it at present; it is a light absorbent, and will emit the light just as long in the dark as it has been exposed to light."

I was certainly astonished, but not extravagantly so. I had for some time been suspecting something wrong; indeed it was impossible when always sitting with the same medium not to do so. It is true this caused me many an anxious moment, and induced that moody silence referred to by Thomson, but I had fought against my suspicions, until they were confirmed by an authority I could not question.

That same night after completing our arrangements in the town, we found it necessary to make a journey by rail, and through some unfortunate oversight the driver of another train, not observing the warning signals, dashed almost at full speed into the front part of ours, which was standing across a line of metals ready to start. Not much damage, I am glad to say, was done, except to the rolling stock, which suffered considerably, while one or two of the passengers met with slight contusions, and the rest with a good shaking.

The accident, however, completely shunted the train of thought which rather oppressed my mind, and Thomson too assisted in the diversion, being now doubly amiable and amusing. But when again left to myself that night, the train returned with increased energy. Here there was an end to my high aspirations, for though a part were true, yet the other part robbed it of all its lustre. But the more I considered the matter, paradoxical as it may seem, the more was I pleased at the knowledge I had just gained. Many times I had been unfavourably impressed with the surprising levity displayed by the spirits; although I found that every medium had his Peter, Frankie, or Irresistible to perform the lighter parts of the séances, also to bring out in stronger relief the action of the higher spirits when they condescended to appear. I had often found, too, that their statements did not agree, amounting sometimes to positive untruths, the latter occasionally causing me to think that I had enleagued myself with the powers of evil, for such an undesirable economy, as regards truth, had shocked me, and I could not understand that such mendacity could emanate from Heaven—that is, the higher spheres—but now, the spirits, at any rate were exonerated from that charge, and a complete justification was afforded by their intermittent visits.

Had I followed the strict line of duty, I should at all hazards have freed myself immediately from such a connection; but perhaps a compensation is found in the fact that if I had, these communications would never have been made, or if made, would have been of no practical value as a complete and truthful testimony.

At last, worn out with anxiety regarding my future, I fell asleep, and the curtain of night descended upon the second act of this sad but curious drama.

CHAPTER IX.

IN THE COUNTRY.

THE following morning we were up betimes, and soon began to prepare our plans for an extensive campaign. I readily entered into the work, for I was now as eager to prosecute the subject further as the most enthusiastic beginner. I was anxious to compare the genuine when it came with the counterfeit, and wished to be fully convinced by ocular demonstration, now that I was admitted behind the scenes, for I found that after all, the results of my first investigation were not so conclusive as I had imagined, and that the groundwork of my new faith was in some respects unstable, and required a better foundation. I had relinquished the faith of my early training, and I clung with desperate energy to the new love, which, if that too were wrecked, would leave me on the cold and barren shores of a wretched materialism. Like an ocean traveller, who had exchanged from one bark to another, I felt an earnest solicitude for its competency to perform all that for which it was advertised, and I agreed to assist the manifestations, if the power were weak, or if the spirits failed to appear. But it was understood that we should in every case wait a few minutes, and pray for their arrival before doing anything ourselves.

We called upon the various leading spiritualists in the town, to inform them of our intention to place our services at their disposal. They seemed very pleased at the prospect of having a medium of such reputation as Thomson in the vicinity, and they willingly promised their support.

The conversation with those we had visited turned upon the exposure of the lady medium referred to in the preceding chapter, and they one and all condemned the action of the gentlemen who had seized the form, as well as the conduct of the officials of the association for admitting them. They expressed their belief that the medium had been subjected to unfavourable conditions, induced by a promiscuous attendance, and that her innocence was beyond a doubt thereby clearly established.

One gentleman, a Mr Gordon, upon whom we called during that day, agreed to come, but considered it almost useless to trouble for merely one séance, for the fresh sitters not being *en rapport* with the medium would retard the operation of the spirits, as witness the first séance we had given in the town, and at which he had been present. He therefore stipulated for half a dozen for himself and family, and for the next six days we were to hold ourselves entirely at his disposal; we were not, during that time, to sit with anybody else, because of Mr Gordon's fear that two sittings per day would exhaust the power, and one of them must suffer considerably.

We assured him of our intention not to give other séances, but to consider ourselves bound by the agreement with him; but sitters propose and mediums dispose.

"Didn't I tell you that all the spiritualists would stand by that medium? Of course the exposure won't hurt her," said Thomson to me, when we were preparing for the arrival of Mr Gordon and his family.

"I don't know that," I replied. "If she came here now, I question if they wouldn't look askance at her, spite of all their faith in her honesty."

"Oh dear, no! they believe that they are right. If every medium were to admit that they had been cheating all the time, the spiritualists wouldn't take their word, but would immediately declare that they were under the temporary control of evil spirits."

"I hope we shall have a good séance with Mr Gordon; he'll most likely have more than six in that case."

"You may depend he will; leave that to me, Joey generally manages to keep such people as long as he likes."

"He may not be satisfied, and perhaps won't see the force of paying the fees unless he gets the genuine."

"Don't you trouble about that," advised Thomson. "£50 or even £100 is nothing to such a man. He may not have the real séance until the sixth, and that will cause him to have six more. I have sometimes gone on for a long while without the spirits, and then, just when I have been on the point of being caught out, up they come and bring off a rattling séance, which drives everybody nearly crazy, and they send off long accounts to the papers, and talk of it to all the world, and then everybody else wants to see the same. By the way, you will have to be introduced as a medium now; otherwise people won't understand why you are with me."

"But they know I am not a medium."

"That doesn't matter; you are developing with me. You may be physical, healing, trance, or anything you like."

"How are you going to manage with Mr Gordon?"

"You must have these things in your pockets; they may want to search me, and they won't think of you."

"Why?"

"Because you look so awfully innocent."

"How splendidly they shine," I exclaimed, when the illuminated articles were given to me; they were of a pale bluish tint in the daylight, but in the dark they shone beautifully white.

"Yes. I put them up on the curtains of my window this morning, so they have been in the sun all day. Now don't you get nervous to-night; when I want the things I will give you three taps on the knee. You must arrange the circle so that you sit at the end nearest to me; but if you can't hand them over quite safely keep them back. Always better have a failure than an *exposé;* bear that in mind."

"What few things you have!"

"Yes. A medium should never have more than he can comfortably carry in his pockets, and never, by any chance, leave anything in his trunks when travelling; that is where

Morton was foolish. When any little row occurs at a séance amongst people that you don't know much about, the first thing they do is to go to the hotel and search your boxes."

"But how did you manage when you were searched?"

"I always manage somehow; it all depends on circumstances. If I have reason to fear a search, I can easily cram these few things in the back of a sofa on which I may be sitting before the seance begins, and then when I want to use them I can come out of the cabinet in the dark and get them."

"But if the spirits come and there is no need for them?"

"Then I watch my opportunity and get them when I can. I remember once, when I went to give a séance in Paris, I tucked the roll of drapery under the mattress of a sofa, and that night the spirits came and I had no need for them: but I'll be hanged if I didn't forget all about them after the sitting."

"What should you have done if anybody else had found them?" I enquired.

"I should have disowned them, of course; but in this case I made a visit the next morning, and was ushered into the same room in which the séance had been held, and while waiting for the mistress of the house, I got back my things. That's where young Lou was so handy; she always places them under her petticoats and gives them up when required."

Soon afterwards Mr Gordon and his family arrived, and we sat down, first, for the physical manifestations, but nothing particularly worthy of note occurred, and we broke up that circle and prepared for the materialisations. Just before we commenced, Thomson asked if they would like to search him; upon which Mr Gordon and one of his sons went upstairs with him for that purpose, but soon afterwards returned and declared themselves perfectly satisfied. Thomson then went behind the screen, no tests of any kind being used, and we sat down outside and blew out the lights.

According to our agreement we waited for several minutes for the spirits to come; but although I prayed from the very depths of my heart, they came not, and then I received the preconcerted signal and knew that I must act. Slowly and cautiously I drew out the drapery from my pockets and held it in the direction of the cabinet; all the time my limbs shook with a great fear, and I dreaded every moment to hear my nearest neighbour in the circle ask what I was doing. If I had been spoken to I dared not have answered, for I am confident my voice would have betrayed the intense excitement under which I laboured.

But my fears magnified the danger; the medium was on guard, and quickly snatched the roll from my shaking hand.

At the same time Joey and Asoka maintained an alternate fire of wit and wisdom, occasionally interrupted by a deep groan or sigh from the medium.

I felt a little relieved when I had safely accomplished the first part of my duty; and when Joey asked in a lively manner how I was and why I was so silent, I was enabled to answer with tolerable composure that I was quite well, and did not wish to take up any time with my questions then, especially when I could see and talk to him every day.

. We were then requested to sing, and during the course of that, the gorgeous form of Asoka appeared before us. Silent and motionless he stood for a few brief moments, and with a solemn motion of his right hand he slowly retreated behind the screen.

Joey then shouted his command for a renewal of the interrupted singing, and quickly I received back the roll from Thomson, and soon we were informed that nothing more could be done for the present, but that to-morrow the spirits thought that they would be thoroughly in accord with the circle, so that grander things might confidently be expected, and the usual farewells having been exchanged, the séance came to an end.

When our visitors had taken their departure, Thomson said, "Well, you managed splendidly; you are the coolest fellow I ever saw."

"But why did you not retain the things?"

"Because it was just possible they might have wanted to search me again, and it would look bad to refuse.' Oh, no; you be guided by me, and all will be right."

"Suppose you lost your presence of mind?" I suggested.

"I never suppose impossibilities."

"But if you made a mistake," I persisted.

"That's another thing. Once when in Paris I got so far from my cabinet, that somehow I got 'mixed,' and could not for the life of me remember which was my corner. But I stood silent, and nobody saw me, because I hadn't those bright things on me, and I put my hand on the head of one of the sitters. Of course he called out, and, of course, I soon touched another, and kept on touching, until I touched somebody, whose voice I recollected, and from him I easily fixed the position of my cabinet."

"That was an awful dilemma."

"Even that was nothing to what happened to me once. I was engaged to give a séance to some good old spiritualists, and I used phosphoric oil, and by some unlucky mischance I spilt a little, only a little, but that was enough; it set fire to the drapery, and everything was soon in a blaze!"

"Merciful powers! what did you do?"

"I just kept quiet and risked being burned; naturally the people soon rushed in, and found me—in a trance!"

"Surely you didn't sleep at such a time?"

"Didn't I? What else could I do?"

"Weren't you burned?"

"No; it was all over in a moment, and the report got about that I could stand fire, and it brought me a lot of séances. They said the spirits protected me, and of course I didn't take the trouble to contradict the statement. But I never again used phosphorus, it is too dangerous. Why, I know of a case where a medium using the infernal stuff got on fire, and when the people went to his assistance one man was so scorched that he died from the effects!"

"Indeed; and what did they do to the medium?"

"He didn't give them a chance to do anything; he went off without stopping to say 'good-bye.'"

"I never heard of the case."

"Perhaps not; but you know the medium," and Thomson gave me the name, and some few months afterwards I heard the story repeated by two other spiritualists.

A day or two afterwards we received a visit from a Mr Ashton, who wished to avail himself of our services. He said he wished to have a séance at his own house with a small party of his friends, one of whom was a diplomatist, and a terrible sceptic, and it remained for us to convince him of the truth of Spiritualism. The following evening at 7.30 was the time fixed, and afterwards he said he wished to have a series of séances for himself and a lady friend.

"Now, to-night, when the Gordons come we must have a failure, unless the spirits themselves come," said Thomson when our visitor had departed.

"What do you mean?"

"I mean that I shall do nothing. It does good to have an occasional failure. Human nature can always be tickled by liberal promises. If we give everything straight off, nobody would come again."

"I believe you are right."

"Oh, I haven't had more than ten years among the spiritualists for nothing. I can read people just as easily as I can walk about a room in the dark, and the best of it is, they always set me down as an innocent. Now I'll wager anything, I can make the Gordons come fifty times if I wish."

"And make them pay every time?"

"Pooh. I tell you that money is nothing. Only make

people believe they are special favourites of the spirits, and they never think of such a thing."

Spiritualism behind the scenes was revealing itself to me in a far different light from that which it formerly presented, and I kept silent, and observed closely every new phase as it passed in array before my eyes. Exactly as Thomson had enjoined, we remained quiescent when the Gordons came for their séance. Nothing occurred beyond Joey informing us from the cabinet that the medium was not well, and that we must have a musical box, as it was so difficult to keep the circle singing, and without music of some kind they could not proceed; and then Joey suddenly said to our lady visitor Mrs Gordon—

"Oh, you *is* so pretty. I do like you, and I shall be so sorry when you don't come no more."

"But it is no encouragement for me to come unless you let me see what kind of a boy you are."

"I'll come, soon as ever I get my dress made. We are getting up some grand manifestations for you, and it is of no use to spoil everything by giving you common manifestations; you be patient, and you'll get a reward. I must go now; good-night. Wake up my medium."

When they were gone Thomson said—

"Now you see how easily I can manage them. To-morrow afternoon, when they come again, we will give them a little, but only enough to make them wish for more."

"Won't they soon get disgusted?"

"Oh no, we can't keep them for a long time, as we have to go to Mr Ashton's afterwards, so we must hurry it over."

"Do you know when a genuine séance may be expected?"

"Sometimes I do, but not always."

"How can you tell?"

"Oh, I feel fidgetty and cold for days sometimes just before they come."

"Have you felt any of those symptoms of late?"

"Yes, a little; I expect the genuine will come one day next week, and one of these two parties will get it; I don't know which, but it lies between them."

"I hope the Gordons at any rate will get a good one, for they are thoroughly good people."

"They will get one right enough; but when the spirits do come, you must remain perfectly quiet."

"How shall I know?"

"Don't ask such a question; you don't suppose that all this joking and tomfoolery is carried on when it is genuine? When they are present, they do a hundred things that no medium could do, even if he were at liberty, and had a hundred confederates."

"Do you really think that darkness is an absolute necessity for the spirits?"

"Certainly not; they can come as easily in the light as in the dark."

"Why do mediums always demand such complete darkness, then?"

"Don't you see that as the spirits can't be depended upon, there must be some sort of cover ready to hide the tricks. People bother their brains to invent tests, which after all are sheer nonsense."

"Nonsense!"

"Ay, nonsense; don't you think it just possible that with my ten years' experience I can outwit any conceited booby who brings his tests?"

"But if you can't outwit him?"

"I do outwit him; if his tests are too severe, I do nothing, and the blame of failure is cast on him, and if I succeed he is laughed at. If the mediums were always compelled to sit in the light, you would soon see a different order of things."

"How about trance mediums?"

"If people like to believe in the twaddle that those fellows talk, they have only themselves to blame."

"Then you don't believe in trance speaking?"

"Not all."

"What do you intend to give to Mr Ashton and his friends to-morrow?"

"It all depends on circumstances; but as there is to be a sceptic present, he will most likely want a test; so I must now give you a few lessons so that we may be prepared."

"What lesson do I want?"

"Oh, you don't know anything yet; but I must say, you are an apt pupil, and a plucky one too. I tell you I think it will be very odd if two such brains can't astonish the natives a trifle."

Thomson gave me a few lessons, such as a code of signals, by which we might constantly communicate with each other without attracting attention. The code was worked by conversing with the spirit, in which all the circle would join, but there were secret words which would be perfectly unintelligible to any one but ourselves. He also taught me a few little unimportant tricks, which were merely the A B C of the craft.

CHAPTER X.

DEVELOPING.

"NOW I must give you another lesson," said Thomson a few hours before the Gordons came the next day. "Sit down," he continued, "and take hold of my hands; shut your eyes, and fancy yourself at a genuine séance."

I sat down opposite to him and obeyed his directions, but I was keenly alive to every movement, resolving if possible to find out the method myself.

He now began to start and shudder, just as at a séance; and in less time than it takes me to write this, he was touching me on the head and shoulders in precisely the same way as do spirits in the circles. He next told me to open my eyes, which when I did, I found he had one hand quite free.

I thought that if I could be deceived, who was on guard, there was no room for wonder that those unacquainted with the secret should be so easily outwitted.

"Now this may appear a difficult matter to you, until I have shown you the way," said Thomson. "Of course it could not be done in the light; darkness is the key to the whole mystery."

"But how on earth did you free your hands?"

"Take hold again, and this time keep your eyes open. Now you notice, our hands are like they are at a séance, a little apart; but when I begin to have these starts, which the sitters think is the spirit controlling me, I gradually draw up my hands until they are close together, and then when everybody is singing I just snatch one of my fingers away, and thrust in a finger of the other hand, and the sitters on either side hold a finger of the same hand, and with the disengaged hand I can do what I want, and then replace it afterwards."

"That seems simple enough."

"Not so simple as you imagine, and you must not attempt it until you have had plenty of practice with me, or you will bungle it altogether. That is only one way of doing it; there are others, which I will teach you when you have mastered this. And then you will find that it sometimes depends upon chance what you must do. Many an accident at a séance has enabled me to do something which otherwise I never should have thought of; so you must be alive to everything."

"Is this the way you do with our present visitors?" I asked.

"Once or twice, but it is very difficult to shift the hands with such a small company and such a large table, as the hands are so far apart. You must be very cautious, and bear in mind what I told you the other day. Always better have a failure than an *exposé.*"

"By the way, how did you manage with that copper-wiring round the table?"

"I had false shirt sleeves, and when I was wired up like the rest I could easily draw out my arms when the lights were turned out."

"Are we to have the usual manifestations when the Gordons come this afternoon?"

"We shall see; you must have the things in your pockets in case they want to search me."

"Will you do anything at the table?"

"Do you know why I have cut the bottom out of the tambourine?"

"No," I answered. I had thought it strange at the time, and almost began to think my partner had a mania for mischief, when I saw him deliberately cut out the parchment leaving only the ring.

"Well, with this ring on the table, which I can throw over my head with my teeth, I can shuffle the guitar into it, and then with a pencil in my mouth strike the strings, and also wave the instrument about; at the same time, of course, my hands are fast held."

The Guitar.

"That's very clever; but will you not give them Asoka from the cabinet?"

"Yes, but we must hurry it over, as we have to go to Mr Ashton's directly afterwards, and we shall have none too much time."

Towards the evening Mr Gordon and his family arrived, and one of them suggested that as nothing had been obtained at the table the last time, we should begin with the materialisations without further ceremony. But as this did not meet the views of Thomson he negatived the proposal, and said that one séance was no rule for another, and we had better keep to the usual custom for fear of disturbing the aura.

The company on this occasion did not think it necessary to search the medium, and we soon sat down to the table.

"Oh, thank you, dear spirits, that is very beautiful!" exclaimed one of the circle, when, after the lapse of a few minutes, the guitar strings were struck, while the instrument itself was raised up and moved gently to and fro, apparently, over our heads.

"Can you touch me with it?" asked one of the sitters. "Oh, thank you," he quickly added, when the guitar had gently tapped him on the head; and away again started the instrument, and then in a short time was thrown with a crash upon the table.

We were not long in rearranging ourselves for the second part, and when sitting before the cabinet, in the dark, I received the signal. I was enabled with a comparative absence of fear to hand out the drapery, which was quickly seized by the medium.

"Please keep the music going. What is the matter?" said Joey.

"Something is wrong with the box," I answered; I held that on my knees for the better convenience of attending to it.

"You don't understand how to manage it. I'll send out one of the spirits to put it right. You won't see him, because he is not thoroughly materialised; but he has power enough to do that little job."

And then came out a hand and quickly removed the obstruction, when the usual lively sounds were again poured forth.

"Is Asoka coming out to-day?"

"Yes," answered Joey, "and he is going to spare enough power for Lily to materialise. I don't know if they will succeed; but if not now, they will another time."

This intelligence was thankfully received, and after a little more conversation Asoka stood before us in his celestial looking garments, and observing the customary silence he waved his draped hand, bowed, and disappeared.

"Is Lily coming now?" enquired we spiritually-thirsty mortals.

"I am so sorry," said Joey, mournfully.

"What is the matter, Joey?"

"Asoka's gone and used up all the what-ye-call-it, and poor Lily hasn't enough to make a dress, so she can't come out to-day."

"Never mind, Joey, perhaps she will succeed another time."

"Oh, but I should so like to please you, dear Mrs Gordon, because you's so good, and kind, and so lovely; but I will manage it another time. Good-bye all, and God bless you."

When we were again alone we prepared for the visit to Mr Ashton. The drapery was rolled up and I put it in my coat-tail pockets, in order that Thomson could get at it in case the circle insisted upon holding my hands during the materialisations. We took the guitar, the tambourine ring, and as a suspicious person was to be present, we resolved to be prepared with a test of our own rather than have a new one suddenly sprung upon us. To that end we carried the sack, and although I knew not the mode of his escape as yet, I was to be informed on that point at the first opportunity.

A small party of four met us when we arrived, including Mr Ashton himself, two rather elderly ladies, and the sceptical gentleman, who was in some way connected with diplomacy. He acknowledged us in the most courteous manner possible; indeed I could not imagine so noble-looking a man being anything else but gentle and courteous. He told us in the course of a little conversation that he had sat in several circles, and with most of the noted mediums; but that he had never seen anything of sufficient importance to forcibly or favourably impress him. In short, the great majority of manifestations which he had ever witnessed, he could easily reproduce himself. He considered all mediums, from Slade and his *confrères* in America, to Morton and his fellows in Europe, to be absclute humbugs; of course present company not included.

The room in which the séance was to be held was a very large one, with many big old-fashioned windows, which were not, as we found afterwards, very carefully shaded. Nothing less than unadulterated darkness would evoke the guides of Thomson.

We first sat for the physical manifestations, but as nothing occurred, I was told to strike a light, and when I did we found to our surprise that the spirits had been silently working for us. A chair stood on the table looking as innocent as possible, and the tambourine ring had been hung on the arm of Mr Ashton, who, of course declared that he had faithfully maintained the circle. We looked at the chair, but nobody seemed to understand the mode of its elevation; and we canvassed the possibility of matter passing through matter as in the case of the ring, but nobody could understand that either, so we believers promptly credited the spirits with the work.

After settling those points to our satisfaction, we gave our serious attention to the next part of the meeting. Thomson inquired if they wished for tests. Mr Ashton professed himself quite content to trust to the honour of the mediums, but upon second thought he said that as there were unbelievers present, it might be advisable to employ them. Thomson then brought forward the bag, which he said was a test that had met with universal approval, and if they wished, he would voluntarily submit to be tied and sealed in it; at the same time, he considered it degrading to give tests, as it implied an intention to deceive on the part of the medium. Very carefully and very completely was the tying and sealing performed, and we assisted the medium to a chair behind the screen, and we went and sat ourselves down about ten feet distant outside.

The little roll of drapery had sorely oppressed me; I was anxious to let Thomson have it, but saw not the least chance of so doing; he had not been searched, probably because everybody had forgotten to propose such a course.

I could not imagine how he was to get it, because he could not come and take it from my pockets, as the room was not chemically dark, and a figure stealing behind me would surely have been observed; neither could I myself hand it over; and I had made up my mind for a failure, when the inexhaustible fertility of Thomson successfully declared itself. The cabinet was fixed in a recess lighted by a large window, which had been so carelessly darkened, that the light from outside freely found an entrance; this discreditable state of things had not been noticed at the first part, because the table sitting had taken place at the other end of the vast apartment. Thomson had been only a short time in the cabinet, when his practised eye discovered the enemy, and he quickly turned it to a useful account. He called out that there was too much light, which we had better see to before beginning, in order to avoid a failure.

Mr Ashton himself went to settle the mischief, but being unsuccessful he requested my assistance. This was the opportunity! Thomson gave me a signal which I easily understood; and when I had finished with the curtains, in walking close to the sack I slipped the roll in the top at the neck, and then resumed my position in the circle, trying to look as innocent as possible.

Even then I had some doubts as to the success of the sitting, for the sceptical gentleman, who knew a great deal about these things, had so securely fastened everything that it seemed impossible to overcome the obstacles; and that roll of drapery, too, began again to exercise my mind, for if he couldn't really get loose it would be discovered; however, these fears were perfectly childish.

" Good evening; glad to see you all," shouted the gleeful Joey.

" Are any of the spirit friends coming out to-night, Joey?" we inquired.

"Yes, if you are good, Asoka will come; but will you all faithfully observe the conditions?"

"Yes," answered everybody present.

" Well then, he will come," replied Joey, and immediately after imparting this information, we saw Asoka, who silently moved a few feet in our direction, and taking off his girdle flung it out, and allowed the Sceptic to handle it. What the compound was which could emit so brilliant a light in the dark, and yet betray nothing of its origin, by smell or any of the senses, he could not imagine. That it was a spirit light he would not admit, although he was solemnly assured that such was the case.

After standing before us for a short time, the form withdrew, and then came out again, and finally it retired for the evening, and Joey told us that if we would be patient a little longer, Cissy would try and materialise.

We sat quietly listening to the music from the box for several minutes, until Joey again spoke, and informed us that they found it impossible that night, at any rate, to do anything else, and suggested the propriety of adjourning the meeting, when they would succeed at the next.

The Sceptic closely examined the sack, but could not find the least evidence of its having been touched, and then I had a sharp knife ready, and quickly cut loose the medium.

The members of the circle, with the exception of Mr Ashton, were interested, if not puzzled, but would not outwardly admit their belief in spirit agency.

"I should certainly like to see more of this," said the Sceptic.

" We shall be very pleased to afford you the opportunity," we returned.

" Thank you; when would it be convenient for you to give me a séance at my house?" he inquired.

" We shall be disengaged to-morrow night."

" Will you say the same time as this of to-night?"

"Yes, that will do very well for us," we answered, and having satisfactorily adjusted this, we soon afterwards left.

" Do you know what Mr Ashton wanted when he called me aside?" asked Thomson when we were going home.

" I haven't the remotest idea."

" He has made arrangements with me to have a series of séances, commencing the day after to-morrow, at eleven o'clock in the morning."

"Won't Mr Gordon's séances suffer?"

" Of course not; what right has he to lay an embargo on us? I wouldn't bind myself to any one person under 1000 a-year."

"I don't think it is right, though, to endanger his chance of getting a genuine séance," I declared.

"You keep easy and leave these people to me. Mr Ashton and his lady friend, Miss Willis, in the morning, and the Gordons in the afternoon, will be very nice."

"Yes, so long as it continues."

"Oh, I'll guarantee that Joey will keep them at it as long as he likes; if he can't, I'll set John King at them."

"This will give us plenty to do now."

"Not so much but that I mean to get hold of another party for a late séance; two séances a day is good work but three is better."

"Why are you so anxious for me to cut loose the tapes so quickly, and always blaming me for being slow?"

"Never mind that now, I'll tell you everything some other time, and then you will understand why."

"You have told these people that I am a good medium."

"Yes, I have told them that you throw off a deal of power, and that you are a splendid physical and healing medium."

"I am afraid they will find out the contrary."

"Are you going to tell them?"

"No, of course not."

"Don't trouble about it, then. I told them that you are developing as a materialising medium too!"

"You did?"

"Yes, why not? You will soon be as good as any of us if you keep sitting with me."

"But I am afraid I shall never get the genuine."

"That will come too, if you stick to it, and are patient. You keep at it like I have for ten years, and you will get enough genuine."

"I sincerely hope so," I fervently replied.

"Then don't hope any longer!"

"What do you mean?"

"It comes of itself; but let us not waste any more time talking about this now, we have all the evening before us, which will enable us to prepare for to-morrow."

CHAPTER XI.

STRANGE MANIFESTATIONS.

THE two parties who had engaged our services were not our only clients; we had been busy corresponding with others, one of whom, a Mr Wilson, strongly urged upon us the necessity of gaining the goodwill of the press. He informed us that he was acquainted with several of the most influential journalists in the town, and if we would give a free séance at his house, and allow him to issue free invitations to them, he was sure that if they became convinced we should be trumpeted forth from the columns of their chief journals.

We consented to the proposal, only stipulating that not more than half a dozen should be invited,—which, with his own family, would form a compact little assembly.

In consequence of this new engagement, we had three séances for the next day—one in the afternoon to the Gordons, one in the evening to the Sceptic, and the other late at night at Mr Wilson's to meet the press. Punctuality was one of the virtues of Mr Gordon, and true to his time he came up the following evening, but the manifestations were not of a striking nature, the power was still developing, and the spirits told them of their anxiety to give abundant satisfaction. Asoka came out with his usual brilliant apparel, waved his flowing drapery over our heads, and then disappeared. Joey gave us to understand that the manifestations would soon assume a startling character, and until the power was ripe, it had better be kept in reserve.

" Now, we must manage to bamboozle this Sceptic of Mr Ashton's this evening," said Thomson, when the Gordons had taken their departure, and we were preparing for the second sitting.

"What do you mean to do?"

"I can hardly tell yet, because he is very 'cute, and it requires great care. We must be guided by circumstances. But don't you attempt to do anything; for the present you must leave everything to me, I shall hit upon something."

"You will take the sack?"

"Oh yes, we must if possible always have our own test; although, if he proposes anything else, we must not refuse to submit, whatever it is."

Shortly afterwards we started taking our usual things, and we managed to arrive at 7, instead of 7.30, in order to give ourselves more time for the last meeting, although Thomson's invariable rule was to be very late. One of his reasons was that such a course gave less time to the curious to suggest searching or applying new-fangled tests. But if anybody did propose any particular test, Thomson always submitted with sublime indifference. If he could surmount it easily, the manifestations were never interrupted; but if he thought detection would follow, then he contented himself with going into a trance, from which I had to restore him.

The fees were not affected by the quality of the séance.

The sitting with the Sceptic could not be considered a brilliant affair, neither was it a failure. At the first part Thomson fixed himself between the Sceptic and a lady, whilst I was placed opposite between Mr Ashton and the other lady. They had succeeded this time in obtaining perfect darkness, and everything looked thoroughly propitious.

I was not surprised, therefore, when the guitar was suddenly lifted from the table, and swept over our heads with a loud strumming noise: falling upon the table with a terrific bang, which half startled us out of our wits, it remained there, and we waited in silence for something else.

The musical box was next seized with a rambling desire, and while still playing, apparently visited every part of the room; and then we were entertained with a series of bright flitting little spirit lights, darting about with weird and awe-inspiring effect. Invisible hands also began to touch and stroke us in a mysterious fashion. The circle was kept in unbroken style, for upon the question being put by Mr Ashton whether every hand was joined, the answer was a decided affirmative.

At the materialisation the sack was again requisitioned, and the appearances of the form and the voice were much about the same as on the previous evening; and at last having concluded with this party we quickly hurried off to the third meeting.

"I expect the power will be weak for this sitting," I remarked on our way thither.

"What matters if it is? Weak or strong we shall get nothing for it; and you now understand the risk is too great to give free or half-price séances; and those who pay nothing are mostly those who create disturbances."

"When are the spirits coming? They haven't been yet, and we have given more than four sittings."

"Don't worry about that; they'll come when it suits them, I suppose. Sometimes they do keep away for a length of time, and when they re-appear they stay for a good many sittings."

"You managed to free your hand from the Sceptic all right," I replied, turning the conversation, for he appeared irritated at the allusion to the spirits.

"Of course I did. When you want to make music sound clear and loud, or soft and muffled, you must open and shut the lid, and swing it about, but mind that the swaying of the body doesn't betray you."

"What were those flashing lights?"

"Only a match head; that also must be done neatly, or the smoke from the phosphorus will be seen. One time I used steel filings, but I haven't any now."

"You promised to tell me how you escaped from the sack."

"Well, I can't tell you now, but I will to-morrow. Have you got the drapery all right?"

"Yes, in my pockets."

"Mind and be careful, then, that nobody takes liberties with your pockets in the dark; this kind of people whom we are now going to see are likely to play any trick, so be alive," admonished my *confrère*, who used often to laugh at those who thought him not much better than a half-witted fellow; but I suspect he could buy and sell all those who so considered him, even in their presence, and before they would be aware of the transaction. Thomson always appeared smiling and simple, but at the same time he was swiftly and keenly observing all men and things around him.

At length we arrived at Mr Wilson's, and found that his ideas of half-a-dozen were not derived from orthodox arithmetic, but were sufficiently elastic to embrace about twenty eager and athletic fellows, with whom we were crowded into a little parlour, designed, apparently, with a view of but comfortably accommodating a young married couple with no encumbrance. But we did contrive to dovetail ourselves inside, making everybody feel as if he were incommoding everybody else.

That nothing would occur there, was clearly demonstrable to me; and as if to add a fresh weight of iniquity to his over-burdened shoulders, our delinquent host had completely neglected to provide darkness.

But we sat long without uttering a word of complaint, and looked at everybody eyeing his neighbour suspiciously, as if he held him directly responsible for the failure. Even the all-devouring enthusiasm of Mr Wilson could not bear this in silence, and at last he induced a gentleman to sing a pretty little song about the moonlight and the silent-flowing river. When it was finished and nobody else would or could sing, we broke up our beautifully designed circle—none but an artist was able to get us all seated—and the company separated with many expressions of regret and disappointment.

"I am very sorry," said Mr Wilson; "if those press

writers had been convinced they would have made your fortunes."

"If you had attended to our directions they would have been convinced," returned Thomson; "but twenty people in a small room like that, and with twenty different dispositions, not to speak of twenty hostile thoughts, which in a larger room can harmlessly dissipate themselves. Thought is material, and evil or antagonistic thought will always shut out my guides."

"I am very sorry," replied the culprit.

"Now, Mr Wilson, do you think you could make a ladder in a crowded little room like that?"

"Of course not."

"Then, as you require room in which to perform physical labour, so do spirits want room for their work."

"Just so. I see now I was wrong; there were too many. But," added he, regretfully, "they were representative men possessing large powers."

"I think you overrate the powers of these gentlemen," said Thomson, "for, admitting their willingness to help, they dare not say anything good about us in their papers for fear of popular prejudice, which you know scorns our noble cause. To tell you the truth, we care very little for the press—we came solely to please you; but as you did not give the proper conditions, you have nobody but yourself to blame."

"If you will come again I will do better next time; but why is darkness such an imperious necessity?"

"You know the photographer excludes certain rays from his developing room?"

"Yes; of course I know that."

"Very well, then, light has a decomposing effect upon the spirit aura just as it destroys a portrait before it is developed."

"But the photographer does not exclude every ray."

"No, he can do with yellow, and we can do with dark blue."

"Well, I shall know better now; but I am afraid those men are offended, and will attack you in their columns," said Mr Wilson.

"Never mind the press, Mr Wilson, let them attack us; they must do that in any case, and we are so used to it that we can laugh at such trivialities."

"Trivialities!" shouted our enthusiast, "why, they will make an awful noise about this failure."

"All the better; human nature always runs after a noise to see what it's all about; it will be a good advertisement. But don't let us talk any more about them; we are going to have a week of public meetings—will you come?"

"When is it?"

"We begin next Monday."

"All right, I'll come and do all I can to help you. I'll get your bills printed, and advertise you in a paper in which I have some influence, and do anything in fact," said our friend, who was nothing if not everything, but we gladly accepted his offers of assistance.

Although we had had a hard day's work, and it was getting late, it did not prevent us finishing the night at the theatre, and by the time we reached home we were thoroughly tired, and glad of the rest which should fit us for the arduous and dangerous work of the next day.

Before Mr Ashton came in the morning Thomson said—

"Now we must do something to astonish our friend Mr Ashton; he is a first-rate man, with plenty of money and high connections; he is worth all these newspaper writers put together."

"It would be very good, though, to gain them over, and we might give them a séance," I replied.

"I would not give a fig for their good-will, because they dare not do otherwise than sneer at us. Let us now arrange what we are to do with Mr Ashton; he comes at 11.30, so we haven't much time."

"You have told him I am a medium. He may ask me who are my guides; what shall I say?"

"Anything; better choose some name from the Bible. What do you say to Isaiah, or Daniel?"

"Don't be blasphemous!" I exclaimed, shocked at an audacity that considered nothing holy if it were saleable.

"You needn't fly out at that. Look at Miss Morel in London; you know she claims St John the Evangelist and the Archangel Gabriel as her guides."

"She is worse than an Infidel."

"I thought you had got rid of all your religious nonsense; but please yourself, only take a high-sounding name, and one that people don't know much about, or they'll be testing you."

"I know; if he does ask, I can say Asoka."

"Just as you please," returned Thomson unconcernedly.

"Mr Ashton brings a lady, doesn't he?"

"Yes, but that's all the better. This table is almost too big to free one's hands because we shall be so far apart; but we must do something to astonish Mr Ashton. I know what we'll do," added he reflectively; "we will make the table float up!"

"How can we do that with such a heavy table and our hands held fast?"

"Easy enough if you are sharp. We shall sit opposite to each other, and when I give the signal you put your knee under and keep up your side. You have got tolerably long legs, and I'll guarantee to have my side up; let's try," said Thomson, and we immediately sat down, one on each side, and began our practice.

I found it was possible to keep up my side, and Thomson, with his short neck, could kneel down, and with his head perform his share, but it would require care in the execution. We tried several times, and always with the same success.

"Of course I can't speak with my head under the table," said Thomson; "so if anybody addresses me, you must at once break in and answer to divert attention from me. I think this will please them."

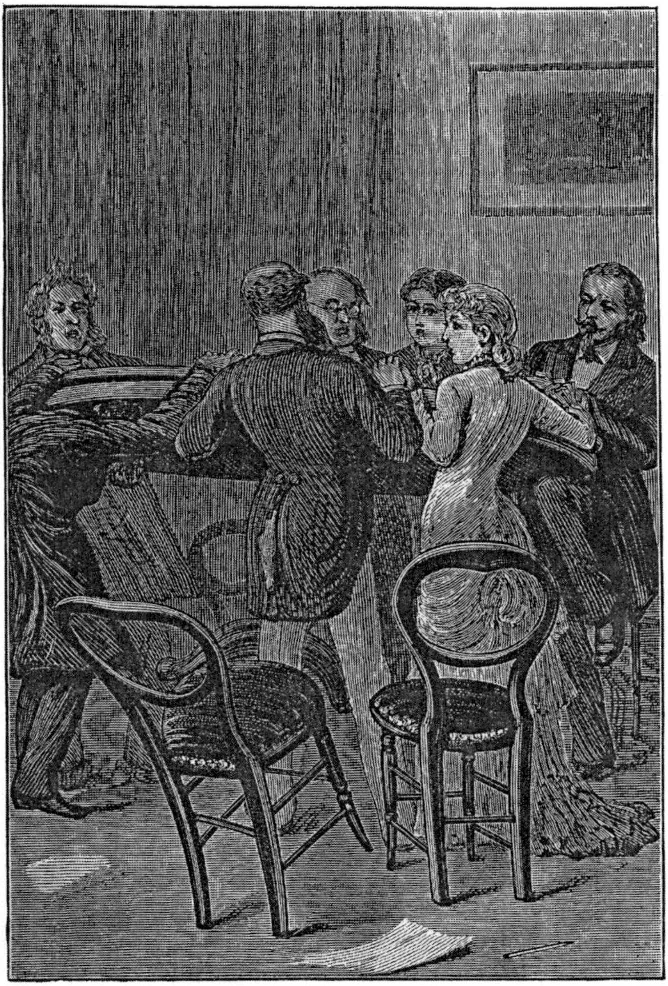

Mr Ashton and his lady friend were now announced, and we soon commenced the sitting. The lady had brought with her a little musical box, small enough in fact to be carried in the pocket, and soon it was wound up, and from the table it tinkled forth its merry music in quite a pleasing manner; but we were all equally astonished when the little thing was seized with a mania for playing antics in addition to music. First it began to move about, and then it floated right off, and apparently quite out of the room, for we could hear its faint melody vibrating in the far distance, and at last it dropped down on the table before us, and rattled away as if in high glee at our surprise. And then the table slowly, and as if with great difficulty, raised itself up on one side and then the other, until it was fairly off the floor; higher and higher it rose, and it floated breast high; no further could it go, for the power was limited.

"Thank you dear friends, thank you; this *is* a test Mr Thomson. Do you think it can go higher?" asked Mr Ashton.

"Look at that star!" I hurriedly exclaimed.

"Where? I don't see it."

"Right over your heads now; can't you see it, Miss Willis?"

"N—o, yes; I think—No, I don't see it?" she replied hesitating, and then the table, after a little swaying, gradually settled on the floor again, and the raps told us to change for materialisations.

"Would you like me to sit under test conditions?" inquired Thomson.

"Oh no; but stay—yes, I think it would be better, because I can then speak of it to outsiders," answered our ingenuous old friend.

"Then I will use the sack," said Thomson, "and if you have a seal you can imprint it on the knots when I am tied."

Carefully and critically our visitors arranged the test, and then we helped the medium behind the screen. It had not occurred to Mr Ashton to search him previous to sitting, but he was quite prepared if such a course had been adopted.

Joey obtains Music.

In a short time Joey began chattering, and he told the lady that he did like her, she was so good and kind to think of a musical box, and if she would make him a present of it he would do lots to please her; and when the lady gracefully acceded to his modest request, he was profuse in thanks, and told her if she would come again, she should see something wonderful; and if the Sceptic would come as well he would be astonished by manifestations even more startling than the floating table.

Asoka now made his appearance and Joey withdrew. He went through his customary genuflexions, and waving of drapery, but not for long did he stay; he slowly retreated, and when safely behind the screen he addressed us in his heavy and rather melodious voice.

"Great and wondrous things are on the eve of accomplishment," said he; " only have a little patience, and a full recompense for all your faithfulness shall be given to you."

" Is Joey there?" asked Miss Willis.

" Yes, I'm here," answered that gentleman after a slight pause.

" Oh, Miss Willis, you *is* so good, I do like you."

" But I like to see my friends; why don't you come out?"

"I can't come now, because Asoka has used all the power, but if you will come to-morrow at the same time, I'll try very, very hard to please you."

"Very well, we will come, but don't you forget."

"All right; but we must go now; the poor medium is tired; good-bye all," said he quickly, and the groaning of Thomson, intermixed with "wake up, do; wake up, now then," from Joey told us that the séance was ended.

" This has been a very successful séance," said Mr Ashton when we had examined and found all the seals and knots all right. " I can speak of this with confidence to my friends; now to-morrow I'll come again at the same time, and bring my friend (the Sceptic) with me."

" Thank you, Mr Ashton, you are very kind," returned Thomson gratefully; " but your friend did not succeed very well after we were gone the other day; he tried to reproduce the same phenomena."

"Indeed," said the astonished Mr Ashton, "how on earth did you find that out?"

"Joey stayed behind and saw it, and told us all about it."

"Well really, now, that is a test; but it is quite true my friend did try, and did one or two of the things very well, but not all."

"It certainly is astonishing; however, I must go now. Good morning, gentlemen."

"How did you manage to work that musical box like that?" I asked as soon as our clients were well out of earshot.

"I lifted it up with my teeth and dropped it on my chair, and then sat on it," answered Thomson quietly.

"It sounded really very funny; of course your sitting on it muffled the sound?"

"Yes; but didn't I get it out of Miss Willis beautifully?"

"You did indeed; but when the table is up, you must not move about, or you will pull me over. I have only one foot to stand upon, remember, with the other holding up the table."

"You performed your part very well."

"Oh, you were going to tell me how you get out of the sack, to-day," I suddenly reminded my partner.

"I haven't time now. You see we have our hands quite full with these public meetings; the first comes off on Monday next, and I must go to town on Saturday morning, because I want to get something very particular, and which I can't get here."

"What is that?"

"Some of the illuminating powder. There's only one place where I can get it, and that's from Paris, through an agent, who knows all about it."

"What do you want more for?"

"I intend to make a big covering, so that the form is all light, from head to foot."

"That would look nice, decidedly; but what shall we give to the Gordons to-night?"

"Oh, the floating table and a few other things; but I want to take you to a fine place for luncheon, where I have discovered they sell excellent stuff. Upon my word, you look as though you wanted something. I don't know how it is, but after every séance you look quite worn out; why, your face alone is then enough to make people believe in Spiritualism. You look like a ghost."

"Come along then, and let us go and test their wine; you know I am quite a judge of drinks now," I answered.

"Yes, I'm glad you gave up that stupid teetotalism. When I knew you first you wouldn't touch a drop at any of the houses where we used to go; I thought then you'd soon give up that folly. A man isn't worth anything if he can't take a glass of liquor."

"I never felt the want of it."

"Pooh, life isn't worth having if one can't enjoy oneself."

"Do you consider drinking a glass of wine the chief enjoyment of life?"

"Come along and don't argue," said Thomson, impatiently, and we soon found ourselves at the place he had discovered; and when taking up one of the papers he began to laugh, and saying—

"Those fellows are having a slap at us;" and he read from the Journal: "'The two mediums, Messrs Thomson & Parker, are doing a good trade; their séances are so numerous and well attended that it is difficult to obtain their services. We have been promised a sitting, but as yet it has come to nothing; perhaps in a few days we may speak more positively about these curious and entertaining gentlemen.' There, that's good, isn't it?"

"I can't say I am proud of the notice," I rejoined, for I did not like the obvious sarcasm in the paragraph.

"Why, if they keep on at this rate we shall have half the town after us. Oh yes, we'll give them a séance, and bamboozle them too."

"They may 'bamboozle' us if we are not careful."

"Will they? I don't think so. You seem awfully sensitive about this sort of thing. Just wait a few months and you will laugh at it like I do."

And I am bound to say the prediction came true, for I grew quite hardened enough to thoroughly enjoy criticism, whether favourable or otherwise.

In the evening our clients, the Gordons, came according to custom, and found us duly prepared for them.

At the sitting the table floated up, and remained suspended in the air for several moments. The guitar and musical box indulged in eccentric flights, etc., and gave the best satisfaction, after which we sat for the materialisation. None of the Gordons had ever hinted at the desirableness of employing tests, and when we ourselves started the idea, Mrs Gordon opposed it, saying that as no professional mediums were present, and as we were all friends, she preferred not to have an element of suspicion introduced, which would spoil the harmony of the proceedings. This generous confidence, however, did not deter us from deceiving them to the utmost of our ability, and the séance went on.

"Are you fond of flowers, Mrs Gordon?" called out Joey.

"Yes, Joey, I am very fond of them."

"Have you any at home?"

"Yes, I have a conservatory full of beautiful flowers. Would you like to have some?"

"Oh yes, yes! please bring me some."

"What can you do with flowers?"

"If you bring some my medium can smell them, and then I also can enjoy them through him."

"Very well, I will bring them as soon as possible."

"Can you bring them to-morrow? I am so fond of flowers, and it is so difficult to get any here in the middle of winter."

"I don't know whether I can to-morrow, but I won't forget."

"Thank you, but don't send, I want you to bring them; and now you must break up, and I will ride home with you, and leave my medium for the present, so I shall bid him good-bye instead of you; good-bye you two, I'm off to dinner with Mrs Gordon."

Before our clients left we told them of our projected meetings, and as we expected, the idea did not meet with the approval of Mr Gordon. He deemed it very dangerous to place ourselves in the power of a possibly hostile audience, and it might end very disastrously; at any rate he intimated his intention of staying away during the following week, but would come again in the morning, and might come when we had finished with the public.

Thomson would not have mentioned the affair at all, but that it was unavoidable. "Honesty's the best policy," he said, and acted accordingly; in fact I never met a more honest man when it paid him to be so.

"Never mind," said Thomson. "It won't much matter for a week; if we are successful we can do without them; and if we are not, why they'll come again."

"I think if the spirits intend to come they ought to do so to-morrow, for the Gordons deserve a genuine séance; they are thoroughly straight themselves, and they think everybody else is."

"Don't trouble, they'll get one; it lays between them and Mr Ashton. But to-morrow the Sceptic is coming, and we must astonish him."

"Suppose the spirits come!"

"We must suppose they won't, and act accordingly; if we relied wholly upon them we should do nothing. You don't think these people would have kept coming for nothing?"

"Why were you so pressing about those flowers with Mrs Gordon?"

"I want some," said he, and added significantly—"You wait and see."

CHAPTER XII.

THE POWER INCREASES.

"GOOD morning, Mr Ashton."
"Good morning, gentlemen; I have brought my friend to sit with you again, and I hope he will be converted."

And the Sceptic came forward and saluted us courteously, as was his wont. He told us that he did not consider the manifestations which he had before witnessed in our company to be absolutely beyond anything which might be produced by other means than spirit agency, but he would be pleased to witness more conclusive facts.

We assured him that we could not blame him for desiring further proofs, for such a wish plainly indicated that he was perfectly unbiassed, and we felt confident he would be amply rewarded for the expenditure of his time and trouble.

It did not take much time that morning to arrange ourselves, and we were soon sitting round the table in the dark. Thomson sat between Mr Ashton and Miss Willis, while I was placed opposite between that lady and the Sceptic; and soon the guitar commenced its aerial flight, while luminous hands partly materialised appeared over the table, and once a Rembrandt-like face suddenly glowed out of the pitchy gloom.

At this juncture Mr Ashton inquired if we were all in our proper position, and receiving an emphatic assurance of our unbroken condition, he further suggested that the mediums should each place his feet between those of his male neighbour, to render it even yet more impossible to assist the manifestations. But the new test did not hinder the work; on the contrary, the power increased every moment; and at Mr Ashton's request, the table rose up until it floated breast high, and after a minute's suspension it slowly descended again.

The Sceptic then declared that his chair had disappeared, and that somebody had fixed something round his neck! In fact, nearly all the chairs had vanished, and with nothing to sit upon, we each stood or knelt as it best suited us.

Swiftly and mighty grew the power; the room seemed to be full of industrious spirit workmen, intent on rearranging everything to suit more sublime tastes, and "Oh good gracious! what's that," from the lady, as a heavy rumbling sound was heard, as if the sides of the room were closing in upon us, showed that poor Miss Willis was sadly terrified. She earnestly begged for a light, but the spirits were obdurate and sternly forbade any change. Nearer and nearer came the thud! thud! thud! until it touched Miss Willis, and after that we were permitted to light up.

We were hardly prepared for the sight of disorder that reigned: the chairs were solemnly standing on the table, the tambourine ring hung around the neck of the Sceptic, and one chair had in some mysterious manner slung itself on the joined hands of Thomson and Mr Ashton; how it came there nobody could understand, for they both declared that no unlinking had occurred: "Ah, that is matter passing through matter," and thus we left it.

But the crowning marvel of all was the cause of the sound which had so seriously alarmed us: that innocent sideboard had advanced to the middle of the room, and there remained to excite our wonder. The manifestation puzzled us, and disconcerted the Sceptic, and he admitted his inability to explain the circumstance; nor was his astonishment abated when, having kindly volunteered to assist in replacing it, he experienced its huge weight and unwieldly form, and he stated that had he not been present he could not have believed it.

The materialisation next claimed our attention, and again

the sack was accepted, after the Sceptic had more closely examined it, and Miss Willis had announced her intention of taking it home, that she might have plenty of time to scrutinise it.

"Hulloh; what did you think of my work?" asked Joey from the cabinet during the materialisations.

"I think it rather extraordinary; but did you do it all alone?" inquired the Sceptic.

"Yes, of course, I'm only a little boy spirit, but weight is nothing to me."

"But do your companions make you do it all?"

"No, they don't *make* me, only if I didn't do it nobody else would. Great spirits like Asoka don't trouble about such things, they attend to the trance and materialisations; but, bless your heart, lifting those heavy things is nothing to me."

"Your mediums must be very good, I never witnessed such things before."

"Oh, yes, the magnetism is greater since Mr Parker has been with us, he gives off a terrible lot of power. I did intend to plant that sideboard on the table, but I'm afraid the table isn't strong enough."

"I should like to see that done; never mind the table, I'll pay for it."

"I don't care about breaking the table, nor the sideboard, but you wouldn't like that big thing to fall over on you; would you now?"

"Now, Joey, are you coming out to-day?" broke in the impatient Miss Willis, and prevented the Sceptic answering, and so we never knew whether or not he would like the sideboard to fall upon him.

"No, I shan't; Asoka is coming directly. Ah, Miss Willis, you ought to see our beautiful summer-land where we live! All sunshine and flowers!"

"Flowers! I am fond of flowers, Joey. Do you ever materialise any?"

"Often. Would you like to have some?"

"I should indeed; but when will you bring them?"

"I'll try to-morrow; but Asoka's coming now," and before he had time to say another word, forth came the dazzling form, and hushed us all to silence.

But this impressive presence did not continue long, for after flinging out the long folds of its drapery, and bowing, it vanished, and Joey again began his chattering. He told us that giving the form under such awfully stringent conditions was a very difficult thing, and could only be given once at each sitting—that was why he couldn't come now —so we must break up and liberate the poor medium, who was suffering very much. This command was quickly obeyed, after we had first seen that his position was the same before as well as after in all respects, and our guests soon afterwards departed, well pleased, and greatly astonished.

"I think we nicely bamboozled *him* this time," said Thomson, alluding to the Sceptic. "You are improving any way; I heard you plant those chairs on the table splendidly."

"How did you contrive to send that sideboard waltzing about like that?"

"Sit down and I'll show you. I got my foot behind and purchased it out thus; whenever I can get a fair leverage I can move anything. I mean to have that sofa on the table next time, as well as the sideboard."

"You mind and don't hurt yourself; that sideboard is no joke," I warned.

"I have done much the same thing hundreds of times; but I find I must run up to town. I want to give the proper lights over the table; match heads are all very well for a make-shift, but they don't give a light clear enough."

"Could you really lift this sofa on to the table during the sitting?"

"Yes, I'll try; fortunately it isn't very big nor very long. See, I can weigh up one end and swing the other over, so!" and clear on to the table lighted the sofa.

"When will you do this."

"Next week; it won't do to give them this until they are getting tired of the others; always keep on giving something fresh."

"By the way, Thomson, do you remember that spirit weighing-machine, about which there was so much excitement in London some time since?"

"Yes, I ought to know something about it, seeing that I put Harvey up to the dodge."

"What do you mean?"

"Well, when the affair was first designed, of course they intended it as the finest test ever used. Harvey was the medium whom they were going to engage, and he came and told me all about it. Did you ever see the machine?" asked Thomson turning to me.

"No, but I remember the diagrams, and the articles that used to be written about it at the time."

"Well, then, you know it was simply an enlarged weighing machine, with a self-registering apparatus, showing the increase or decrease of weight in the body."

"Yes."

"Poor Harvey was in a terrible state about it, and said he didn't know how to bring it off."

"I thought Harvey was so clever?" I rejoined.

"Clever! he's an awful bungler. You know very well that machine was invented to show the exact amount of power taken from the medium by the spirits, and when different spirits appear while the medium is in the body of the machine, of course the register must give a different weight, for some of them may be children, and if the medium himself comes out the register would betray him."

"Quite right; didn't Harvey know what to do?"

"No; what would you do in a similar case?"

"I really don't know."

"Well, I told him to get two gimlets, and screw one in the machine and the other in the floor, and then to fasten a piece of stout cord to each, and take it up or let it out, to show any difference he liked."

"That was a clever idea; and you mean to say that two gimlets deceived those scientific men?"

"Scientific men! pooh. I am sorry for science if some of those are its representatives; although I always say I would much rather deal with scientific men than with tradesmen. But the reason why Harvey was caught out was this—he forgot his gimlets one day, and, of course, the people at whose house the machine was found them; but I think they were true to Harvey, and kept his secret."

"Did they; then how came you to know?"

"Well, of course Harvey told me; but it was kept secret in the 'swim,' I mean."

"And that's how that mighty test was overcome?"

"Yes, and your scientific men were beautifully jockeyed. Oh yes, give me scientific men to sit with; you can play on them as easy as blind men. You are just as safe with them as with a gentleman. Now, there's the Sceptic, he gives his word to keep the conditions, and being a gentleman, of course he won't break his word."

"How did you get out of the cage at the hall?"

"Ah, I must have that cage again, that's a splendid test; you remember the maker himself offered to give it to anybody who could get out? Well, I got out easy enough."

"But how?"

"That's the secret. You know there were three padlocks hanging outside, one at the top, one in the middle, and the other at the bottom. Well, I used to pull up the top lock and unfasten that, and then I could push open the door far enough to get at the other locks in succession, and open them as I wanted. But the second night there was one lock you found undone; the simple reason of that was, I forgot it until too late, and I trusted to your sharp eyes; I knew you had got wit and sense enough to cover it up."

"And at the time you tried to make me believe it was my own fault."

"Yes, what else could I do. You were a bit of a fool then."

"It was very clever; but it must require great skill and coolness; and in the dark, too."

"You will find, that with plenty of practice you can do anything as well in the dark as in the light; only you must be careful. By the way, speaking of that, we must mind Miss Willis, she's as sharp as a ferret. I am half inclined to offend her. Did you notice how I made her ask for flowers?"

"Yes; but ——"

At this moment our enthusiastic friend, Mr Wilson, burst into the room, and, without ceremony, began to deplore the failure of the séance at his house with the gentlemen of the press.

"You needn't trouble about their criticism, Mr Wilson; we enjoyed it immensely," assured Thomson.

"Enjoyed it! Well, you are funny people, upon *my* word," said Mr Wilson, opening wide his eyes.

"You see, Mr Wilson, my reputation is made, and when once a medium is established, all the press of the world couldn't shake him; that is because people believe more in the hereafter than they do in the present."

"Ah, well, I suppose you can afford to laugh, but if you are not really angry with them, you might give them another séance."

"By all means, with pleasure."

"Because I'm afraid they will have another cut at you; they are threatening now, and I really should like you to get the press on your side."

"Hang the press."

"Thank you."

"Of course I don't mean you," said Thomson. "I know you are a sensible fellow. Will you be chairman for us next week at one of our public meetings?"

"Yes, with pleasure," eagerly exclaimed our friend, who was a man of vast power and importance; and by a little judicious flattery, we knew he would do almost anything for us.

Withdrawal of Clients.

He stayed chattering away until we informed him that we expected a party to come up shortly for a séance, and if he would excuse us for the present, we should be glad to have the pleasure of his company any other time he liked.

"That's a blessing," said Thomson, when our verbose friend had gone; "I'm always suspicious of a man who talks so much."

"He means well," I answered.

"No doubt; so did that engine-driver mean well when he cut into our train the other night."

"That was want of care."

"Just so; but now let us be prepared for the Gordons. What shall we do?"

"I must leave that to you; suppose we do the same as for Mr Ashton?"

"Suppose we have a failure."

"No; let's do something for our money."

"Very well; we'll float the table and the sofa. But I mean to astonish them yet."

"How?"

"I can't tell; but I have a notion that I shall startle them, and I am never deceived in my impressions."

When the Gordon's arrived we sat down at the table for the first part; we were still developing, for the power was yet too weak to show the outward and visible grandeur of the oft promised manifestations. True the table floated as with Ashton, but that was not grandeur, and a few other little trifles occurred; and better still, when we obtained a light, we saw that the spirits had not been idle: the sofa had arisen, and was leaning in an intoxicated sort of way on the table, and a chair also had gone up, and appeared to have been assisting the sofa in its potations.

These manifestations were accepted in all good faith by everybody except ourselves. As for me, I could only watch and wait.

"Ah, Mrs Gordon, you haven't brought my flowers," said Joey regretfully, from the cabinet, when we had changed to the second part.

"I couldn't bring them to-day, because I left home early, and they would have faded, but I'll try and let you have them another time."

"Won't you bring them to-morrow?"

"We are not coming to-morrow!"

"Oh, dear; of course I had forgotten."

"Yes; you know we are afraid that sitting too many times will injure the medium."

"It doesn't hurt him when he sits with people like you; it's rough and raw people who hurt him."

"Well, Joey, we haven't many good mediums, and we must take care of those we have."

"Yes, you are very kind, I wish everybody was like you. Oh, didn't I enjoy myself when I went home with you, and didn't we make the table jump about?"

"I am glad you were pleased, Joey."

"Oh, I just think I was, and I saw your beautiful conservatory. Ah, Mrs Gordon, I wish you would keep evincing; we are developing something very good for you."

"We will come again after next week, but we won't overtax the medium; he looks rather ill now."

"We will reserve the power for when we meet again. What did you think of the sofa, chair, and table floating about?"

"We thought it wonderful."

"I did all that just for your sake, dear Mrs Gordon. But that's nothing to what we will do yet; we will float the chair with the medium on it to the top of the table, and then we will send the table up! And we are also making new 'light' dresses for Asoka, Lily, and me, and we shall appear altogether, just as we look when we are at home in the summerland! Oh, so, so lovely, and so sweet. But I must go now. Don't forget my flowers, Mrs Gordon. I do like you! Good-bye all, and God bless you."

CHAPTER XIII.

MORE PUBLIC MEETINGS.

"WE must be very careful with Miss Willis," said Thomson, just before our clients again made their appearance. "She's as suspicious as a monkey; she thinks she will find out something about that sack; that's why she wanted to take it away with her."

"Are you afraid she will find out anything?"

"Not a bit, she's very sharp, but not sharp enough for me. She will perhaps sew up the seams, so we must be prepared; get a needle and cotton, and stick it up behind the cabinet."

"I think you are as suspicious as she."

"I'm not going to be outwitted by her; and there's one other thing: you are much too slow in cutting the tape after a séance, and you sometimes cut the wrong side. You should always be ready, and directly they have examined the sack, you ought to cut at once; first the hands, and then the *left* side at the top. You have many times almost bowled me out when you have been slow, or cut the wrong side."

"I'll be more careful for the future, but you can't sew in the dark."

"Can't I? I can do anything in the dark," said he; and he told me of some strange adventures that he had met with in times gone by, and while listening to his recital, Mr Ashton and his friend arrived.

"I have brought back your bag, and have thoroughly examined it," said Miss Willis.

"Are you satisfied?" asked Thomson.

"Yes, quite so, and I thank you for letting me take it

away. I am sure a trickster or a conjuror would not have been so obliging."

"Of course they wouldn't," replied Thomson, earnestly, "but I should be sorry to descend to conjuring."

And with this we prepared for the sitting; and Joey soon told Miss Willis, in reply to a question regarding the materialisation of flowers, that the state of the atmosphere was against him, and the medium, too, was not in his usual health, but he did mean to get her the flowers, for she was so good. She asked him if he couldn't "levitate" a bunch; but Joey, with virtuous indignation, repudiated any such intention, for in that case he must steal them from somebody, and he would never do that. He would materialise some very shortly, and that would be much better.

We had been more than usually careful over the seals and knots with the bag this time, and when Asoka appeared in his bright costume it gave unqualified pleasure, for it afforded additional proof of our integrity.

I did not forget Thomson's injunction when the séance was over, and directly the word of satisfaction was uttered, no time was allowed for it to be rescinded, for I cut away immediately according to my instructions.

We did not expect Mr Ashton would continue his séances, thinking that his probable temporary withdrawal was due to the same cause as that which drove away the Gordons. But Thomson said it did not matter, for much more money could be made before the public than with a few private friends.

"Of course," he said, "they believe that it is weakening to a medium to sit more than once a day, and if we told them that we could give a dozen sittings in as many hours it would spoil us, so we must let it alone. We shan't care a fig for the loss of two customers, for if we don't succeed they'll come back, and be doubly pleased to think they are right; and if we do succeed they'll come back all the same."

"You are going to town you say to-morrow?"

"Yes, I must run up, everything else is ready, and I must get a few really necessary things. I think I shall bring the cage; I know it would take."

Thomson was continually harping on that famous test, and I could not help thinking with him that it would be highly successful. Few people would deem it possible to get out, however closely they might examine it; but the danger of using it in a mixed audience was very great, for several minutes were necessary to secure the locks after showing the form, and exposure would inevitably follow if any mischievous person should rush forward to effect a seizure; and that this phenomenon was possible we full well knew from existent facts; and when on the following Monday Thomson returned without the cage I was rather glad than otherwise.

The town in which we were to lecture and exhibit spirit powers was a few miles from that in which we dwelt, and when we reached the place we found the friends awaiting our arrival, and I believe rather disappointed that a few well-developed spirits had not journeyed in front to herald our approach. They were a mixed lot decidedly. One in particular was a phenomenon himself; and when after tea we walked along the streets to the little hall accompanied by this eccentric curiosity, he appeared evidently anxious to impress us with a sense of his great spiritual powers, both dormant and active. He would occasionally shudder, and look wildly around as if looking out for a handy point from which to levitate himself, Mrs Guppy fashion, and then he would shake his head violently and mutter, "Get out! get out, can't you!"

"What is the matter?" I asked, though I well knew the cause of his seeming disquietude.

"My guides won't let me alone," he seriously replied.

"What kind of medium are you?" I queried.

"I'm a healing; and my guides will develope me greatly now that I'm under the influence of such a medium as Mr Thomson."

"You are a mesmerist, then?"

"Yes; and I do understand it a little; leastwise my guides do," returned the phenomenon knowingly.

I was not surprised at this confidence, for books on mesmerism and magnetism are easily obtained, and it was nothing new to hear such a statement from people like him; but the worst of it was, they often had an unquenchable desire to operate upon us, and if we declined their services they were grievously offended. This gentleman (a collier or navvy) was brawny enough in all conscience for a mesmerist, but I wondered how he had managed to master all the technicalities of the subject; judging, and perhaps wrongly, that his mode of life was not one best suited for the attainment of any great scientific knowledge. Regarding his mode of expression, I must give a translation, for I do not think I am equal to a phonetic rendering of his speech.

"How long have you studied the subject?" I asked.

"About three months."

"Have you read much about it?"

"No; my guides tell me everything, so I needn't read. But I'll show fyou what I can do," said he when we had reached the hall, and found one or two friends inside. "There's a young man standing there; I'll have a go at him."

"Be quiet," whispered Thomson to me, "and you'll see some fun, but don't laugh, or he might have a 'go' at you. We have but to flatter these people and they'll do anything for us; that fellow now will be worth a regiment to-night, if anybody attempts a seizure. Of course they are an ignorant lot, but they are a fair sample of many others who talk of 'objective, and psychology and philosophy,' and all that, but there's scarcely one who knows the meaning of them."

"Hoy, Mr Thomson! come on, this young man says he has been mesmerised, but could never feel anything," shouted the phenomenon; and we walked to the other end of the long room where stood the mesmerist, confronting his frightened victim, who had consented under protest, 1 do believe.

"Stand there," said the operator sternly to his patient, who obeyed apparently with fear and trembling, while the other commenced making passes as if he were trying to catch gnats. "Do you feel anything?" roared he, when he had been snatching away for two or three minutes.

"No," feebly answered the subject wincing, and looking at us, as if for protection against his assailant.

"All right; wait a minute, I'll make you feel it," shouted the phenomenon vengefully; and he seized his unlucky patient, and shook him as a terrier does a rat. "There! do you feel anything now," said he, blowing with excitement—rage, to me it appeared.

"Yes, a little."

"Hold up, I haven't done yet." And again he grasped him, and in the struggle that ensued, they lost their balance and rolled over on to the floor; but quickly picking himself up, the operator called, "Do you feel anything now?"

"Yes," replied the bewildered subject.

But my colleague, who had cautioned me against laughing, was now himself attacked by the malady; much to my surprise, too, for he had a marvellous faculty for keeping his features under control; but he had never bargained for such a severe trial as the present, and exploding with laughter, he crammed his handkerchief into his mouth, and hastily withdrew to the sanctuary afforded by a small room adjoining the hall.

"What is the matter?" inquired the phenomenon, still keeping a determined hold of his subject.

"You throw off so much fluid," I answered.

"Yes, I know I throw off a wonderful deal; my guides tell me so; but I forgot that such a great medium would feel it."

"It has affected him certainly. You must be more careful; you are a very powerful mesmerist. Too much so, in fact, for some subjects, particularly those who are physically weak."

"Well, I can generally make them feel my mesmerism; I've got a particular way of my own."

"Yes, I see, but don't you know there are two kinds of mesmerism."

"What are they?"

"Muscular mesmerism, and magnetic mesmerism."

"Which is mine?"

"Muscular, of course."

"Mus'k'lar!"

"Yes; but that kind has sometimes an irritating effect upon the patient, and when it does it is likely to produce unpleasant consequences for the operator."

"Would you like for me to try you?" said he, making a step in my direction.

"Oh no, no, no; thank you, the muscular is too strong for me, in fact, the magnetic is almost too powerful," I hastily replied, retreating from my dangerous-looking interrogator; and just then catching sight of Thomson peeping through the doorway, and convulsed with laughter, my own gravity was nearly upset, but fortunately I was able to master my feelings.

"Ah, very well, some other time then; I *should* like to try you. But as for that fellow (indicating his patient), he is not very well; I believe some evil old 'sperrit' has got hold of him; but I'll master him if I break his very neck." Whether he referred to the neck of the spirit or the subject, I was at a loss to determine; in any case, it was a black look out for the latter, who almost had sufficient reasons to swear the peace against the phenomenon.

Further conversation was prevented by the entrance of several of our brotherhood, and the mesmerist, triumphant at having made his poor little subject 'feel it,' entered with heart and soul into the business in hand, and rendered very welcome and efficient aid. The platform was at the end opposite the door, but Thomson was greatly displeased that it was so very low.

"We must have this platform raised," said he to me; "a high platform is some sort of protection." But as it was impossible to do that at once, we were compelled to put up

A Conceited Tailor.

with it for one night, and a few people straggling in, we withdrew to the little room for a time.

We could soon see that our audience was not likely to be a large one, which we attributed to the snow and cold, and we came out, and placed the members of the spiritual association in two rows of chairs, without a gangway, before the platform, in order that strangers should not have the chance to approach too near, and then we opened the meeting with a hymn.

In lieu of the lecture which I had so carefully constructed, I gave an impromptu address, after which we announced that the manifestations would begin, and we requested that the very best order might be observed, for the conditions under which the spirits worked were so extremely delicate, that the least disturbance would probably prevent a successful issue of our attempt to give the blessings of Spiritualism to the public.

We also informed them that we intended to give a test, to convince them of our honesty, which was the sack test, and the medium would allow himself to be fastened in that, under the supervision of two referees from the audience.

Some little disturbance was caused at this point by a conceited little tailor, who refused to believe in the *bona fides* of the referees chosen by the majority of the audience.

I believe, if I remember aright, we had allowed him to come in at half-price, and he gave us to understand that he meant to have the full worth of his sixpence. I refused to have him on the platform, but Thomson told me to let him come up, as he couldn't hurt.

When the little fellow came up, he was asked to see that the knots and seals were in proper order, but being apparently a quarrelsome sort, he refused, and said—

"No, I don't never trust to nobody, I want to tie them knots myself."

We allowed him to have his own way in everything, and then he professed himself satisfied, saying, as he looked cunningly around—

" There, he won't get away from that."

I believe the tailor stood in more danger now than he suspected, for I fancied the phenomenon seemed much inclined to try his muscular mesmerism on him, and I confess I experienced a sharp longing to bundle the little fellow out of the place; but I checked my feelings, and drawing the curtain which enclosed Thomson in the cabinet, we requested every one to take his seat, and the tailor to take off his hat.

As the conditions appeared highly antagonistic, I did not anticipate a very successful meeting; nor was I deceived, for although the physical manifestations were just as striking under the knots and seals of the tailor as at other times, yet the form itself was not vouchsafed. The guitar strummed, the bells rung, and a small harmonium was vigorously played; and to finish, the coat of the medium came flying over the top of the curtains into our midst, and then I was pleased to hear Joey's voice, telling us that the spirits could do no more.

We had allowed a light strong enough to see everything that was passing in the room, and I sat down in the front row of the audience, so that no charge of complicity on my part could be sustained; and the tailor, when he was requested to come forward again, was much puzzled to find that all his cleverly contrived knots and seals had neither prevented manifestations, nor had they been touched. He scratched his head, perhaps to hoe out an idea, and he succeeded, for he asked if we would give him permission to take the bag home. Thomson willingly gave him his desire, and we both thought we should never see that bag again; we expected that he might cut it to fragments to find out the secret, and if he had kept his hold of the bag, we should not have deplored its loss, seeing that we should also lose him for the following meetings.

But I owe the little fellow my sincere apologies, for he evinced no particular desire to pick or to steal, but faithfully returned his charge the next evening, at the same time admitting that he could find nothing to warrant his belief that it was a trick sack.

A Chattering Chairman.

We hoped now that our efforts to please him would produce better behaviour; but his lordship of the needle and goose was just as captious and disagreeable as before.

We had for this night secured the services of our enthusiastic friend, Mr Wilson, to act as chairman; also two gentlemen from the town in which we lived had accompanied us. Neither of these two latter were spiritualists; but they both acted in a perfectly straightforward manner, and fully bore out Thomson's axiom, that "a gentleman's word may always be taken."

The audience was even scantier than on the previous evening, and although our friends who came with us were intellectual enough to satisfy the most exacting speaker, I had no heart to deliver a lecture, and instead I determined to give another impromptu address.

A chattering chairman is always a nuisance. His duties should be a simple introduction of those on the platform to the audience; but not so thought our able and eloquent president, for he rambled nearly all over Europe to find tropes and arguments to prove the truth of Spiritualism, and of our particular integrity; although he knew less of Spiritualism, and not more of ourselves, than did his impatient listeners, who silently protested against the notion that they were there to hear a history of either, however grand.

He floundered about, and in short I do not think he knew how to stop; but at last the wearisome oration began to falter, and after a few spasmodic gurgles, died away.

I have been frightened at an audience, but never before ashamed. Our friend, whose only fault was his over-kindness, had spoken of me as possessing such superlative powers, that I was meditating an abrupt retreat to the sideroom, when he finished, and I courageously faced my hearers and completely gave the lie to the splendid *éloge* of my chairman.

And then the manifestations were about to commence, and our elumbated tailor came forward to distinguish himself again. He almost eyed the bag with an air of proprietorship since he had once taken it home; but after some little squabbling he again professed himself satisfied, though not before he had told one of the two gentlemen with us (a banker) that he was in league with "them Sperritcherlists." But as little notice as possible was taken of this curiosity, who was quite bewildered and very angry.

Precisely the same occurred as on the previous evening. The physical manifestations were very lively, but we were not given any materialisations, and for this reason I believe the Association were very angry; they had bargained rather hardly with us for the little hall, and yet considered themselves in the light of free guests, though we did not by any means object to this, for they formed a little body-guard for our protection. They were bitterly disappointed because they did not see a materialisation; they did not want the physical, they had plenty of that.

After this meeting Thomson said to me—

"Well, I have been a medium for over ten years, but I never before fell into such hands; that secretary ought to have told us of these people, and then I wouldn't have gone near the place for anything."

"Could you have escaped from the bag with that man's tying?"

"Don't talk nonsense; of course I could, but I was afraid they would attempt a seizure of the form."

"I did not think so once, but I think now that it is much too dangerous to offer this to the public. I don't think the secretary is to blame, for in a mixed audience we are sure to have such undesirable customers."

"Are we?" sneered Thomson, who was in a bad temper.

"That is my opinion, and now it is supported by facts."

"Oh. Well I have given great numbers of public meetngs in England and on the Continent, and never met such a lot. Do you know, that in America, if a little snob like that were to attempt such antics, he would be quickly flung out; and then look at the meetings we gave in London, how pleasant and orderly everybody was."

"It certainly has been an unfortunate venture, and to tell you the truth, I'm not sorry."

Thomson Disgusted.

"How much have we taken?" asked Thomson.

"Last night we took 12s., and to-night 5s."

"And our expenses altogether?"

"About £5."

"I thought as much."

"Yes; it will be quite that, and we haven't paid for that hall yet. I suppose the association will charge for the full week, whether we use it or no, and then the secretary paid a few shillings for some small hand-bills."

"And as I consider he has deceived us by not letting us know the character of the people, he may whistle for his money."

"Oh, but we must pay."

"You may if you like, but I declare I won't."

"Well, I suppose I must if you won't."

"More fool you. I shall call on our old friends to-morrow and get them to come again. I think while we stay in this part of the country we will stick to private séances; they pay better and there's less danger."

CHAPTER XIV.

EXPLANATIONS.

AFTER the preceding events we maintained a quiet attitude as regards the public, and contented ourselves with the custom of our two clients, with whom we had again arranged to visit us.

Not that Thomson was long satisfied with them alone, for he soon afterwards again vigorously asserted that private séances were not good enough for our purpose, and he aspired to dazzle the public with a series of brilliant spiritual entertainments.

"We must have young Lou here," said he one day; "we can do anything then. You have no idea how clever she is; and yet as with me, people look upon her as a poor harmless child, almost an idiot; but she has got her wits fully developed, and no mistake."

"What do you want with her?" I inquired.

"We must give these people something fresh, or they will soon be tired of this game. We must vary the manifestations, and with Lou we can do almost what we like. But of course nobody must know that she is here; she will have to go into another room during the séances."

"What good will she be in that case?"

"You will see. I think I shall send for her at once."

"By the way," I rejoined, "you were to show me how you get out of the sack, but you keep putting me off."

"Very well, then, I'll tell you now. There are three or four modes of egress, but I always choose the easiest. You remember I asked you for a needle and cotton the other day. Well, I had that stuck up behind that picture over the cabinet, to be prepared for any emergency. Now if we were professed conjurors nobody would dream of asking permission to take anything home for private examination, but being mediums, we must submit to all that sort of thing. I don't care who overhauls that bag, they won't find anything wrong; it isn't a trick sack at all, and yet it is by a trick that I get out. When Miss Willis took the sack home the other day, I expected that she might, to satisfy herself, sew every seam over again, and sure enough she did. By that dodge she shut up one way of escape, but when the manifestations occurred as before, she was satisfied that we must be genuine. Now you'll laugh at the simplicity of the way I generally manage. You see this seam at the top; you know that the tape is run through that, and when I get in, it is pulled up tight round the neck, and both ends are at the back when they are tied and sealed. You see also this little hole in the seam at the front. Now, when they are busy pulling up the sack behind, I put one of my fingers in that little hole and pull out a piece of the tape, and fasten it to a button of my vest, and if I want more, I fasten it lower down; that is why I always have plenty of tape, so that a little more one way or the other is not noticed; and so when I wish to come out I loosen the tape, and let free the neck of the bag."

"That is simple enough so far; but how can you free yourself when your hands are tied and sealed?"

"The hands are never tied in reality, that is, to anything else. You have noticed when my hands are tied so tight as almost to stop the circulation of the blood, and the knots sealed as carefully as if life depended upon them, there are always two long ends left on each hand for me to pass through the little holes at the back of the bag when I am in; they are then tied to the chair. Very well, those ends are never passed through; I always have a similar piece of tape in my pocket ready, and as those outside the bag don't know and can't see what is going on inside, I pass that through which is tied in all good faith, thus leaving my hands perfectly free. Of course you must be very cool and careful, for the least hitch would throw you out; and again, you must never forget to cut off the two ends on the hands, because as the sitters think they are cutting you loose, they would at once notice if you came out of the bag with those ends as long as when you went in."

"I can see it is very simple."

"Yet it is simple certainly, and for that reason I like that way best; always choose simplicity, and you may play your games before the 'cutest eyes. But to show you that it requires a little dexterity I will do it first, and you shall then try your skill."

And Thomson performed the trick before me as when our clients were present. It seemed so easy and so simple that I was glad when my turn came, in order that I might show him I was clever enough to do it to his satisfaction; but I over-rated my power, and found that it was no such easy matter, and, need I say, I utterly and ignominiously failed.

"Now," said Thomson, laughing at my rueful visage, "you see it requires practice to do that simple little thing. Suppose you had to do it before regular sitters, which is quite different from a trial with me, and you muddled it like that. Of course you would be detected and laughed at. But don't trouble, you can practice until you can satisfy me, and then you will do."

"How did you manage when Miss Willis sewed the seams over again?"

"When she brought the sack here again, I saw in a moment that the little hole in the seam at the top was closed up. On that occasion I did actually pass the right ends of the tape on my hands through at the back, but I had taken care to have very long ends, and I twisted the tape once round my wrists when in the sack, but still leaving plenty for them to tie; and then when I wanted to come out, I unwound that tape, and could then reach my pocket knife, and I cut and tied both ends together. My hands then being free, I set to work on the tape round my neck, which I had also allowed to be drawn up tight, and turned the sack so that the knots were in front, and with the needle and thread I sewed another piece of tape on that near to the knot, and then I cut, and with the piece sewn on, when I wanted to draw it back I could do so, and sew it all right again. Now you can understand why I am always blaming you for being so slow in cutting me loose. I know it was your wish to please the sitters, but always leave them to please themselves, and they will like you all the better. And you see, too, when you sometimes cut the wrong side you placed me in great danger, because I must cut with you, so that I can get hold of the piece that's been sewn, and avoid the danger of anyone seeing it."

" Can you sew in the dark?"

"I can do anything in the dark. I have told you so before. Do you know why this bag is made of such thick stuff? I could do the same with calico or linen, but this is easier. I have had sometimes to cut my way out and sew it up again so that nothing may be seen. It would be far more difficult to do without the bag, which is, in reality, only a blind to hide the hands. Mr Ashton is coming again to-morrow with Miss Willis, and I shouldn't be surprised if she wants the bag home again; she is very sharp, but I don't think she has wit enough to cope with me. A medium of experience can always out-wit a looker-on even more than a conjuror, because a conjuror would not be allowed to play the antics which we can; and then we can always fly off into a trance if anybody is troublesome, and they are blamed for the failures."

The simple methods which Thomson selected to help out the power astonished me. I had often wondered how it was possible to escape from such positions; but now another part of the mystery was revealed, and in all sincerity I confess that this dangerous kind of life began to please me. I enjoyed the adventures that daily befel us, and the cool daring necessary to successfully carry on our practices.

I still believed that Thomson was a genuine medium, and that the spirits would eventually come to our assistance; but this hope grew fainter, or to speak more correctly, I thought less about it, for any reference to a genuine séance always irritated my partner. How could I absolutely disbelieve in his mediumship? Far abler and greater men than I had pronounced in his favour. He had been tested by all that their scientific ingenuity could devise, and had emerged in triumph from every ordeal. And the results of his remarkable skill were on view at more than one place, not the least amongst which the spiritual association of the highest authority, or claiming to be such, exhibited in their rooms several articles of his guides' handiwork, and exultantly pointed them out to visitors as indubitable evidences of spirit power.

Shortly after our conversation regarding the sack mystery, our friend Mr Wilson called, and forthwith began to impart some strange news he had gathered respecting the séances at which Mr Ashton's friend, the Sceptic, had been present. We did not consider his tidings of much importance, but it was evident our friend regarded it as super-excellent. I will let him tell the story in his own way.

"Now, gentlemen, you have achieved one of the most extraordinary conversions of modern times. What matters if the enemy sneers at you. You can point him to this grand and lasting monument of your spiritual powers; it is something of which to be proud. It is magnificent. It is the most splendid evidence possible to obtain of spirit communion. You may remember that you met this gentleman at Mr Ashton's, when also some ladies were present. But it is not with the ladies I have to deal, although I have the most supreme respect and the profoundest admiration for them. I have one at home, and several growing up, yet I must on this occasion pass them by, not because they are of no importance, but because they do not come within the range of this particular story. Well, then, this gentleman at the first sitting did not think much of what passed; in fact, after you had gone, and as I told you some time ago, he guaranteed to reproduce the very precise manifestations, which to some extent he succeeded in doing. At the second meeting with you he did not witness enough to convince him; but at the third and last, although he gave no indication of his feelings to you, yet was the grand triumph of his conversion effected. He was in correspondence with a gentleman living in a town fifty miles away, and this gentleman has forwarded his letters to me, with a request to send you on to him. In the first letter he sneers at you, and says he has seen better tricks with Slade and Morton, and all the other great mediums with whom he has sat, but he never witnessed anything with anybody worthy of the least consideration before he encountered you. Listen to what he says in his last letter:—

'Dear Sir,—I hasten to inform you of another séance I have lately had with Messrs Thomson and Parker. I do not wish to mislead you by any hasty conclusions of my own, but I may say that these two gentlemen are the most inexplicable media I have hitherto met. The manifestations I witnessed with them astonished me beyond measure, and cannot be accounted for by any of my own hypotheses. I am almost driven to the confession that they were due to spirit agency.'

"There, gentlemen!" continued our friend, who drew himself up to the full extent of his 5 ft. 1 in., and, wildly flinging his arms about, presented a picture enough to astonish a Greek, while he thundered forth his superlatives in a most moving manner; "there, that comes from a gentleman who has investigated Spiritualism as much as most people, but never before found anything worth mentioning. These letters are sent to me under the strictest confidence, and to nobody else would I reveal their contents. Now, your fortunes are made. I am proud of you, and, like the prophet of old, I say unto you, 'Go and prosper.' He who sends me these letters wishes me to have a sitting with you, and if I am satisfied, I am to send you on to him. Money is no object to that man. Why, if he is worth one penny sterling, he is worth £50,000! There ! You will have to go to his house, where you will be treated like princes, all expenses paid, and your full fees."

"We should not go anywhere for less," said Thomson, bluntly.

"No; of course not. But this man won't mind what money he spends so long as he can be convinced of the truths of Spiritualism. Money is absolutely the very smallest consideration that influences him. When can you give me a séance?"

"Any time you like; but I am afraid we shall not be disengaged for two or three weeks," replied Thomson.

"Now, there's another thing. Several gentlemen of the press with whom I am acquainted are very desirous of testing your marvellous psychological powers. You know that they have already sneered at you, and severely criticised you. Now, take my advice, and let them come and see your wonders, and they will trumpet you to the four winds of heaven."

"You may bring them when you like; but as for their praise or blame, I have told you before I don't care a fig for either. My reputation is made."

I considered Thomson was both unwise and ungrateful—the first, for refusing to meet those who expressed a not unreasonable request to see before pronouncing judgment; and the second, for the sake of our friend, who, spite of his little eccentricities, was really a very kind-hearted man, and was putting himself to a deal of trouble to further our interests.

"I know," replied Mr Wilson, "that you have a great reputation, and the eyes of all in the place are upon you; but there is one other little thing I want to ask. Have you offended any of the spiritual societies in London?"

"I may have offended all for aught I know or care," said Thomson. "I daresay some of them may not like it, because I would never bind myself to them. You see these associations like to get hold of a medium who will sit for the benefit of their funds; but if you ally yourself to one, you will offend all the others, so for some years I have held

A Peculiar Post-Card. 143

aloof from all alike. There was a time when I was always sitting with and trying to please them, and I believe I am a member of one of them now, but I never by any chance go near their place."

"You astonish me," exclaimed our friend.

"Well, it's like this. There is one association in London considers itself the light of Spiritualism. Then there's a man, with a little weekly paper, who thinks he is the life of all; and another fellow, who has hired a house, and has christened it a big name, he also has a paper, in which he is always whining for money, and quarrelling with everybody because they don't support him better. Well, he imagines himself to be both light and life combined."

"Really!"

"It's a fact; and then they all hate each other like poison, and never join, like other public bodies, to work hand in hand. If one proposes anything, the others are sure to deride it. They would sooner sink the ship than work side by side, so you can't wonder if I refuse to have any dealings with such people. Those three I have mentioned are always in a state of triangular battle, and perhaps I may have received the fire from one of them."

"You certainly have; but I daresay you won't care much."

"What *are* you driving at, Mr Wilson?"

"Well, it appears a gentleman wrote asking one of these companies where Mr Thomson was?"

"Well?"

"They answered, 'Mr Thomson is staying in your vicinity, but he is not very particular—in paying his way.'"

"What!" shouted Thomson, springing to his feet.

"Fact, I assure you; but that is not all, they say nothing about your mediumship, they attack your private life; but, gentlemen," vociferated he again, getting excited, "that communication was sent on a *post-card!*"

"A post-card!"

"A post-card," quietly answered he, and asked, 'Who is

the secretary of that association? I notice some of them incline to ladies. Is this a lady or a gentleman?"

"Neither," said Thomson, wrathfully.

"What do you mean?"

"Do you think a lady or a gentleman would do an act like that?"

"Well, I don't think I should; but what do you intend to do?"

"What can I do, but grin and bear it. Send them a packet of envelopes and a dozen stamps, faugh! they might have had the decency to use an envelope. They're a precious lot! Of course, if I brought a criminal action against them, that would not benefit me, and whether it would or no, I am not so vindictive as to want to imprison them; and if I entered a civil action, what jury would award a medium a farthing damages even?"

"Well, I must be going. I don't think I should trouble much about that evil post-card. Good morning."

When he had departed, Thomson said, "I told you it would do us no good to have anything to do with associations of any kind, but you had such a great desire for it that I gave way, though against my better judgment, and now you see the result: we have offended them, although they can't mean you, for you have always maintained their usefulness, and they know very little about you."

"That is true, but it's an unpleasant incident; let us forget both them and it. If they had had said aught against your mediumship I could have understood it."

"Oh, they won't say that: fishmongers don't usually cry 'stinking fish,' but if you offend a spiritualist, he is bound to have a 'fling' at you. They are constantly deriding the Christians for being intolerant and mean, but I don't believe a Christian would have been guilty of this."

"You will find if we don't pay this little bill for the hall we had last week they will condemn us."

"I don't care; I will not pay a farthing. Besides, if they want it, let them come here for it; if it's worth having, it's worth fetching."

A pleasant reunion was that when our friend, Mr Ashton, came up at his usual hour the following morning, but I was very sorry to hear him complain of a bad attack of lumbago, though Thomson turned it to good account; he assured him that the spirits could easily cure him, and after the physical manifestations, we would induce them to exercise their powers.

While sitting round the table that morning, we saw a luminous appearance suddenly float over the table. Mr Ashton declared that he could discern the features, and he asked if it were the spirit of his son?

"Yes," was the answer, and which, as may be imagined, evoked strong emotion from our client, who was further informed that the son had come back, and would materialise in order to cure him of his complaint.

The manifestations which that morning occurred were not of much importance, speaking from a test point of view, as there being only three persons round the table, and two of those interested parties, the third person could not easily guard against deception. The principal reason of my reference to this particular séance, is because of the luminosity being so confidently identified. The circumstance does not prove that Mr Ashton was any more gullible than vast numbers of other spiritualists, who are, so to speak, on the alert to claim anything as a relative. When we had seated ourselves before the cabinet, Asoka's voice was quickly heard saying that if we would solemnly promise to remain perfectly quiet, he would himself come out and magnetise the lumbago away, and afterwards he would send out Mr Ashton's son.

We cheerfully gave the demanded promise, and very shortly out came the gorgeous form, and without speaking it bent over our client, and commenced rubbing his back, continuing this vigorous treatment for five or six minutes, Mr Ashton the while keeping his word, and not attempting in any way to disengage his hands from mine.

About a minute before Asoka had concluded his magnetising, Mr Ashton peered up into his face and said—

"Yes; I see the dear spirit's features, they are as dark as those of an Oriental; and I feel very much better already, I am very thankful indeed."

"You will be quite well after a few more magnetisings," said Asoka from the cabinet, whither he had retreated.

"I feel confident I shall; but is my son coming out to-day?"

"Yes, but you must preserve the same conditions as before, you must keep the chain unbroken, or I will not be answerable for the consequences. You know it is extremely dangerous for the medium, if anybody breaks the circle."

"Yes, dear friends; I think you may trust me."

"We are not afraid to trust you, but we fear you may not be able to govern your feelings, however we will risk it; so join hands, and your son will come out in a minute."

And the form once more stood before us, this time in the character of our dear old friend's lost child, over whom he exhibited such emotion that it was communicated to me and I had great difficulty in controlling myself, and I was very glad when the séance was finished, and Mr Ashton had departed.

"If ever you do that again I shall make a disturbance," I exclaimed, flaming with anger.

"Why, what else could I do? directly he saw that illuminated drapery over the table he claimed it as his son."

"You should have said that it was not."

"And if I had he would have been so bitterly disappointed, that most likely he would not come again."

"If you do it again, you will have yourself to blame, if the end doesn't please you. I could scarcely keep my seat, to witness his emotion. To palm off yourself as a spirit whom nobody knows is quite bad enough; but his only son!"

"What a fuss you are kicking up! why I have seen people declare to Jesus Christ himself, and the medium in that character has blessed them. And you talk of excitement, why I have seen people half-mad sometimes over forms admitting themselves to be Abraham and Isaac; and sometimes even Adam and Eve have appeared, and the medium dare not say anything or it would perhaps ruin him. I am not so bad as that."

"Well, ruin or not, I can't stand a scene like this again; rich people like our clients don't mind spending a few pounds in the investigation of this subject; but let me beg of you not to play with such sacred feelings again—it is too horrible."

"Well, I won't do it again; so be quiet. But I have sent for Lou, and as we must keep up the excitement you will see what she can do when she comes."

"I do hope our friends will each have a genuine séance; they certainly deserve it for their generosity and kindness. When do you think we shall have one?"

"I don't know; but it lays between the two. I can't say who will get it, but don't worry about that; they will come soon enough," answered Thomson, and with this I was forced to be content.

CHAPTER XV.

THOMSON FURTHER UNBOSOMS HIMSELF.

SOME two or three weeks now passed away, and our time was fully occupied, giving sometimes two and three séances each day, Sundays included. Mr Ashton had become so engrossed in the pursuit, that he often came twice a-day, mostly accompanied by Miss Willis.

The Gordons also continued visiting us, as usual, in the evenings, besides several séances given to other people who were anxious for our services.

Mr Ashton had such confidence in the truth of Thomson's mediumship that he inserted an advertisement in the local journals, setting forth the wonders that were to be witnessed, and challenging the attention of scientific men who might, if they chose, through us, investigate the subject.

I need hardly say that this bold announcement evoked sundry sarcastic allusions from the gentlemen of the press, on Spiritualism and Spiritualists in general, and ourselves in particular.

Knowing some of those gentlemen personally, I often felt ashamed to meet them, for we had frequently broken our promises regarding a sitting with them, and my most earnest persuasions were of no avail in fixing Thomson to keep his word. I argued that they were gentlemen, and would keep the conditions; but he was obdurate, and declared that he never, if he could help it, acted in opposition to his impressions, which told him that they had prepared a trap for us; and, therefore, as we could afford to laugh at their sneers, we must put them off with promises, which were never kept. Although they announced in a paragraph that they would shortly publish an account of a projected séance, yet it never came to anything.

One evening the Gordon family came according to their custom, and Mrs Gordon had brought a beautiful bouquet of choice exotics, which she presented to us for the spirits, and by a strange coincidence, at the séance which followed, Joey gave a remarkable clairvoyant test, which was regarded as a reward for the flowers.

When we had been sitting a few minutes, Joey suddenly exclaimed—

"Where's Olaf?"

"What do you mean?" quickly asked Mr Gordon.

"There's a spirit lady here, she was very dark on earth, and she is asking for Olaf?"

I was myself quite ignorant of the meaning of all this, but when I saw the expression of intense interest exhibited by our clients, I knew that Thomson had obtained information sufficient to touch their keenest sensibilities, and at the end of the séance I asked what it all meant?

"That just shows you what a medium can do if he keeps his eyes and ears open," said he. "Olaf is an all-absorbing name with this family, and very few people know anything about it. It is a sort of cupboard skeleton, and you noticed how I coupled the name with a dark lady? Those few words I said meant, to them, a whole volume; and I just said enough to set them on fire for more."

"But what does it mean?"

"Well, I met Mr Blackfold the other day, and he, as you know, is not aware of the kind of work we are doing. I managed to bring up the name of Gordon, and he said he knew them, and from him I got that information. That's how these celebrated clairvoyant tests are done. Of course as we are comparative strangers to the Gordons, and as that is a subject of which few people know anything, you can understand their amazement."

"I think we must be careful. Mr Gordon is a keen man, and wouldn't much relish this if he found it out."

"The chances are a million to one against detection. If there had been any likelihood of that, I shouldn't have given it to them."

I was fast becoming, with careful practice, a proficient, or rather, developing, so that I could now successfully assist the power, which on all suitable occasions I did to the utmost of my ability.

When Mr Ashton called again for another séance, he was accompanied by Miss Willis, who had again taken the sack home to re-examine it ; and in order to be prepared for any trap, we again stuck a needle and thread up on the wall behind the picture to help out the manifestations.

At this sitting Miss Willis said, " Joey, I have asked you several times for some materialised flowers ; I wish you would let me have them to show to my friends."

" Oh, Miss Willis, you have been so good, and we have grown so much in harmony, that I will let you have them to-day."

" Thank you, I shall be so pleased."

" Very well, then ; but what sort of flowers do you want ? "

" I should like some that are in season."

" What flowers are in season in winter time ? "

" Camellias, azaleas, and stephanotis."

" They are not in season, they are only grown in hot-houses."

" Well, I don't care, I should like to have them."

" All right, so you shall, get a light, and look before you."

When the light came, Miss Willis found a bunch of flowers, containing those requested, besides a few other sorts, which gave unbounded pleasure. After the flowers had been examined, and found to be quite fresh, in fact, actually wet with what we were pleased to imagine dew, we placed Thomson in the sack, and sat down for the materialisations.

Extra care had been taken this time to secure him, and

our friends remarked that if a materialisation occurred under such stringent conditions, it would be evidence beyond question.

My own thoughts on the occasion were,—" If Thomson succeeds in getting out this time, he is a clever fellow;" and he did succeed, for in about ten minutes there stood the form revealed, and after going through the customary motions, he retired, and soon afterwards the séance terminated.

Everything was found to be quite satisfactory, and Mr Ashton then informed us that some of his friends, to whom he had spoken about our wonderful gifts, had expressed a strong desire to see for themselves, so that we were to hold ourselves in readiness, as they would invite some of the principal people in the place to meet us, and he would let us know in a day or two when we were to go.

After our friends had taken their departure, Thomson said—

"I am very sorry to lose that bunch of flowers, but we must keep the game alive."

"How did you get them on to the table?" I asked.

"Easy enough; you saw me place them in that glass of water in the side cupboard just behind where I was to sit in the circle, and when the lights were out, I soon began to 'fish' for the request, and one or two things I said made her think about flowers."

"You certainly managed it very cleverly. But how did you get out of the bag this time?"

"I had to cut my way out, and sew it up again."

"It was done very neatly, and very quickly too, but do you know how other mediums perform their tricks when they help out?"

"Not all; every medium has a way of his own, of course I don't know all their ways any more than they know mine; you can perhaps understand now why mediums are so jealous of each other? Naturally every one wishes to do the greatest trick. I daresay you wonder how I got free from those belts and straps which that party in London used when they locked me to the stove? It was very simple to me, because I can pick almost any lock that's made, and fasten it up again."

" And you picked those padlocks ? "

"Just as easily as walking," said Thomson, and he gave me a few instances of his skill in this direction.

" It seems to me that most séances are 'helped out' by the mediums," I rejoined.

" Either by themselves, or by their confederates; but I prefer to trust others as little as possible; you remember that séance with Morton in Harley Street ? "

"Yes, was that genuine ? "

"No, don't be ridiculous. Morton sadly wanted to get hold of my illuminated things that night when we were both in the cabinet, and he was angry because I wouldn't let him have them; but I told him where to get the stuff, and I believe he too now uses it, but not in the same way that I do."

" I always considered Morton a fine medium; in fact, before I knew you, I saw some rather startling things with him."

"That goes for nothing," declared Thomson. "If you had seen them in the light, you would have laughed at your own simplicity. There is hardly a manifestation that I know of which I have not succeeded in doing, and they have been written about in all the spiritual papers."

" But how about the genuine ? "

" Oh, they are so scarce that no medium dare trust to the spirits. You remember after that séance with Morton, when we left the house and were walking along the streets he called me back to say something privately? Of course you don't know what it was ? "

" No ; what was it ? "

"He wanted to know if you were 'in the swim,' and I told him, that as yet you knew nothing. And you also remember when we were talking about those public meetings of ours, Morton said, 'If you want a third man, here's one, but no conjuring;' that last was to throw you off the scent."

"I recollect once at a séance in London, when we were all friends, or, at any rate, there were no paid mediums present; some flowers were brought into the room after the doors had been locked, and we had been sitting full half-an-hour."

"No paid medium present? Was there an interested medium there?"

"To a certain extent, yes. There was one who wished, I believe, to have his powers made known."

"Then that mystery is explained: were the people of the house rich or poor?"

"Poor."

"Then you needn't trouble any more about it. They were all, or nearly all, in league to deceive you."

"What could they gain by deceiving me?"

"At that time you were very friendly with the editor of the *Spiritual Magazine*, and because you saved him from being sold up, when he had the brokers in the house, he would print anything of yours in his paper, and these people considered that if you were favourably impressed, you would write glowing accounts of their séances for that paper. Most of these mysteries can be easily explained. Did you ever read in the magazine about a wonderful test that John King gave to a gentleman in Paris through two Mediums at different times? The real truth was this: I was sitting daily with a gentleman when Morton came to Paris, and he wished very much to have a séance with my client; so I coached him up, and when his séance came off, his John King corroborated me about some private matters. Our client considered this so wonderful that he sent accounts of it to the spiritual papers. So it was wonderful to anybody but to the mediums, who might, if they were not so jealous of each other, play into one another's hands and amaze the world. Instead of which, they hate each other like wild cats. A very funny thing once happened through this very jealousy. There were three media all claiming John King as their guide. Thorp, Colton, and Fletchman. Thorp was Dr Ayton's protegé, and sitting one day with the Doctor, his John King made statements which were flatly contradicted by Colton, who gave a séance at the same place a day after, and when, Thorp being absent, John King absolutely denied any knowledge of séances with Thorp. Well these two mediums kept on for some time; each giving, at different times, séances to the Doctor, and each time contradicting his opponent; John King, through both, solemnly declaring his ignorance of the other.

"At last, to settle the matter, the Doctor called in Fletchman, and then John King swore that he never by any chance manifested through any body but his present medium, who was in every respect so superior to anybody else, and if a spirit had come through any other medium calling himself John King, he was a lying evil spirit.

"This puzzled the poor Doctor more than ever; he believed in all three media, and continued for a little time to have all three at his house, but it got so bad at last that the Doctor was eventually obliged to end this 'Battle of the Mediums;' so he bundled off Colton and Fletchman about their business, and Thorp got the victory, for he remained with the Doctor. I don't think Colton is doing much now, but Fletchman is chief trance prophet to the 'Grand Universal Association of Light.' All three wanted to drag me into it, but I kept out of the squabble."

"It was quite a comedy."

"Yes; but that is nothing to other things I have seen. However, don't let us stand talking here all day. I expect the train by which Lou is coming will soon arrive, so let us go and meet her."

A day or two after that conversation, when Thomson and Laney had gone out, leaving me at home to finish a lecture for one of the Spiritual Societies, a lady called, and when she entered the room began—

"Mr Parker, I presume?"

"Yes, madam."

"Eh—er—"

"Take a seat, if you please."

"Thank you," softly and slowly.

"What can I have the pleasure of doing for you, madam?"

"Er—ah—you are a mesmerist, I understand?"

"Quite true."

"Can you mesmerise?"

"Yes."

"Eh—ah—you are a spiritualist?"

"I am."

"And you give séances?"

"Yes."

"I called here the other day, but—you were out. I want to have a séance. When would it be convenient for you to come?"

"I see by my diary that we are free to-morrow night. Will that please you, madam?"

"Yes," answered the lady, who now began to speak without halting; "but I cannot have the sitting at my own house, as my friends don't believe in spiritualism, so I have made arrangements to have it at the house of one of my tenants."

"How many will be there?" I asked.

"Only three ladies besides myself. What are the conditions which I am told mediums require? I don't understand much about it myself."

"We require the room to be perfectly dark, and we will engage for the other conditions," I answered. "But we don't usually give séances to strangers unless we have some guarantee that they won't break the conditions."

"I have been sent to you by Mrs Thornleigh; and as for the conditions, I don't know what they are."

"We have the honour of knowing Mrs Thornleigh, and her reference is quite sufficient; but the particular conditions to which I now allude are, that the members of the circle must remain perfectly quiescent—that is, if they wish for a successful séance."

"What would happen if those conditions were broken?" inquired my visitor.

"I dare not say; but it would be extremely dangerous to the health of the medium, irrespective of the fact that the sitting would be a failure."

"What is your fee, Mr Parker?"

"Two guineas, madam."

"And do you guarantee a performance?"

"We do not guarantee a manifestation."

"I beg your pardon; I am so ignorant about it. But do we have to pay in the event of no manifestation?"

"Certainly. We do not control the spirits; they control us; and if the conditions are strictly observed, no doubt something will occur."

"Are you always successful?"

"We have nothing to do with success beyond observing the conditions; but if the circle is devout and harmonious, you will be successful. We make no promises; sometimes nothing whatever occurs."

My visitor remained for over an hour, and seemed to be much interested in the subject; but there was something mysterious in her, which I could not fathom. She appeared to be putting leading questions for the purpose of drawing me out, and in consequence I was guarded in my behaviour. I was almost inclined to think that she was a lady detective, but the reference she gave was so good that I discarded that idea. Still I was not easy, and soon after she had departed Thomson returned, to whom I related the conversation.

"We must be very careful," continued he, "for she may be engaged in a plot, although she has given Mrs Thornleigh's name. To-morrow night, you say? Well, we shall have a full day with Mr Ashton in the morning, the Gordons in the evening, and this lady at night."

"What do you intend to do with Mr Ashton? He is always asking when the 'double form' is coming."

I asked Thomson this question, for he had been so confident about giving them astonishing marvels with Lou, and

Promises.

now she was with us, she was apparently of no use, for none of our customers knew that she was in the town, because whenever they came she at once disappeared.

"Don't you trouble," answered Thomson. "I'll tell him to-morrow that he may expect the 'double form' in a day or two, and we'll manage it all right, never fear."

"But of what use is Louey? We can't have her at the séances, and as they would inevitably see her if she were secreted in the room, I don't see, unless the spirits come, how it is to be accomplished, and you may depend he won't be satisfied much longer with promises."

"I can manage it very well, both for him and the Gordons, and even if I couldn't I can keep them as long as I like. I know more about these things than you do."

Mr Ashton had, for several days, been asking that he might see two spirits at one time come from the cabinet, and he had received innumerable promises from Joey that they were developing the power; and the prospect of witnessing this manifestation kept him sufficiently excited to continue his visits, until at last he was rewarded with the "double form."

CHAPTER XVI.

THE DOUBLE FORM.

"QUICK, Lou; run away upstairs. Here's Mr Ashton!" exclaimed Thomson, hurriedly, when our client again knocked at the door. And away she scuttled out by one door, while Mr Ashton and Miss Willis entered by another.

"I think," said Mr Ashton, "if we are to expect the double form to-day we had better use good tests, so that there may be no room for doubt when I speak of it to my friends." And at our request he locked the entrance door of the room, also the folding doors which opened into a bed-room, and afterwards we soon began our proceedings.

"Will you be able to do it this morning, Asoka?" asked our client, when we had been sitting for some time.

"I have tried very hard, friend, but I shall not be able to succeed to-day; we are developing, and to-morrow I think you may expect it."

"Well, we won't exhaust the power for any other manifestations, so I think we had better break up now," advised Mr Ashton.

"Yes, that is a very wise proposition, and we will now say farewell."

The next sitting which followed, with the Gordons, was likewise hurried over, the excuse of the spirits being that the medium was very fatigued and not in good health.

This story aroused the sympathies of Mrs Gordon, who was not like many others whom we had met. They had a dozen different prescriptions for every ill, real or fancied, under the sun, and were offended if we did not, at least, give one of them a trial. But this lady's kindness took a practical form, as pleasing as it was graceful. Thomson told them that there were various little delicacies to which he had been accustomed when in France, and he fancied that the want of them made him ill; but he didn't know where they could be procured.

Upon Mrs Gordon learning the names of one or two of these delicacies she obtained them for him at once, and hoped they would increase his comfort: in fact, the whole family gave him their sympathy, which he received in a mournful kind of way, that nearly caused me to lose control over my features; not at their kindness, which was as real as it was spontaneous, but at the sublime assurance and promptitude of my partner in turning everything to account. The truth was, he had made himself too familiar with the brandy bottle the night before, and was suffering from its effects, although this was the only time I ever knew him to transgress the strict rules of sobriety; but "always make people do something for you; they take an interest, and like you all the better for it," was another of his rules.

When the time came for us to go to the address given by my mysterious lady visitor of the preceding day, Thomson said—

"Now we must be very careful with these people; she may be a lady as you say, but she may also be a decoy lady. I have a good mind to do a failure."

"Oh no, let us do something for the money; I'll take the things and hand them to you in the cabinet."

"You are always talking about the money: that's the very last consideration with those who have séances and are wealthy; while with those who are poor we needn't trouble about. The only thing is, to be careful. You were very foolish yesterday when you left those things in the window to get the light, because if the landlady or the servants were questioned by anybody, they might tell about them. I am always telling you never to leave anything behind."

And with this admonition ringing in my ears we entered the house of the mysterious lady.

"I hope we have prepared everything to your satisfaction," said she.

There were three other ladies present, all equally mysterious; and we did not like the appearance of things at all, neither in particular nor in general; but we quickly arranged everything, and began as usual with the "physical" and blowing out the lights. We found too that they did not, or perhaps would not, properly understand the science of "darkening" a room. The light from outside streamed through the cracks and crannies of the window in a more free and easy manner than we felt inclined to endure, but we would not disturb ourselves; we told them we would see what our guides would do. Thomson could have got his hands free, but every moment revealed surrounding objects more clearly to the sitters, whose eyes were growing accustomed to the gloom, and such a feat would have been instantly detected. Seeing that course was shut up, Thomson gave the signal to float the table, not in the usual way, for the disappearance of his head would have caused surprise, if not alarm; we both raised it on our knees and kept it suspended for a few moments, and then gently lowered it to its legitimate position, and agreed to sit for the materialisations.

Our company of ladies was not only mysterious, but very suspicious; they wanted a reason for every movement of ours, and I saw that my partner's patience was rapidly dissolving.

In the formation of the circle for the second part, I was placed, as was our custom, at the end nearest the cabinet, but the ladies demurred to this; and then Thomson told them, if they wanted a successful issue they must not disobey the spirits, who knew their business; and if I were not allowed to sit there the power would not be sufficient.

It was easy to see they would have preferred their own way, and, for a wonder, Thomson was obstinate to have his way, and they consented to be guided by us; and we sat down before the cabinet, into which Thomson retired.

But how to let him have the things was the next question! The ladies, "what's that?" every time I stirred an inch, made me think of Thomson's axiom, "Always better have a failure than an *exposé*." I could not, at first, even extract them from my own pockets, for one hand was a prisoner of the lady sitting at my right side, and although the other was not enslaved, it was required to hold and keep the musical-box at its work. That little rebel, as if to increase my agony, insisted upon making frequent rests, which anybody could tell were not in the tunes it was so intermittently gabbling through.

Moreover, I knew that Thomson could not reach them, for I sat facing the cabinet, and there was too much light to perform the experiment with safety. At last I did manage to draw the troublesome goods out, and I held them with a signal in his direction, but it seemed as if the very demon of mischief were abroad that night, and Thomson neither took the things, nor responded to my signal.

"What are you coughing for?" inquired one of the mysteries.

"Because the withdrawal of the power affects my uvula," I answered, and immediately dropped the things on the floor to my left, where nobody was sitting; for I had seen the glowing light quite plainly through the folds of the drapery that enclosed it, which had become loose, and I was afraid they would see it in my hand.

"Where is your other hand?" next asked my tormentor.

"Here, holding the box. Why are you so suspicious? Don't you know that destroys the power? You are constantly breaking the conditions," I returned; and the conviction grew upon me that they were lady detectives, in fact, I thought one was a man.

"I am very sorry, but you are so fidgetty."

"That is because I am affected by the power; a moment since it touched my throat, and then it caught my hands, while it has now gone to my left foot," I replied; and in an instant I felt the signal "all right" on my knee, and soon a part form was visible, but it stayed only for a minute, and finally disappeared.

"Was that a spirit?" inquired one the ladies.

"No; it was only a part of one," exclaimed Joey. "You have not provided the right conditions, and we only give this little, just to show you what we could do if everything were harmonious and devout. We are going now. Good night, and go home all of you."

And we departed, feeling as if we had escaped from a trap, glad to be once more in safety; when Thomson began—

"I'm sure they were detectives, and they were using the one who called here as a decoy."

"I don't think so, because they would have seized you in that case; but I wonder you did anything at all. I dropped those things so that I might kick them to you, but I began to think you wouldn't notice them."

"I couldn't help seeing them; they were shining on the floor like a little lamp. But why did you keep on coughing? that is such a plain signal, and would make anybody suspicious."

"You didn't notice any other signal, and those ladies terrified me; I was afraid they would be awkward—one of them looked like a man."

"Yes, I thought the very same; and I kept the guitar close by to give him muscular music like your 'muscular mesmerism.' Oh, I was on guard, but you see they didn't offer the fee."

"Why didn't you ask for it?"

"How stupid you are! Never appear anxious for money; always tell people what is your fee beforehand, and if they offer don't refuse, but never ask for such a thing."

One of the virtues of Thomson was early rising, and the next morning he was up betimes, in order that we might prepare for Mr Ashton's "double form."

I wondered how it was to be done, and I asked him how and what he intended to do.

"It will be difficult," said he, "but I can do it, as I have several times before. I shall introduce Lou through the folding doors after the séance has begun."

A Cool Proposal. 163

"But Mr Ashton locks the doors and holds the keys."

"That's nothing; I can easily get over that."

"The doors will creak when you open them," I objected.

"The joints and jambs can be well oiled."

"Eh, but you forget; we sit in a dark room, and if you open the door the light will come in."

"Oh dear, no; that room will be as dark as the one in which we sit. I know exactly what to do."

"You seem to be up to everything; but don't you think when you leave your cabinet to open the door they may speak to the spirits, and getting no answer will suspect something?"

"No, the spirits will be 'working up the power,' and must have silence for several minutes, and you must keep that musical box going; fortunately we have a fresh and a large one."

"I shall be very nervous all the time."

"You needn't be anything of the kind, and if Mr Ashton should attempt a seizure, you must knock him over with the guitar."

"What! Why, you are a demon. Hurt that dear old man," I shouted, horrified at the cool cruelty which could rob and then injure a man; it struck me that we were no better than burglars.

"Well, if you are so squeamish, and he seizes the form, we shall be exposed."

"We shall be exposed a thousand times before I would hurt him, or stand by and allow any one else to do so. But I don't think there is any cause for alarm; he wouldn't think of a seizure, so don't mention it again."

"You are an awful booby. Once when I was giving a séance in Manchester there was an unbelieving old gentleman present, who broke the circle, and when I was 'floating' the guitar he tried to catch hold of it."

"How did you know that in the dark?"

"Oh, I always know when anything is wrong. I knew

he was standing up, and I, too, stood up, and gave him such a lesson he never forgot."

"What did you do?"

"I brought the flat part of the guitar down on the top of his head, and it stuck on; and didn't they have a job to get it off again? Of course when the lights came I was joined in the circle with the others, so they couldn't say I did it, although he offered a reward. They all said the spirits did it; but wasn't he wild? and didn't he look a beauty, bonneted with that guitar? I like a guitar; it is so handy for protection. I should like one of these exposing fellows to try his games on me; I'd give him an exposure enough to last him a few minutes, I can tell you."

"Did you hurt that old gentleman?"

"He was more frightened and angry than hurt. It was quite a treat, though, to see him vowing vengeance, and I standing by and helping the old boy; it cut him a bit, but he soon got over that, and never troubled to investigate Spiritualism again."

"That was a terrible revenge; but why didn't you have a failure?"

"It was no more than he deserved. I wasn't going to have my séance spoilt by anybody like that. If he didn't like it he could have kept away."

The Lights and Shadows of Spiritualism, as swift as they were varied, were coming and fading in such rapid succession, that my life was now one of kaleidoscopic character.

Our elaborate preparations for the great event were as careful as they were complete; nothing was forgotten to insure success, and obviate detection. The door-posts and locks were oiled until they moved as if hanging on velvet hinges. Both rooms were equally dark, and to prevent the folding door being opened by anybody before the séance, it was bolted inside, and if Mr Ashton had requested to look in we intended to disown the room entirely. The fire-irons were placed upright to prevent a noise from an accidental touch when Thomson went from cabinet to door to bring out Louey.

The screws and hinges of the musical box were next thoroughly examined and oiled, to expedite its movement and to keep it from playing antics, as musical boxes are sometimes accustomed to do. By the time we had finished, Mr Ashton and Miss Willis were announced and entered the room.

"How are you this morning?" said Mr Ashton, warmly. "I hope the power will be sufficient for a success."

"I cannot say we shall succeed. I can only hope for the best," replied Thomson.

When Mr Ashton had locked the entrance doors and that opening into the room in which sat Louey waiting for the signal, we tried a few moments for the "physical," but nothing occurred, and we changed to the second part for the supreme manifestation—the "double form."

But the moment the light came to permit of the variation, we discovered that the spirits had not been idle. The sofa had travelled up, and was on end and resting on the edge of the table; and, to my surprise, Thomson gave a warning signal, accompanied with a look of great alarm; and happening to glance in the mirror, I saw that by using the tambourine ring with which to strike the strings of the guitar, the paint had come off, and left two moustaches like streaks of black colouring on my face.

I was barely in time to turn round, and while Thomson kept the attention of the others busily engaged, to dip my handkerchief in a tumbler of water, and erase the awful traitor stains. No one besides ourselves had noticed anything wrong, because Thomson's keen eyes had seen the mischief, and in a moment it was removed. The feelings of our visitors were worked up to a high pitch of excitement; hitherto they had, with us, seen only one spirit at a time come from the cabinet; but now, if we succeeded, it would be accepted as a most triumphant and crowning display of spirit power.

We again took our seats, after Thomson had gone behind the screen—not under test conditions—and with the musical box clattering away at its several tunes, we sat and silently wished for success—I with full confidence in Thomson's power, and our clients with equal faith in the spirits.

But we were doomed to disappointment. Louey, who was in the next room, refused to answer the signal and unbolt the door from the inside; and although Thomson could have opened it if she had, even his skill was not sufficient to cope with this dificulty. We could see a streak of light piercing the keyhole, which told us that Louey would not come. Joey angrily referred to that light, and severely scolded whoever was there for not extinguishing it. I was afraid, because I thought our clients might wonder why gas light should be needed on the noon of a brilliant sunshiny day, but they were quite unsuspicious. We sat there until Asoka deplored the want of power, but said if they would come again at three o'clock in the afternoon, he felt sure of success; and on these terms we broke up.

Louey told us afterwards that she became nervous and frightened; and I verily believed the poor little thing when she said, she knew, if she had come in, she must have spoilt everything through inability to control herself.

It was a great disappointment to us all—to our clients who had so confidently expected it, and to us because of the waste of all our trouble.

Mr Ashton had, however, asked if we thought the power would be enough to give a séance at half-past seven in the evening to a party of his friends. We were informed that the party would include several local magnates, and if we thought it could be done, we were to go at the time mentioned. Naturally no objection was raised from our side, and they left us until three o'clock. We were not to have a success even then, for Thomson was so angry with his little cousin for her " obstinacy and cowardice," that he said, as she had made one failure, he would make another; and true enough he did, for when Mr Ashton returned, we had the sitting, but it came to nothing, and a fresh appointment was made for the next morning at eleven o'clock. I fully expected that our client would be annoyed, but his serene temper was not ruffled in the least, and he again departed, after reminding us of the engagement at his friend's house.

The number three séance of that day with the Gordon family was likewise a failure, or rather the power was still developing. They asked Joey to be more explicit regarding "Olaf," and he told them that he had instituted inquiries in the spheres, and directly he got any information he would at once communicate to them its tenor.

A short time before we were going to dress for the fourth séance, our friend Mr Wilson came in and hurriedly exclaimed—

"Now, then, I told you a little while ago that a gentleman whom I know wishes to retain your services. He is enormously rich, worth anything; and he doesn't mind money one bit. He writes me—ah, here's his letter—yes, I am to have a sitting with you, and if I am satisfied, I am to send you on to him at once. Now, then, come on—Oh, this gentleman is my manager," and he hastily introduced a quiet looking man, in direct contrast to himself. "Now, then, you give us this sitting at once, and I'll telegraph to my friend that you are coming on to-morrow."

"Why, really, Mr Wilson, we have barely enough time to dress for an evening party, and——"

"Never mind that; let them wait, it will do them good."

"But I am afraid it won't do us good."

"Oh, just sit at the table for a few minutes, it won't take long—come on." And he bustled us to our seats. Fortunately it did not take long to darken up; and in a short time we had everything ready, and commenced—a not very difficult task, to convince him of our power.

Louey sat with us this time. There was no particular reason for hiding her from Mr Wilson; on the contrary he must know, for if we were to go to his friend's house, it was necessary that he should know of her existence. We began our séance in a most convincing way as far as force went. We bumped the table up and down, we flung the chairs about in a manner which suggested that the spirits were labouring under a furious desire to convince our friend.

When we had almost dislocated some of the furniture—the table in particular—Mr Wilson stopped us, and declared that he was abundantly satisfied.

"That will do, that will do; if you can only give my friend such wondrous manifestations your fortunes will be made."

"When do you want us to go?" we inquired, for we almost began to imagine his friend meant to divide his wealth between us.

"Oh, to-morrow morning by the first train."

"Impossible! we have to give a most particular séance to-morrow morning, and——"

"Never mind then; go the next day."

"Yes, we can go then; but how long will this gentleman want us?"

"A month perhaps. You will go to his mansion, and be well cared for; and then, if you like, you can come back here again. I'll go and telegraph to him at once, and——"

Our friend's further speech was summarily cut off by a furious knocking at the door, and Mr Ashton came in, hurriedly exclaiming—

"Why, really now, do you know the time? I have a carriage waiting for you; everybody is waiting."

All right, Mr Ashton, we will be ready in five minutes; take a seat please. Good night, Mr Wilson, you may depend upon us, we will be there at the time mentioned." And we bundled him out, and were soon ready to accompany Mr Ashton. Lou had disappeared as soon as his voice was heard.

As far as material prosperity went, we had nothing of which to complain; three, four, and (to-day) five séances per diem were good conditions, and the prospect of a continuance of the like pleased Thomson amazingly.

"Won't the power be short to-night?" I whispered to Thomson in the carriage.

"Shut up; you'll have them hear you," he snapped in a whisper.

In a short time we arrived; and when removing our overcoats in the hall I again whispered—

"Do my pockets look all right? I'm afraid they bulge out."

"No, they are all right; but don't be whispering to me now, keep as far off as possible."

The company to which we were now introduced was composed of about twenty individuals of both sexes, the majority of whom were quite ignorant of Spiritualism, and they eyed us with great interest, not altogether unmixed with suspicion. We soon, however, took our seats round a large oblong table, which barely possessed sufficient capacity for the accommodation of all. Thomson and I were seated as usual opposite to each other, he between Mr Ashton and Miss Willis, for they were *en rapport* with his guides, and would not injuriously affect the free display of the power. I sat between two ladies, and having received a signal from my partner to attempt nothing, I composedly submitted to let them grasp my hands as tightly as they pleased. If holding me would have prevented manifestations, they would have succeeded remarkably well, for they gripped me so hard and fast, that I would have asked them to relax their hold a little; but on account of their enormous suspicion of the least movement, I endured the punishment, although the pain was hardly compensated for by the fee.

A clergyman too was present, and sat two distant from Thomson; he was very suspicious, but he received a tolerably good test. When we had been sitting for a few minutes, he exclaimed that somebody was touching him, and others also experienced the like.

The guitar now suddenly began its aerial flight; and when the clergyman inquired if all hands were joined, he received an unanimous "Yes," accompanied by a thump on the head from the flying guitar.

Thomson could have easily freed both my hands, but he did not seem inclined to give them too much; and after sitting for about an hour, we lighted up, and found a chair hanging on the linked hands of Mr Ashton and Thomson.

How it came there was the question. Nobody could answer, for each person declared that the circle had not been broken for one instant.

We saw that they were puzzled, and we determined to leave them in that state; and when the hostess asked if we were not to sit for materialisations, we informed her that we felt it to be of no use with such a large company, but we should be pleased to come another time. The fact of no form being given was a sad disappointment. We told them that if they insisted we would try for it, but we were confident nothing would occur, and at last they had to content themselves with what we had given to them.

Our mysterious lady was also present, and to our surprise she was extremely friendly, and did not forget to hand us the fee for the sitting we had given to her.

When we left the place, I asked Thomson why he would not sit for the form.

"Because," said he, "it is too dangerous in such a big company of strangers, and then there was the parson. I am always suspicious of that cloth, but I think I puzzled him. He couldn't make out how that hand could pat him on the back like it did; I was strongly inclined to box his ears."

"What for?" I asked in amazement.

"Because he broke the circle, and stood up as well."

"How do you know that?"

"I can always tell, but he couldn't understand how that chair got linked on our arms."

"Do you think he meant mischief?"

"I don't know. I always give the church a wide berth; it is not to be trusted."

I did not consider that séance a success, but I hoped that Mr Ashton would not be disappointed with the double form. Nor, indeed, was he. When he came up for it, we had everything prepared, and no time was lost, but we quickly arranged ourselves before the cabinet in our usual manner.

I had charge of the musical box, with strict injunctions to force the wheel round if it showed signs of insubordination, for it might stop without rhyme or reason, and just at the critical moment when its music was most needed to assist the power. During this sitting I was in an agony of fear. I heard every slightest movement of the medium, even above the din of the music machine. I knew by a sort of nervous intuition when Thomson pulled off his boots, and when he gently shifted the screen in order to pass round to the door to bring out Louey. I was conscious of every footfall, though it must have been as soft as a cat's, and I *felt* him reach the door and open it, and then return with the duplicate form—of Louey.

It seemed now as if the worst part of the work was done, and I breathed more freely.

The first appearance was Asoka, who once came out, and when he had retired he told us that, in spite of all difficulties, they would succeed; but we must all solemnly pledge our sacred word of honour to observe the conditions, for now the medium was in such a critical position that the least infraction would seriously jeopardise his health, if not even his life. We earnestly consented, and shortly afterwards Asoka again appeared, and by his side stood—the double. Strong emotion was evoked by this gorgeous and fascinating sight, and spite of my own knowledge of the secret, I was in some measure affected by the epidemic of belief.

One after the other, Mr Ashton and his friend were allowed to walk into the cabinet, and view more closely the wondrous spectacle, while I was posted on guard also inside, and standing to the right of little "Joey," whose form, draped in long flowing guaze, and illuminated by the girdle and mirror, was plainly visible. I saw dimly the serious face of the child, as cool as on any ordinary occasion; she was standing rather to the back of Thomson, who was entranced and sitting on a chair. When he thought we had been long enough in the cabinet, he gave me a slight kick, thereby to indicate that we were to leave him, and a few spasmodic groans supported my suggestion that we must retire.

Mr Ashton was highly delighted, and I think Miss Willis

too shared his belief and happiness; he was fully convinced that it was no dummy form, but a veritable personage, separate in every way from the medium. He had felt the little hands, and contrasted them with those of Thomson; he had also placed his hands on the two heads, and satisfied himself that it was "Joey," and at the end of these external observations we again took our positions outside.

Asoka at once spoke out again, and told us that he was about to restore the fluid of the form, and we must remain perfectly still until the end. I heard, as before, every movement, and knew as well as Thomson himself when safety had been assured by the removal of the girl; and after a few words from Joey and Asoka of farewell to our client, whom he informed of our projected visit to another place, and that we intended to come back again, and having received the assurances of Mr Ashton that he was abundantly satisfied with the manifestation he had just witnessed, we prepared to separate. He bade us God speed in our work, and a promise of his assistance if needed, and a wish that we might meet again.

And we left the trustful, generous, and courteous old man, who, after all, had never received the genuine séance, though he had seen an indubitable "double form."

CHAPTER XVII.

LOOK INSIDE.

AFTER a cold and dreary journey by rail we arrived at our destination the next afternoon, and found awaiting us on the platform three or four gentlemen, who were introduced to us as the principal members of the Spiritualist Society of that town.

This was not according to the programme. We expected to meet the wealthy man of £50,000 value, and he was there too in the little group, which was a matter of great surprise to us; but we thought that perhaps his carriage was outside; its absence, however, was another surprise. For myself, I was anxious to get to his house, for I was suffering many molar agonies.

We left our luggage in the station, and were ourselves conducted to a small stuffy place, which the wealthy man tried to delude us into the belief was a hotel; but we objected to the imposition, and seeing that there was some misunderstanding or something else which we could not fathom, we demanded to be taken to the best hotel in the place. That request being granted, we soon found ourselves within the cosy precincts of a proper resting place; and by the potent aid of spirits from its vaults, my toothache rapidly subsided, and when I was asked if it were better, I was enabled to reply that, thanks to the spirits, the pain was considerably allayed.

Our enthusiast, Mr Wilson, now appeared on the scene, and informed us that the town crier had been sent round to notify to everybody whom it might or might not concern, that Mr Parker, of London, would lecture in the hall the same night on Spiritualism, and the celebrated medium, Mr Thomson, would afterwards sit for manifestations.

Protest was useless, and soon we were ready, and found ourselves at the time specified confronting a large and orderly congregation, who appeared anxious to see the curiosities. Fortunately I had two or three MS. lectures, one of which I delivered to a most attentive audience, and afterwards the seance was held, but with no degree of success, which was attributed to the fatigue of the medium.

When we were going to our hotel we were accompanied by the chairman of the association, and passing by his house he kindly invited us to go in for a while to talk over plans for the séances; while there, we found how much the enthusiasm of Mr Wilson had misled himself and us. The person whom he represented as being so wealthy kept a small shop, and wasn't worth £50,000 at all, nor would his position in life justify him in spending much money in the investigation of Spiritualism.

Nothing remained for us but to make the best of it, and in this town, although we made no pecuniary success, yet I enjoyed the stay much better than at any other place before or since our travels. Our entertainer, I soon discovered, had been an active member of the church to which I had formerly belonged; and we talked of our Christian experiences, and of the various men whom we had known and appreciated. I could not tell him what I knew regarding Spiritualism; but at that time if I had spoken out it would have done no good whatever, for a revelation would have been attributed to a quarrel with Thomson, and I had yet no evidence to offer that all was trickery, and half a story would have been laughed at as "old news." Moreover, I knew that when once a man lets his ideality run loose, there is no limit to their journey, nor to the persistency with which such a man will fight for the "cause;" besides which, I was reduced from the high position I had formerly assumed, to that of a mere investigator, as intensely anxious as any man could be to get the truth, however small, and the lesson I had learned, in the rapidity of my conversion to Spiritualism, taught me not to relinquish it until my reason was fully satisfied, by absolute daylight proof, that all the manifestations rested on no better foundation than folly and fraud.

"I think you are very foolish to give your lectures as you do," said Thomson, when we were again alone.

"What do you mean?"

"Why don't you shut your eyes as do other mediums, and give them off under control?"

"I couldn't do it."

"Nonsense! You don't suppose that those fellows who go chattering about are really asleep under the control of spirits?"

"Yes, of course."

"Then you're a bigger fool than I thought. See here, you don't seem to understand the way to go to work; if you would give such lectures as yours under control, you would soon be considered a medium indeed. It doesn't matter a bit what rubbish a man talks in the trance; he could make more money thus, by reciting the alphabet than you would with ever such a grand discourse given normally. I have seen Fletchman rehearsing his lectures, and he used to say, 'This is the way I do it,' and I don't see why you shouldn't do the same."

"It would be impossible to me."

"Nothing is impossible. Just shut your eyes and chatter away; say you are controlled by some great personage—Martin Luther, Judas Iscariot, John Wesley, anybody."

"I don't think I shall try it; but do you know how that medium managed to handle red hot coals?"

"No; I don't know all the tricks of other mediums, but because one can't explain it, that is no reason why one should credit the spirits with its performance."

You don't appear to be so much of a spiritualist as I am."

"You wait a little. Now let us talk of our position. Of course we have been let in by our friend. His wealthy man turns out to be nobody, while we are coolly foisted upon the Society.

"Well, it is rather droll certainly; Mr Wilson is a wag, I should think."

" He may be twenty wags for aught I care; but he won't play off on me again," said Thomson viciously.

" I don't think he meant wrong."

"It's of no use to speculate on what he meant; the only thing is to get away again as quickly as possible. I can see we shall lose money by coming here."

" We shan't take much hurt. What a fine fellow is the chairman of this Society where we have been to-night."

" Yes, he's all right," said my partner unconcernedly.

" It was like old times for me to talk with him; he is a true type of a Class Leader—earnest, upright, and enthusiastic. What a lot of men Spiritualism takes from the churches, particularly dissenters; to tell you the truth I'm sorry for it, but I fancy if they knew all, at the onset they would remain true to their first love."

" Yes, I've known great numbers of men who were once among the Christians, but you see, if they find out anything, they stick to Spiritualism for very shame. But now, what are we to do? Never mind the Christians or anybody else," snapped Thomson impatiently.

In my own mind I absolved our friend Mr Wilson from intentional wrong; he simply took an exaggerated view of things, including himself. I suggested that we should go back again, but to this Thomson emphatically objected. He said that we must give them a little rest, and they would be more hearty in their welcome when we did pay them another visit; and that we must give the people here a few séances, and afterwards go on to the next large town, about forty miles away, where he knew several wealthy friends who would be glad to secure our services.

This course we adopted, and the chairman of the Society insisted upon us all making his house our home. He saw that we had been misled, and although it was no fault of his, yet he made full atonement, and rendered every assistance to us in our work, that is as regards the preparations for the meetings, and at the end of a few days we bade adieu to our manly entertainer, and leaving Lou under his care, we went on to pastures fresh.

The prognostications of Thomson were fully verified; when we reached our destination we found his old clients, one of whom—a Mr Lilley—quickly made arrangements with us for a series of séances to take place in his own house, where we ourselves were to stay during their course.

Thomson did not like the latter part of the contract for fear of having to submit to a search, but our client never hinted at such a thing, and I don't think he ever thought of it. Thomson also informed me that Mr Lilley's family were much opposed to Spiritualism, and when we arrived at the house we hardly anticipated a favourable welcome from those who considered that through such people as ourselves the head of the household had been seduced from the faith of his youth, of which he had been a firm and liberal supporter; but I am bound to say that we received every attention at their hands.

The first séance which we gave to Mr Lilley was much like many others, except that instead of Asoka, John King came, and told our client that if he would prepare the necessary things they would give him wax moulds of spirit faces and hands, similar to those obtained a few months before in London, respecting which a chapter will be given in due course in this work to reveal the mystery.

During this séance I had fresh opportunities of witnessing the ingenuity of my partner. Some of the questions which our client addressed to the spirits relating to Philosophy and Theology I considered beyond the range of Thomson's ability, but I reckoned without knowledge. Other questions regarding private matters which had passed between John King and Mr Lilley through different media, were even yet more difficult, for Thomson could not know what occurred when he was absent; but he was fully alive to the exigencies of the occasion. To all those things of which he was ignorant, John King from the cabinet would utter in confidential and sententious tones, "Look inside."

This convenient way of disposing of a difficulty was as effectual as it was comical. Mr Lilley received it all in perfect good faith, and with a pleasure that was apparent, perhaps because of the spiritual confidence existing between them, from which I was excluded.

To every question propounded of a deeper import, or of a more difficult character than usual, back would instantly come the flattering but thundering "Look inside," to which Mr Lilley would answer, "Ah yes, John; you're right John; that is the place to find it."

At the end of this sitting, at which only we three had been present, we descended to the drawing-room, where Mrs Lilley and the family were, the former upon our entrance saying—

"When I passed the door of your séance room, and heard you all singing, and the musical-box going too, do you know of what I was reminded?"

"Haven't the least idea," answered her husband.

"Of the Priests of Baal calling upon God to help them!"

"But we obtained our desires, Madam," I quickly answered.

"Bravo, Parker!" exclaimed our host; but Thomson gave me a warning look, and I said but little afterwards when the conversation turned upon the exposure of the lady medium in London. I found too that Thomson was abundantly right in his knowledge of spiritualistic human nature, for although that *exposé* was as clear as light, yet Mr Lilley was bristling with arguments in defence of that particular medium. I allowed the conversation to drift along without taking any part in it, for I gathered that I had already gone beyond the bounds of prudence.

The next morning we went out with our client to arrange for the séances for the wax moulds. He caused a large galvanized iron vessel to be made to hold the liquid wax, in which the spirits would dip their faces and hands in order to get the moulds.

When everything was prepared for the evening séance, we parted from Mr Lilley, ostensibly to view the town and look up old friends; in reality to be alone to talk over our plans, and also expose the girdle and mirror to the sun, or they would not emit light at the sitting.

"Now there's one thing you must observe here," said Thomson, "and that is, you must know nothing."

"What do you mean?"

"Well, last night in Mr Lilley's room, when he began talking about Spirit Philosophy and Theology and what not, you, like a fool, showed him that you knew more than he did, and have thereby offended him."

"Why, he asked me certain questions—"

"And you answered them; that's where the mischief is. You must be as ignorant as a pig unless you give them as spirit messages, you must, with such a man, let *him* know; never mind what he says. I know these people of old; with flattery you may do anything with them."

"I was awfully tempted last night to support Mrs Lilley in that discussion; I thought she was too much 'shut up.'"

"Then I'm glad you didn't give way to your 'awful' temptation; you made a very foolish remark about the priests of Baal."

"I think she is much too sensible a woman to mind that. It struck me that she held her own very ably in that argument, and that seemed to make her husband rather sharp upon her."

"Don't you ever interfere in such cases; Mrs Lilley is quite capable of taking her own part."

"Yes, and I think her husband might very profitably take a few lessons from her."

"Perhaps so; but he won't take lessons from anybody except John King."

"Do you think he will get genuine moulds?"

"Yes, I think so; if he doesn't, we must make them."

"How?"

"I know how; I have made them before for him, and

don't consider myself any worse than a tradesman who adulterates his goods; or a man who writes articles about Hindoo languages, and knows no more about them than a Hindoo knows about skating; and others who write about the mathematical or astronomical meaning of the Pyramids, when they are as ignorant of mathematics as a Zulu. They just copy it all from books, and give it as their own."

" How long have you known our friend Mr Lilley?"

" Oh, for several years. He has heaps of money, and I don't think his wife minds him spending a few guineas over his hobby; but she don't like mediums ever since he took home Long, who is a very curious sort of man, with nothing of the gentleman about him; he got asking questions of the servants, and bribing them, of course she soon heard of it, and really she couldn't stand it so broad, so that I believe it came to a question of either she or Long leaving the house; and he had to go. But we must never speak to the servants; that's where Long always made a mistake, for at every house where he went, he always tried to get at the servants for his clairvoyance. You remember Mrs Thornleigh saying she had strong suspicions of his attempting to bribe them at her house."

" Were you here at the same time as Long?"

" Yes, about six years ago. Old Rushton used to live here then, and I'll tell you a queer thing that once happened to Long and myself with Lilley and Rushton. John King used to come through both of us, but that made no difference to us; we were great chums, and had many a spree together. You know that for several years the spiritualists have written and babbled about a new era, or dispensation, or some such nonsense, just on the eve of arriving, and every spiritualist thinks that he will be the Messiah to lead this new dispensation affair. Amongst others, Lilley and Rushton considered themselves eligible. Well, one day I gave Lilley a séance, and I couldn't think of anything fresh; so John King began to talk about this era business, and he told Lilley that in a short time there would be 'wonderful changes,' and everybody would worship according to the new religion; in fact, it was to be the millennium. Lilley, of course, began to put leading questions. I knew what he meant, but I tantalised him for some time by telling him to 'look inside.' At last John King came out, and blessed him, and spiritually anointed him to the dignity of 'Logos.' He told a long rigmarole about anything he could think of: to be faithful and deserving of the great honour conferred upon him, and always to 'look inside;' that the spirits for a long period had kept their eyes upon him, and that they had just held a grand meeting in the spheres, and had unanimously elected him the chief—the Busiris, before whom all must bow: and, of course, John King didn't forget to recommend the medium to his care. He told him that the instrument through which the spirits send their messages must lack for nothing, so when that séance was over, I got an extra £5. Lilley always behaved well to me in money matters.

"About this time Long had some invention he wanted to bring out, but, like me, he never had any money, although we both made plenty, and he didn't know how to raise enough to get this thing out. I forget what it was, he was always inventing something. At last a thought struck him; he went and asked Rushton for the loan of £50, but the old man wouldn't hear of it; he said he had no money, and couldn't possibly let him have it. Long saw it was no good, and he let the subject drop, and began to talk of Spiritualism. In the midst of the conversation he suddenly went into a trance, and John King came. After a long address, John King began to tell Rushton that the leaders of the new era were being chosen, and the best man they could find on earth to be chief was himself: and further told him, that he must prepare to take his proper position; but in his exalted seat he was not to forget the humbler means used in the battle—he must reward them well.

"The old man almost went off his head with joy, and when Long came out of his trance, Rushton looked at him—you know his smiling way—and said, 'Well, Mr Long, I think

I can oblige you in that little matter,' and at once he gave him a cheque for £50. Long faithfully promised to return the loan, but Rushton said, 'Oh, I don't mean it as a loan. I think such valuable servants of the cause ought to be well paid, particularly when we get messages of such stupendous import,' and Long walked off with his cheque, while Rushton nearly went crazy about his message. The best of the joke, however, still remains. Both Lilley and Rushton were on the very high road of happiness, and began to consider themselves a foot or two higher than the rest of their fellow-creatures, but when they met each other they both received a little check.

"'Mighty events are on the eve of accomplishment,' began Rushton loftily; he had commenced to cultivate a grandiloquent style, and to let his hair grow long, and was in an awful agony to unburden himself.

"'Yes,' answered Lilley simply, who didn't mean to share his secret with anybody.

"'A wonderful manifestation occurred to me the other day,' again babbled Rushton.

"'Indeed.'

"'Well, you see, it appears that every new cause requires an able commander. I don't believe in committees and that like, I believe in having one head.'

"'Well?'

"'And the spirits take the same view, and in the new era just about to dawn on a spiritually dark people, the leaders of which have ——'

"'Here, stop, stop! What do you mean?'

"'If you will let me go on I'll tell you, but to no other living soul would I reveal the communication. I don't mind you, because I think you have a little spirituality.'

"'Thank you.'

"'Yes, I do think so. Well, the spirits have held high conference, and have selected ——'

"'Yes, I know all about it; you needn't say any more. I know they have chosen a leader, but I don't choose to say who he is.'

"'There is no cause, for I know.'

"'What do you know, pray?'

"'I know the leader—the Logos.'

"'Oh, indeed! Who is he?'

"'Humble and weak he is, true enough; but he will endeavour to discharge well the duties of that high office.'

"'I wouldn't be surprised,' said Lilley sarcastically, 'if you are not just conceited enough to suppose you are the chosen leader.'

"'It *is* I!' thundered Rushton majestically.

"'You!'

"'Yes; and what have *you* to say against it?'

"'Oh, nothing; no indeed! nothing in the world; not a word, oh dear no. Logos! humph, fine Logos.'

"'As good as you any day.'

"'Of course; you should get measured for a Nimbus. I suppose you got this wonderful news through Long?'

"Yes, John King gave it through him. I hope you won't deny he's a medium."

"'No; oh, no! but I always suspected that his messages were tinged with his own peculiarities and feelings; but, excuse me, I am very busy. Good morning, *good* morning, Mr—a—Logos,' and he solemnly bowed his visitor away without giving him a chance to answer. Those two used to be good friends once, but I believe they were unfriendly for a long time afterwards. Naturally we two mediums heard of this storm from our respective clients; but we told them both to stand their ground and be firm, so they were both satisfied, and each kept faithful to his own medium, while contemptuously disregarding the other's existence. Of course we didn't care how much they quarrelled, in fact we were glad they did; there was less chance of their getting by the ears again; but you see now, if we play our cards right, he'll do anything for us. When I tell him to 'look inside,' that refers also to some of the great things John King promised him then."

This story, told in sober style, I had no reason to doubt;

in fact, the more I knew of the two men, the more I found by their lofty ways that they deemed themselves much higher than the rest of their fellows. Neither were they alone in their beliefs, for I met several who talked of the new era in such a strain as directed the minds of their hearers to themselves as the leaders.

Towards the evening we returned to Mr Lilley's and found everything ready for the séance, and I thought if ever the genuine could come, now was the time, for surely never were conditions more favourable.

CHAPTER XVIII.

JOHN KING AND HIS FOLLOWERS.

ABOUT seven o'clock in the evening we three entered the séance room, when Mr Lilley showed us several souvenirs of the spirit world. On one wall hung a photograph of Katie King, John King's daughter, but it betrayed such evidence, to my mind, of its being the medium herself, whom I knew, that I was surprised our client did not see it also. There was also a strip of spirit drapery (a piece of the like had, in the days when I was younger, been presented to me, and which I had religiously preserved for a long time), also a few other little things which bore testimony to the robust faith of our client.

The physical manifestations that evening were much like others already described, and after about half an hour spent in watching the spirit lights flit about, and lustily singing hymns, Thomson entered the cabinet.

John King was the first to come out and magnetise the vessels containing the hot liquid wax; after which Joey began his chattering.

Mr Lilley, who was a believer in symbols, christened John the "Master," and John returned the compliment by dubbing him "Lord of the Inner House," the "Busiris!" Joey was content as "Doorkeeper of the Hall of Life," and Asoka was "Chief Pillar," while we two mediums had to put up with our every-day names.

"John," said Mr Lilley, "don't you remember when you came through another medium once telling me something about the 'Spheres of Life.' What did you mean? You promised to explain some time."

"Look inside," roared John, at the same time treading on my toes.

"Yes, John, that is the only place to find it," returned Mr Lilley, and he burst out singing some rhymes about John, Joey, Asoka, and Cissy, not forgetting himself, and after that topical concert we adjourned.

The next morning a telegram came from one of the private secretaries of the E. of ——. The telegram stated that they wished for thirty séances, and would pay 3000 francs for them, also travelling expenses.

"That's good," said Thomson. "Of course you will have to be the medium for the physical manifestations and trance."

"You surely don't mean to say that you have actually played off these tricks upon the Emperor?"

"I should rather think I have, and mean to do so again. The Emperor you will find is the very nicest man you ever saw. People who call him a tyrant don't know what they are talking about. I have been there before and know him quite well; he makes you feel just as if you were at home, and you forget he is an Emperor."

"Do you ever have a failure with him?" I enquired.

"Oh, no, that would never do; you can't talk about bad conditions with such people; they wouldn't understand it, but might take it as a reflection upon themselves, and then it would get some of the court officials into a row, and you'd soon make enemies."

"Yes, I should think so."

"And then again, you must never mention money; they will pay handsomely if you leave it to them. I have had many a 1000 franc bill from the Grand Duke of —— for each séance he has had; and they never dream of tests. I remember once when I was giving one of a number of sittings to the King of ——, one of the nobles proposed a test, but the king wouldn't hear of it; he told them there were no sharpers there, and if anybody was afraid they had better leave."

"What spirits do you have with the Emperor?" I queried.

"I let them find out. I have been recognised as three deceased relatives each time I came out at one sitting."

"Will you give Mr Lilley his moulds?"

"Yes, if I get a chance; but I am now going to answer this telegram, you see they pay for an answer. I shall say I am coming on, so we will wait for an answer, and in the meantime we will go on with these séances. Lilley hasn't paid me any money yet; I shall have to set John King at him."

"You are very funny with your 'Look inside.' I am surprised he is satisfied with such an answer."

"Oh, there are two or three more to whom I tell that tale when they ask inconvenient questions; they like it, because it compliments them. But what a row he kicked up with his howling last night; do you remember what it was all about?"

"I didn't trouble to recollect such a jingle; it seems to me that he looks upon John King as God."

"Yes, I can make him do what I like with John; but you have offended him right enough, I thought you had. When I was alone with him for a little while, he told me he didn't like you, and he wondered I had you with me. Of course he doesn't know that you are so necessary. I told him the power was much stronger since you had been with me, but it was no use; I shall have to make John talk to him," said Thomson; and that same evening John King gave him a little lecture.

The wax moulds were not given however, but Thomson had told me he shouldn't attempt it until the third or fourth sitting. He also told me that a few years before he had given to Mr Lilley some wax moulds, and that he could give a wax mould of a complete head, hand, or foot, without showing a single break in any of them, and yet retain the skin marks; and subsequent lessons from Thomson sufficiently proved that he really could perform these tricks.

At the end of the séance Mr Lilley wanted us to go with him to visit some of his learned friends. We had no particular wish to go, but were compelled by reasons of policy to abstain from showing any disinclination to accompany him.

When we arrived we found three or four nice old gentlemen—retired tradesmen—who spent their time in confusing themselves over questions which the want of early education prevented them from properly understanding.

But they talked for an interminable time, until we were both completely bored. I saw that Thomson was trying to comfortably ensconce himself without showing any appearance of fatigue, but it was almost impossible, and he began to nod and open his eyes alternately, and trying to look as innocently wide awake as the circumstances of the case would allow.

I too felt exceedingly drowsy, listening to their weary and monotonous rumbling, and at last, spite of my utmost efforts, I found I was gradually losing myself, and fancied myself in an immense bottle full of bees.

But I was aroused by Thomson's voice saying—

"I hope you will excuse me, gentlemen, I don't feel well, and I must go out into the air."

How gladly I welcomed the contrivance for escape; but to my horror the company agreed to let him go, but said that I could remain. However, Thomson was loyal in this instance. He told them that he felt lonely without me; and they allowed the plea, thinking that a medium must be eccentric; and so we obtained our liberty, when Thomson said—

"Well, what do you think of them?"

"They are a queer lot. They have been reading Swedenborg, from whom they have got those ideas about the 'grand laws of correspondence' and 'Divine Light,' and they mix up Swedenborg with Darwin, and John Stuart Mill, and others, until they make such a hotch-potch that they don't know what they are talking about. I was afraid you were going to leave me in their clutches."

"I had a good mind, just to teach you patience. These men

have loads of money, and so long as they will pay, you mustn't mind their little oddities. You remember that man in London who used to come up and give us long lectures about the 'Human Machine'? Well, I didn't like to hear him any more than you did, but when he put down £5 for a séance, I considered that paid for his lectures and my séances. You must learn to put up with these drawbacks."

"I wonder you didn't then?"

"Oh, I can do anything here; they look upon me as half an idiot."

"I scarcely liked to join in their conversation for fear of giving offence somehow."

"You might have joined in and said anything if you had given it off under control; they'll swallow anything from a spirit, when they'd quarrel like cats with anybody else. But we must try and give Lilley his moulds to-morrow. He hasn't given me any money yet, but I'll have it or know the reason why."

The next afternoon when I was in Thomson's room he called to me—

"Shut the door and come over here; I want to show you something."

"What is it?" I answered, and walked over to him, where he was turning some things over in his portmanteau.

"Have you shut that door carefully?"

"Yes."

"Then speak low; we don't know who may be listening; walls have curious ears."

"What have you there so carefully wrapped up?"

"I am going to show you. There, do you know what that is?" he asked as he unfastened and held up the objects to view.

"Good gracious! why, I thought you told me those séances were genuine?" I exclaimed in astonishment; for the things he held in his hands were the identical plaster of Paris casts from which the face wax moulds were taken in London a few months previous to this, and which at the time created quite a furore among the spiritualists.

"Well, I couldn't let on all at once to you," said he apologetically. "Of course these are the casts of 'Akosa and Lilly,' and we must try and do the same over again to-night."

"But how did you manage to show up two forms at once?" I inquired in reference to the appearance and vanishing of two spirits, or, as it was called, "Duplication and Re-absorption," at the same time Louey was sitting with his client.

"You ought to know by this time that the double and vanishing are worked easily enough. You know Lou has another little sister. I did it with her, but the little monkey nearly laughed outright when they almost worshipped her. It was the same with you when we appeared at that séance just before you joined me. Lou can always keep her face, but I was always afraid of the other. She is a perfect little fool."

"I don't see how it can be done to-night; it is so difficult not being in your own house."

"That's just it; consequently if we succeed now, it will be all the better test for them. We must do it somehow, for I want some money, and he hasn't given me any yet. You don't seem to care whether he pays or not."

"Oh, he'll pay all right. I'm very sorry if I have offended him as you say, because I like him very much. I believe he is generous to a fault."

"Yes, he has paid me a lot of money at different times. But come on, tea will be ready by now; if we are long up here together they may suspect something."

The revelation just given startled me very much, for in my many cogitations or "silent fits" on the facts of Spiritualism my mind had always flown back to the spirit wax moulds as an incontrovertible argument. When at the time I had read the account published which is given in the next chapter, I could see no room for trickery. The writer of that account I knew to be a man of upright life, and one whose wealth placed him beyond the necessity of deluding others. But at a word the whole mystery was revealed: Thomson, assisted by two little girls, aged 16 and 14 respectively, had completely deluded everybody.

In the evening we went again to the séance room to have another trial. Just previous to beginning Mr Lilley was called away for a minute, leaving us alone in the room which was on the same floor as Thomson's bedroom, where were the casts of Akosa and Lilly.

"Now is our time," said Thomson, "the wax is all ready. I'll just step into my room and fetch Akosa; we'll make a mould before he comes back, and hide it ready."

And away he went to fetch the cast, and in a moment returned, and telling me to keep watch he dipped the face in the wax; but unfortunately for us the wax was not of the proper consistency, and after one or two attempts he had to relinquish this our only chance. But he proposed to hide the cast in the cabinet, and do it during the course of the sitting, which would take place, as usual, in the dark. I opposed the idea because of the difficulty of getting it out of the room again after the sitting, seeing that it was much too bulky to carry off in sight of the enemy, though I believed this could have been safely accomplished because of the ingenuousness of our client; but the idea was given up, and Thomson again returned it to its hiding-place in his own room, and re-entered at the same moment as did Mr Lilley.

This séance, like its predecessors, came to nothing as far as the moulds were concerned. John King came and said the conditions were not exactly right, nor the power fully developed, but he felt confident that success would crown our praiseworthy efforts; and after the usual compliments were exchanged, to the entire satisfaction of both parties, we again adjourned.

Several days now elapsed with a séance for each day, but no moulds were forthcoming; nothing but promises and compliments, which, so long as they pleased our client, no one else complained.

Our telegram to the E. of —— remained unanswered for some time, but at last came a letter, telling us that on account of the political disturbances they did not deem it wise or safe to have us there, but we were to hold ourselves in readiness to go, and keep them advised of our whereabouts. This occurred just previous to one of the cruel and dastardly attempts on the life of the Emperor, whom Thomson represented as a man worthy of the love which every good king commands, but which was denied him by a section of his unruly and dissatisfied subjects.

One morning we received a letter from a Colonel Malêt of Brussels, containing a warm invitation to visit the spiritualists of that city, and guaranteeing us several séances.

Thomson had been there two or three times already, and spoke in high terms of their capacity for belief; but this I found afterwards was tempered with a certain amount of wise discretion.

We talked over the matter, and hardly knew whether to accept or no, but finally decided in favour of the Belgians. I was anxious to go, for in that case we should leave the little girl behind, and he would be compelled to confide more in me. So I voted for the journey. But as a description of a voyage across the Channel would not be much more interesting than an account of a walk up the Strand in a high wind, I will invite the reader to study the succeeding chapter while we pass over from the snow, rain, and fog to brighter weather.

CHAPTER XIX.

EXTRAORDINARY MANIFESTATIONS.

THE present chapter, with the photographs, appeared in a spiritualist paper, called the "Medium," in the beginning of the winter of 1879, while nearly two years afterwards a lecture was delivered in London by a gentleman of high social standing on the facts of Spiritualism as obtained, using Thomson as a chief illustration. To this account which follows are also appended the phrenological delineations and the editorial remarks thereon.

The article began :—

"EXTRAORDINARY MANIFESTATIONS IN LONDON."

THE PRODUCTION OF FACE WAX MOULDS BY MATERIALISED SPIRIT FORMS.

Unity, Duplication, and Re-absorption of Duplicated Forms into one.

TRANSFIGURATION AND VANISHING OF MATERIALISED SPIRIT FORMS.

"*All witnessed in a good light.*"

And the writer says: "The above heading of this chapter and record of marvels, however sensational it may read, is nevertheless a simple statement of facts, of which I was privileged to be a witness, the results of which remain in my possession, viz., the veritable wax moulds, from which I had casts made in London, and mounted in plaster frames as medallions. These medallions I have had photographed on wood, and engraved therefrom, so that the illustrations in this paper are a faithful copy of said plaster casts.

The series of séances in which these marvels were displayed was of so extraordinary a character, and so utterly beyond what I had previously witnessed on the plane of physical appearances, that I think them worthy of permanent record, and for this purpose have had the illustrations specially prepared, and now proceed to give an account of the same; and I think I shall be able to prove that the phenomena were genuine, and quite beyond the suspicion of fraud. Of course these rest upon the truthfulness of my testimony, and, in support of this, I must appeal to my character and position, not as an enthusiast ready to gape and swallow anything that is presented as a spiritual production, but as a careful and patient student of occult phenomena in all its phases; and having satisfied myself of the genuineness of such phenomena, I have sought to methodise the same on the physical plane as scientific facts, and from thence I have endeavoured to seek the solution, and to enunciate therefrom a system of philosophy whose ethics may stand the test of sound and enlightened reason, and go a little way towards enlightening the human mind on the grand question of life and its continuance in future states of existence, convinced as I am that the phenomenal aspect of Modern Spiritualism is but the foundation of facts upon which the new superstructure of human society must be based. In addition to this, I have the patent fact of the possession of the wax moulds and casts therefrom, supported by the evidence and testimony of a modeller in London, who cast the figures from the moulds, and who will testify that the moulds were without any air-holes for the nose or mouth, and all in one mask-piece. (Any practical modeller, whose business it is to manufacture casts, will know the value of this.)

Even to myself, who am certainly no novice in the spiritualistic school, these manifestations are astounding, and were it not that I can produce the results in actual form, I should almost hesitate to publish them, fearing that they would be too great a draft upon the credulity of the unpre-

AKOSA.

LILLY.

pared, and (in this specific department) inexperienced human mind, which is ever prone to ascribe to trickery or delusion what is beyond the domain of ordinary experience. Nevertheless, in committing these particulars to the general public, I have the inward testimony of a good conscience, and the knowledge that not one fact or detail is overdrawn, coloured, or falsified; and with this I proceed with the details taken from my notes which I took at the time.

In obedience to an inner impulse (for what reason at the time I had no knowledge or conception) I went up to London, on Wednesday, October 15th, and met a friend at Euston Square, with whom I went to see ——, at his lodgings in Southampton Row, and had a sitting with him by our two selves. At this séance we had some fine manifestations, such as the movement of objects, &c., and the playing of the piano, which was closed, while my friend and myself sat upon the lid, the notes being sounded according to request. We had also the materialised forms; but as they came out singly from the cabinet, that in itself was no proof that they might be other than the medium, and the very naturalness of the figures left me desirous of more convincing evidence of extraneous instrumentality in the production of these forms.

On Thursday (the next day) I went again with Mr ——, and this time Miss —— (a young lady cousin of the medium) was present, and sat with us. At this sitting the forms were of a different size and sex, and on two occasions *two* forms came out at the same time; the phenomena altogether were so remarkable that I determined, if possible, to obtain a series, and knowing that some extraordinary mould-making phenomena had been obtained in Paris through Mr ——'s mediumship, I asked Mr —— if he would sit for us, in order that we might, if possible, obtain some wax moulds. To this he readily assented, and in accordance therewith I procured some paraffin wax for the purpose of our next sitting, on Friday, October 17th.

I may here state, that the cabinet was a small room leading out of the large sitting-room on the second floor, facing the street, and separated from it by folding doors, which, when used for séances, are thrown back, and thick curtains drawn across the opening. There is a door leading out of the small room on to the landing, which was locked to prevent access and egress during the séance, also a window looking into the back yard, which was darkened by thick brown paper and curtains so as to exclude all light; in short, the room was made pitch dark, and the medium was, or supposed to be, reclining on the sofa in a state of unconscious trance, while the manifestations were in progress. I assisted in the process of preparation, which was the melting of the paraffin wax by boiling water in a hand-basin. When this was done, the basin with the hot liquid wax floating on the surface of the water, was placed on a table *outside* the cabinet-room, about a yard from the curtains, in the large room where we sat; alongside we placed another hand-bowl containing cold water, so that the wax mask could be the readier produced, by dipping first in the liquid paraffin, and then in the cold water alternately. It requires three or four dips to make the mould or mask of sufficient consistency to preserve its figure.

The arrangements being completed, Mr —— retired into the cabinet, while Mr —— discoursed music on the piano (which is a general accompaniment in all séances), and I, with Miss ——, sat at the table in the centre of the room. We lit a small lamp, but this was not sufficient to kill the daylight which came in through the windows (it was 4 P.M.), so we blew out the lamp, and sat in a subdued daylight, but quite enough for us to clearly distinguish all objects in the room.

Soon after we sat down there came out from the cabinet a figure draped in white, and, lifting the vail, displayed a state of almost nudity, with a loin-cloth round the waist. It is possible that this figure was the medium, who went to the basins and waved his hands over them and then retired into the cabinet. A voice (certainly not the medium's), which is known as that of " Frankie," told us that the figure was " Glaucus," the leader of the band of attendant spirits who use Mr —— as their instrument, and that he had magnetised the wax and vessels, as they intended to try to give us some face-moulds. However, they were not successful at this sitting, and no attempt was made; but we were rewarded in another manner.

After " Glaucus " had retired (whose figure was about the same in height as the medium's) *two* figures came out of the cabinet, both draped in pure white, and of *considerably less stature* than the last one; one appeared masculine and the other feminine (as I judged), who leaned on the arm of the male form. I was astonished at the apparitions, and called Mr ——'s attention to the fact of the size of these two forms, and who, like myself, decided they were both much less in stature and bulk than the first figure. After they had retired, in answer to my question, " Frankie " said the male figure was " Glaucus," who was reduced in bulk to supply material for the second figure, which was " Bertie."

Being the first time I had witnessed this phenomenon, I contented myself with noticing the fact, and reserved my request to touch the forms until I became more *en rapport*, and more familiar with the conditions; but I had seen sufficient to prove that these were real materialised forms, and I felt shut up to the conclusion that they were genuine human forms, and could not be accounted for except on the suspicion of confederacy.

I mention these details to show that I was on my guard, and although I might be satisfied in my own mind that they were phenomenal, yet the mere seeing them under such conditions would not be satisfactory to outsiders. But this doubt, like all the rest which arose in my mind, was afterwards dispelled by demonstrations that I could not question, as will be seen in the sequel.

The next séance was on Monday, October 20, when Mr —— and myself only were present, as Miss —— went home before the séance commenced. On this occasion we had subdued daylight, as before.

The medium retired into the cabinet, Mr —— took his place at the piano, and I sat at the table, when, in about five minutes, a male figure, draped in white, came out from the cabinet, and after passing his hands over the vessels, retired to the curtains, but instead of going inside, he *gradually melted away*, from the feet upwards, not by sinking through the floor, but as if the form sank down until a little white spot (the crown of the head) was the only remains of what but a few moments before was, apparently, a solid draped human form. This white spot remained for a few moments and then disappeared.

This phenomenon removed any lurking doubt in my mind as to "confederacy," but which was still to be more tried, for, feeling I was too near the forms, I removed my seat under the window about twelve feet away from the curtains, and I had only just sat down when two figures (a male and female) issued from behind the curtains, both being smaller in dimensions than the prior figure who disappeared in the mysterious manner described above. They both went to the vessels on the table. The female was leaning on the left arm of the male figure, who with his right arm held the veil of the female over the hand-bowl containing the liquid paraffin, and with his left hand supported her while she dipped her face into the hot liquid and then into the cold water bowl. This operation was repeated three times— (the correctness of my observation was afterwards verified by the wax mould, which at the edges showed three distinct layers of wax). The two figures then faced round, the male going inside the cabinet, and the female walked across the room to where I was sitting and placed the mould in my hand. The extreme naturalness of this form startled me, as the motion was not a sliding one (which is generally the case with these materialised spirit forms), but a regular step-by-step walk. She certainly was not more than four and a-half feet high, and somewhat slimly built. Yet, notwithstanding what I had just witnessed, the thought came that possibly Miss —— *might* have played the part of the spirit-form, instead of going home as she appeared to have done; but this thought was dispelled at the next two séances, in which she sat in the room with me all the time, —and in fact she was playing the piano while I did the singing part to the best of my ability,—so this proved that *she* and the little form were not one and the same.

After "Lilly" (for such is the name by which this form is known to us) had retired, "Glaucus" and "Bertie" (the same form who had given us moulds of her hand and foot in Manchester through Mrs F—— and Dr Monck) issued from the cabinet, and went through the same operation as the two former ones. After this was completed, the two advanced towards Mr ——, who was at the piano, when "Bertie" threw her gauze vail over Mr ——, and gave him the mould which she had prepared. I was watching the affair, and while the two figures were standing stationary, about three feet apart, "Bertie" suddenly *vanished*, and was *non est*. This was an unexpected surprise.

The above was the first attempt, and consequently the moulds were imperfect, and on noticing the one given to me, I discovered that the mouth was open, *i.e.*, there was an opening where the lips ought to have been. This fact caused another doubt to flash across my mind, inasmuch as it *seemed* to show that, after all, it might be a human being, because such would require the admission of air to the lungs, either through the mouth or nostrils, to support life while the process of moulding the face was progressing, *i.e.*, assuming it possible that any mortal would dip his or her face in hot liquid wax. However, I kept my own counsel, and waited for the next attempt.

My object in mentioning these particulars so specifically is to show that I was quite alive to the objections that might be urged against the absence of so-called *tests*, as our experience in former times had shown us the utter worthlessness of any tests that we could supply on our side, for, do as we would, there was sure to remain some door open for a doubt to enter, and frequently we have had *our* tests rendered useless, and replaced by others of the spirits' own making, which were far more satisfactory and conclusive. Nevertheless, I felt all through that the "application of tests" was on its trial, and I waited the issue not altogether free from some little anxiety. But my patience and confidence were rewarded in due time, as the sequel will show.

By this time I saw that these manifestations were beginning to tell on the medium, but as my time was short, I asked the controls if it would be possible for me to obtain a complete face mould. The reply was, that on the morrow they would try, if I would come at the same hour—four p.m. This brings me to the next séance, which took place on the following day, but as my friend could not be present, Miss —— and myself were the only ones present beside the medium. As I thought the daylight, subdued as it was, was inimical to the success of the moulding process, I suggested a better mode of excluding all daylight, and in accordance therewith we had the daylight quite shut out, and used a lamp instead.

Tuesday, October 21st.—Precisely at four p.m., all the arrangements as to providing and placing the wax and water vessels, &c., being completed, the medium retired into the cabinet, Miss —— took her place at the piano, and I seated myself at the table, about 7 or 8 feet away from the curtain.

In a few minutes "Glaucus" came out, and magnetised the vessels as before, and after making obeisance and partially disrobing, exposing the gauze vail extended so that I might see it, he retired. This figure was about the same height as the medium, and nearly nude when he lifted the deep vail which enshrouded his head and upper parts; the feet and legs were quite bare. Shortly after "Glaucus" and "Lilly" came out, and, going up to the vessels, "Lilly" (whose form was natural, parts of which I could plainly see) dipped her face partly into the wax as before, and then came to the table, and placed the mould before me; but it was only a part face, consisting merely of the nose, mouth, and chin. This was given, according to my request to "Frankie," that "Lilly," if she made another attempt, would give me one without any air-holes. I felt disappointed at not receiving a full face, as this was the second trial. However, for this I must wait patiently, if it was to be had at all. When these two—"Glaucus" and "Lilly"—had retired, I was astonished to see a large, massive figure emerge from the curtains, certainly much taller and stouter than the medium.

The figure approached within about eight feet of where I sat, and, to my amazement, it was "two-in-one," distinct, but not separate. After standing before me about a minute, the male form raised his right hand and drew it down between the joined figures, when the female retired about three feet distance, and stood out separate and distinct from the other. Both figures raised their vails, and I noticed that "Lilly's" face was dark; having done this, and thus given me evidence of the completeness of their forms, "Lilly" drew near to the other, and actually went into the body of the male form, for I saw most distinctly the *gradual process of absorption* enacted before my eyes. The majestic form then retired into the cabinet. In a few minutes, during which we were requested not to let the music or singing stop, out came a male figure of large massive proportions, who went to the table on which the two hand bowls were placed, and I saw him dip his face three times alternately in each vessel, after which he approached me, and, lifting his vail *with both hands*, I saw the wax mask on his face, to which he repeatedly pointed with his right hand. (This was, as I was afterwards told, a sign for me to take it off, but I did not know this at the time.) He then raised his left hand, and with it took the mask off his face, and, placing it on the table before me, he retired into the cabinet.

"As this form was different from any of the others, I asked who it was. The reply was, "Akosa the Greek." Presently the same "Akosa" came out of the cabinet leading "Lilly" by the hand, when both drew near to me and stood opposite each other, holding each the other's hands. "Akosa" then lifted the mould from the table, as much as to say, "This is mine," and on my saying this he nodded assent. "Lilly" then retired behind "Akosa," and both *glided* back together behind the curtains. After seeing "Lilly" safe in the cabinet he returned, threw his soft gauze vail right over me, and then retired into the cabinet.

The production of spirit-drapery is a marvellous phenomenon. In this particular instance the figure emerged from behind the curtains with a somewhat scant white covering over the head and shoulders. While I was gazing he raised this plain white gauze, and, manipulating it, it appeared to become more and more profuse until it enveloped and enfolded his whole form. He then separated it and held out a large square with a beautiful openwork pattern of leaves upon it; and after noticing this it became absorbed in the other part of the robe, which gradually lessened in quantity until it was of the scant proportions that merely covered the head and shoulders. Here was an unmistakeable proof of the manufacture of drapery before my eyes, and which exonerates spirits from the charge of "shop-lifting," which has sometimes been brought against them, as if it were not as easy to make covering as the form to be covered! My ability to distinguish all these things shows that there was a good light during these séances.

Soon after the stentorian voice of "John King" was heard close behind the curtains, and greeting me in his usual homely but genuine style, expressed his pleasure at meeting me, and hoped I was satisfied. I conversed with him in the style of correspondences which he perfectly understood, and then said the power was nearly exhausted and nothing more could be done that day; but if I would stay in London he would give me *his* face. This decided me to have one more sitting, at which I was fortunate to get, not his, but the feminine face which is illustrated.

Wednesday, October 22d,—Was my next and final meeting, at which Miss ——— and myself were again the only sitters beside the medium. Before commencing I suggested to Mr ——— that, in view of publishing the results of these séances, it would be advisable to adopt every reasonable means to prevent the thought of confederacy by those who should read it, and I proposed that I might be allowed to put some gummed paper over the doors in addition to locking them. To this he readily assented, and I placed a slip of adhesive paper over the door joints and marked it with private marks across the paper and door frame, so that if it should be removed or tampered with I could detect it at once. I need hardly add that after the séance was over I found it exactly as I had left it, although for other reasons not specified I well knew that "confederacy" was out of the question. As this was the last séance I made preparations, and, sitting near the lamp, I took down notes as follows :—

At 4.35 p.m., the medium retired into cabinet.
At 4.45, " Glaucus " came out to magnetise the vessels.
At 4.48,   Do.   do.   do.
At 4.51,   Do.   do.   do.
At 4.53, " Glaucus" and " Lilly " came out arm-in-arm and retired.

At 4.55, " Glaucus " and " Lilly," who went to the vessels containing the paraffin and wax, " Glaucus " held " Lilly's " vail over the basin, and I saw her dip three times, going to the cold water vessel alternately. While this process was going on the white covering fell away, and I saw distinctly the back parts of the form, which were of a dull white colour. After the last dip they both turned round and came near to me, standing opposite to each other; they then each raised their vails with both hands, and while so held up I saw the wax mask on " Lilly's " face, who raised her left hand, and taking it off her face, put it into my hand. I thanked them for the successful effort they had accomplished, and requested that I might touch them. "Glaucus" then took my right hand and placed it in "Lilly's" left hand, which was cold and clammy, while the hand of "Glaucus" was warm and natural. I stood up, and thus we were hand-in-hand, three distinct forms to all intents and purposes. I retired to my seat at the table, and "Lilly" going behind "Glaucus," both retired into the cabinet. Immediately "Lilly" came out alone, and, lifting her vail, disappeared again.

At 5 p.m., two forms, "Glaucus" and "Lilly," emerged from the cabinet, and appeared to be stuck together, similar to the other case referred to before, and, approaching me, they separated; "Glaucus" first drawing his right hand between the junction of the forms to sever the connection. "Lilly" pointed to the mould lying on the table, and retiring behind "Glaucus," both *glided* back into the cabinet.

5.10.—I heard a conversation going on in the cabinet between "Frankie" and "Lilly" (the latter's voice very faint), and asking what it was about, "Frankie" stated he was freeing "Lilly's" hair from some of the wax which was left, and it was a troublesome job he said.

"Frankie" then asked me if I was pleased, and said I ought to feel honoured, as "Lilly" would come out and materialise for none but myself. "Why so," I asked; to which he replied, "Look inside and you will see all there, as you will find the whole programme!" He then woke up his medium, who conversed with "Frankie" (who, from the sounds, I judged to be about three or four feet apart), and whose voice gradually declining in strength and power as if he were entering his medium's body, and immediately the colloquy was concluded, out came the medium, looking dazed and rubbing his eyes, at 5.15, which closed the séance.

I then took the mould to Mr ——, the statuary, one of whose workmen cast it in plaster of Paris, and mounted it in the frame as a medallion as shown in the illustration. Mr —— could not understand how I had obtained them, unless

they had been taken from dead people, and he suggested if
I wanted more that he should take them in plaster, as he
could make a much better job; but when I asked him if he
could take them from living people without air being
supplied, he replied, "that would be impossible," so after
paying him I left with my treasures, leaving *him* and his
workmen in a state of mystification, "for," said the worthy
man, "I have been in the trade for forty-five years, but I
never saw moulds made like those." *He* seemed to think
that I had got some new method of taking copies of faces,
and gravely assured me that *he* could do much better.

My object has been to give a plain unvarnished statement
of facts to which I was a witness; in a scientific point
of view, they are worthy the thought and investigation of
the most advanced and intellectual minds, and they offer
a field of research that will amply repay any effort and cost
that may be entailed. Further, I have hinted at the true
value of all these physical and materialised manifestations,
which, according to the ethics of spiritual philosophy, are an
index and representation of the mental, intellectual, and
spiritual states of those and others to whom such manifestations are given.

The one who, during these séances, seemed to take
special charge of the medium and who superintended the
phenomenal part, is know by the *soubriquet* "Frankie," and in
reply to several of my questions he said, "Look inside," this
I would urge upon all students of occult science, for being
interpreted it means, *Try to discover what underlies all these
manifestations.*

I leave the phrenological delineations of the casts to
Mr ———."

PHRENOLOGICAL REMARKS ON THE CASTS.

"Akosa."

"This mask exhibits rather remarkable physiognomical
and phrenological developments. The phrenological student

will read with interest the following measurements:—The mask is 1⅞ in. deep from the highest development of the eyebrows backwards. The height of the forehead at the highest point where the level background is met is 4¾ in.— not 'villanously low.' The breadth across the eyebrows is 4½ in.; width between the eyes, 1½ in.; width between outer corners of eyes, 4¾ in.; breadth of face across the under lip, 5½ in.; width across the base of the nose, 2 in.; length of nose, 2 in.; breadth of cheek across point of nose, 6 in.; length of face, 10 in. The point of the nose is small and sharp when compared with the great width of base; it is also bent slightly to one side, which gives a mean, sinister, and cunning cast to the countenance. The central range of brain organs is very full, as is indicated by the great width between the eyes. The animal forces and passions are excessively indicated by the full under lip and broad jaw. A deficiency of moral and self-restraining power is evident in the short upper lip and undeveloped nose. The perceptive faculties evince much instinctual perception, but not that of the cultivated scientific kind. The intellect is almost wholly in abeyance, but there are marks of great penetration into character and the nature of things in a useful sense, and power to control men.

When this cast was shown to me, and before I had any knowledge of the character it is intended to represent, I said, 'If this man died in a moral condition he altered very much from what he was in his younger days. He was one of those men governed by impulse. When an idea seized hold of him he felt it all over his body like an insatiable thrill, which nerved him to desperate action for the gratification of the demand thus set up. To reason with or endeavour to restrain him by moral considerations would have been futile. For the time being his whole nature was permeated with an idea, and his whole nature would struggle for its gratification.'

I was told that he had been a pirate, and that my delineation was characteristic. But I cannot see that this was radically a bad man. He was a sensitive; one of those large men with immense organic resources, and having the basic elements of mind in excess of the perfecting and reasoning elements. He could not control and understand that nature which he possessed ; but being sensitive, and no doubt badly trained and situated when young, he would become the instrument of spirits who would obsess him and urge him on to the performance of deeds without respect to any consideration, except that of immediate, passional enjoyment. Such men are really maniacs and governed by an excess of inclination in a few leading directions.

This is a man that could be large-souled and generous to those who secured his goodwill, but he had no love of refinement nor ability to be affable, imitative, or accommodating in his manner.

Nature gave him a wealth of vital force, which, with suitable control, would have rendered him a valuable member of society. It is pleasing to know that in the spiritual state this man is being developed into his true self; such spirits when reformed are valuable in a circle where physical effects are being produced. When kindly treated they are faithful and devoted, protecting their medium, and having great power over matter to carry out his wishes, as far as conditions will permit. All such spirits require to be under the control of higher guides."

"LILLY."

" It needs no profound observation to perceive that this form is an embodiment of feminine grace, purity, and perfection; the features are admirable in their regularity and fulness of development; they are much smaller than in the other cast, but much more highly developed, showing that material bulk is not the highest qualification. The expression is rich and full; love is instinct in the ripe lips; the open mouth is indicative of a transcendental ecstasy, and the nose shows firmness of moral purpose; the perceptive faculties are full and in a high state of cultivation, and the intuitions are of that acute, penetrating order which arrive at the inner life of mankind and the adaptive nature of things, in a moral sense, at the first glance; the reasoning powers do not appear full, but the central range of organs is immensely developed, indicating wisdom rather than philosophy. This is not the rationalistic type of mind which theorises and argues by inferences and other logical processes, but it is a type of the perfect woman, who sees truth just as it is, and understands the moral fitness of things, without any other process than that of simple perception.

These two faces are in many respects alike, and yet how different! The man is the raw material—spirit controlled by matter; the woman is the manufactured article—matter controlled by spirit. The one has gross sensations, and uses brute force as a means to his ends; the other has exquisite feelings, and by wisdom attains her ends in accordance with that inner plane of action on which she is developed. Thus on the organic plane heaven and hell meet, showing that 'place' and 'state' are different matters. The one of low development propitiates the flesh and wounds the spirit—is selfish; the higher type saves the spirit and sacrifices the bodily comfort. Brother, sister, reader, to which class do you belong? I may state that I read Mr —— article for the first time after these remarks were in type, so that they are independent expressions."

EDITORIAL REMARKS.

"The thanks of all spiritualists, particularly the readers of the 'Medium,' are due to Mr —— for his kindness in instituting the experiments, and producing the engravings and article which form a prominent feature in this number of the 'Medium.' He has generously undertaken every responsibility in connection with the matter, so that it is, from first to last, a contribution from Mr —— to the friends of this interesting inquiry.

The extraordinary manifestations illustrated and described by Mr —— in this number suggest a few remarks for the benefit of readers who are not practically acquainted with spiritual phenomena. Some will think that they have nothing further to do than to engage the services of the medium, and repeat these experiments with success at pleasure. There could not be a greater mistake—a mistake which has often led to bitter disappointment, and caused excellent mediums to be underrated and traduced.

Remember that the success of a manifestation depends as much upon the other persons present as upon the medium himself. The medium is in all such cases a passive instrument, and only one of the factors in the matter. His organism emits a fluid which the spirits can use, by consolidating it with other elements, to build up the material form; but these 'other elements,' emanating from the spectators, become quite as potent for success or disappointment as the one supplied by the medium. Mr —— has explained this so fully that nothing further need be said.

It is also to be observed that Mr —— had a series of sittings which were not interrupted by the presence of alien sitters. If it is hoped that promiscuous parties can hold sittings and have similar results, these hopes are doomed to demolition. Even if the forms could thus come forth in mixed companies, it would have a tendency to injure the health of the medium, reduce his power, and introduce disturbing spiritual influences."

Nearly two years after a lecture was given on

REMARKABLE MANIFESTATIONS.

"THE PHOTOGRAPHING AND MOULDING THE FORMS OF MATERIALISED SPIRITS."

"On Sunday evening the Hon. —— delivered an address at the Spiritual Institution, 15 Southampton Row.

The theme selected by Mr —— was an account of some of his many and most extraordinary experiences in the phenomena of Spiritualism. Few observers have had better opportunities, or made more good use of them than this talented gentleman has. In addition to his natural abilities, he is not only a ripe scholar and well versed in science, but he has a wide knowledge of the world in almost all the phases of life which it presents. His convictions are, therefore, not lightly formed, nor is he easily misled by semblances or counterfeits.

It was expected that the remarks offered would chiefly bear reference to phenomena observed in America, but an unanticipated treat was enjoyed by the recital of a lucid and well illustrated account of materialisation phenomena which took place in Paris ; being, in fact, none other than the celebrated experiments of ———, through the mediumship of Thomson. These wonderful manifestations have been alluded to, from time to time, in letters to the periodical press of the movement, and copies of some of the photographs have been seen, but a full and connected account of the many sittings, accompanied by a collection of a large number of the photographs, nearly eighty, had hitherto been beyond the experience of the band of old and intelligent spiritualists who had the pleasure of meeting Mr ——— on Sunday evening."

EDITORIAL NOTE.

Mr ———'s Address.

"We were astonished on transcribing our notes on Monday, to find that the report of Mr ———'s address the previous evening, would occupy upwards of eight pages of the 'Medium.' But we felt consoled with the reflection that we could not have too much of a good thing, and so we have given half this week, and the remaining portion, having reference to mediumship in America, is reserved for next week.

It is a grand and lucid summary of spiritual phenomena and explanations, and though it will read, to the novice in the science, like a fairy tale, yet all competent investigators will be able to follow Mr ——— right through. Some of the facts confirm the report written by Mr ——— to this journal nearly two years ago, on which occasion engravings appeared on our first page of the moulds of spirit faces described. The photographs of spirit 'Akosas,' however, which Mr —— showed, do not resemble at all the cast engraved by Mr ——. The photographs to which we allude, were taken in darkness from the spirit-form, and present a much more youthful appearance than the engraving.

The true way to investigate this subject is for a select circle to sit with the same medium in strict privacy, and keep the medium, as far as possible, continually under their guardianship. Sensitives, to be at all reliable, should not be allowed to run loose and sit with anybody."

It seems almost superfluous to enter into explanation of these manifestations.

The wax moulds were not taken from spirits, as alleged, but from plaster of Paris casts, which I have seen and handled. The moulds were all made ready before the meetings commenced—were assumed by the medium and his accomplice while manipulating the bowls of wax and water. The vanishing, etc., was performed by the medium, assisted by *two* young girl cousins. By the use of a liberal quantity of flowing drapery the "Duplication and Re-absorption" was easily accomplished. There was only just enough light to show that it was dark.

The girl who personated "Lilly" was surreptitiously admitted to the séance room after the meeting began. The medium himself has told me with great hilarity how he did everything, but when I say that that medium and my partner Thomson were one, nothing further need be said. If, however, the spiritualists should call in question my declaration that it was all a fraud, I challenge them to reproduce the same things in full light. I know that "spiritual manifestations" cannot be done except under those very conditions which most favour deception, and with those who are *en rapport*, or, in other words, well drilled dupes.

CHAPTER XX.

ON THE CONTINENT.

A DELIGHTFUL change was that from the cold and murky atmosphere of an English manufacturing town, to the bright and crisp air of pretty Brussels, with the sun-rays glinting from the houses, and calling forth a smile of satisfaction from everything. The harmony was catching, and under its influence I soon brightened up, and again braced myself for fresh enterprises and trials. The sun shining upon us as benignly as if we were missionaries of the highest type.

"You will have to leave everything to me here," said Thomson, when after receiving a warm welcome from our hospital host, we had retired to unpack our trunks and dress for dinner.

"What a beautiful old place this is," I exclaimed, while looking out of the window upon the fine old Flemish building opposite.

"Never mind the place now; you will have plenty of time to admire it afterwards. I want to talk business."

"What do you want?" I asked, rather glum at being checked in my enthusiasm.

"You seem to be all life now. Well, let's hope you will remain so. But I want you to attend carefully to my words. When we are in the séance room, you mustn't speak to me at all."

"Why?"

"Because you don't understand French, and they will be suspicious if you speak in English. You must closely attend to the signals, and I shall have to arrange everything. I have told them that you are the medium for the physical and trance, while I only sit for the form."

"When shall we have the first séance?" I inquired, sobered by the serious business in hand.

"Oh, they won't ask us to sit to-night; they'll think we are too much fatigued with our voyage. We shall have dinner first and take a walk in the evening, and perhaps go to some theatre."

Thomson was quite right; when we descended to dinner everybody stedfastly set his face against a sitting for that evening, but told us that a large company would assemble there the following night to witness the manifestations. I found too that the son of our host spoke English fluently, having lived in England a few years, so I was not so much cut off as I had expected.

After dinner, under the leadership of our host, we roamed over the town, and while he pointed out its chief beauties, we listened with enthusiasm and respect. Thomson knew the place quite well from former residence, yet he displayed his policy by giving undivided attention to our guide, who appeared pleased with our ejaculations of delight. Mine at any rate were sincere, for the historical associations of the famous old town awoke many recollections in my mind, and I thoroughly enjoyed the long rambles over boulevards and streets; but at last they ended, and we went home to enjoy the sleep of the worker.

The next evening a party of friends sat down to enjoy our spiritual manifestations. Thomson, who had fixed himself opposite to me, managed to convey a large vase from the chimney piece, and plant it on the table; he also swung the guitar around over our heads; after which we floated the table. He then contrived to shift the piano, and strike the keys with the lid closed down. He always examined —if he saw a chance—every piano wherever we went, to see if it permitted of his manipulating the levers acting upon the wires. After the physical he went into the cabinet for the materialisations, and here I found it extremely difficult, if not impossible, to let him have the drapery, but he came in the dark behind me, and extracted it from my pockets; and in a few minutes John King made his appearance and finished the proceedings.

Asoka was not at all a prominent member of our troupe while on the continent; John King was the favourite, though Joey had to interpret for him, as he was ignorant of the French language. When we were again by ourselves I asked Thomson what the sitters thought of the manifestations?

"Oh they were delighted," said he; "they are going to do big things for us; to-morrow night some people are coming from Charleroi to sit with us. But we have a suspicious character among the sitters. It is very funny, but nobody ever suspects you! they want to tie our hands with tape round the table, and this suspicious character wants to hold me on one side, while another suspicious character is to hold me on the other."

"That will prevent some of the manifestations anyhow," I answered.

"Oh no it wont; I could, but I don't want to get free; you must do this, as nobody suspects you, and I have told them that you are the physical medium; so the quieter I keep at the table the better."

"But I don't know how to get free if we are tied."

"See here, I'll show you; tie this tape round my wrists, and I'll tie yours. Now, with your teeth it is easy enough."

In an incredibly short time he had unfastened the tape, and was free with the exception of the hands that held him, but this also he safely accomplished; and after a few such lessons he pronounced me perfect. At the time appointed, our friends from Charleroi came up, but they wished for no further test than simply holding the hands, and after that séance they told us that they were quite satisfied; and hoped to have the pleasure of again meeting us at their own place; and that as they were delegates from a large Association of Spiritualists, they would present their report, and would let us know when our visit would be convenient to themselves.

At the séance with the "suspicious characters" we were all tied round the table, but true to my teaching, I liberated my hands and performed a few little tricks, such as are by this time quite familiar to the reader.

On the Carnival Sunday which followed, we were not engaged for any sittings, and for the relaxation I was truly thankful; we spent the day—one of great interest to me—in wandering about the town, and watching the merry masqueraders, who, whatever others may say of the wickedness of a Continental Sunday, are not guilty of drunkenness, nor is brawling of frequent occurrence; indeed these two features of an English revel were, to a degree, conspicuous by their entire absence.

We had made arrangements with a M. de Belfort, to give him a series of séances, for the purpose of experimentalising in spirit photography, etc. They were to begin on the Monday, which, when it came, found us duly prepared.

Thomson said that some sort of disguise was very necessary, in order to show up different characters on the plates as they were exposed; and to this end he purchased a wonderful Roman nose, a pair of glassless spectacles, and an imperial moustache; with which he thought it advisable to give Napoleon III.

I must now confine myself to the most salient points of the most prominent séances of this period, for a description of all would involve a wearisome and useless repetition.

We arrived at the appointed time at M. de Belfort's, and found three other gentlemen who, we learned, were anxious to sit, and very soon we began with the "physical." The table was a small oblong piece of furniture, but just suiting our number, which could sit round it without trespassing upon the comfort of his neighbour.

According to our custom, we two mediums sat opposite to each other, and after sitting for a few minutes the table began to sway to and fro, and at last it rose fully breast high.

The Missing Table.

We were all compelled to stand up to keep our hands on the top; the table then rose a little higher, when, through my inability to keep pace with Thomson, who had it fixed on his head, and being a light table, he was able to bear the whole weight by using his hands to weigh it towards himself; it suddenly lurched in my direction, and as I stood at arm's length from my right hand neighbour, there was room enough for it to roll between us, and settle down outside the circle, which as that came to the right swayed slightly to the left, thus we quickly found that it had entirely disappeared.

The members of the circle carefully felt about on the floor, to find the missing thing, which had become so strangely invisible. I could not enlighten them, because of our mutual ignorance of our respective languages. Thomson too had placed my tongue in strict quarantine, and it is most likely if I had told Thomson he would have kept the secret for his own delectation.

There was some excitement over this phenomenon, and the talk waxed fast and furious. Nobody had got it and nobody—except myself—knew where it was, although a great many speculations were indulged in as to the whereabouts of the delinquent. When we had searched for a respectable time, some one suggested that a light would assist us, and the spirits offering no objection, we acted on that idea—and there, outside the circle, about three feet distant lay the innocent table.

M. de Belfort informed us at the end of the sitting that they wished to begin the photographic experiments on the morrow; and for the materialisations, he was preparing a test. It was a wire cage, which would be firmly nailed to the walls up one corner, and its one door would be securely fastened upon the medium, while M. de Belfort would retain the key in his possession.

"I wondered what had become of that blessed table?" queried Thomson, after we had left them.

"Why, it fell between Colonel Florion and me, and then rolled away."

"Well, it was a fortunate accident, and has completely mystified our friends. I thought you had purposely done it; but do you know what they said about it?"

"Not exactly, but I guessed. The Colonel must be rather dull that he didn't notice it."

"Oh, he was too much excited with the floating; but they all firmly believe that it rose up over our heads, and then when it got beyond the power of the magnetism settled on the floor. Didn't I laugh to myself when we were all fumbling about on the floor, and wondering where on earth it was gone to?" and he recited in high glee their surprises and surmises on the marvel, which informed me that I had accurately guessed their meaning.

Just before going up again to our clients, Thomson said he didn't think they would search him, and he would therefore have the moustachios, nose, and spectacles, while I could carry the drapery. This division would obviate the chance of our pockets betraying any evidence of unlawful goods; but as the new test would require skilful fighting, he would be prepared with a pair of pincers; for he intended, at all hazards, to give John King.

We found the same sitters in attendance as on the previous occasion, and we soon began with trying for the physical, but nothing out of the ordinary occurred, and we went on to the materialisations.

They locked the medium in the cage according to proposition, and we took our seats with a musical box that absolutely refused under any cajoling to assist us; and we were ourselves compelled to keep alive the harmony. I joined as vigorously as any body in the tunes, and trusted to the noise to cover up my failure to pronounce the words.

I scarcely expected that Thomson would succeed, and I was surprised soon to feel him at my coat tail pockets getting out the drapery. At first I thought it must be somebody privately searching my pockets, but I was quickly assured, by receiving the usual signal, and in a short time John King stood before us.

He did not stay long, however, and in a few minutes the second part was terminated, but not before the drapery was restored to my pockets. I could not, during the séance, hand the things to the medium, for my hands were fast held in the circle outside the cage, but it did not seriously affect the power, for Thomson was able to do all that was necessary.

The third part, for the photographs, now commenced. M. de Belfort conducted us to another room in which he had partitioned off a portion of the space; in which portion, and up one of the corners, he had hung a large curtain to serve as a screen, behind which the medium would sit. The whole affair was done in broad daylight. The arm of the camera was thrust through a measured hole in the partition, and covered the corner, where hung the curtain. We were not admitted, nor even allowed by the spirits to look into the railed off space during the operations, because of the danger of incurring an injurious admixture of spiritual forces, which would naturally prevent the manifestations.

Thomson had requested that I should be allowed to focus the camera and remove the cap, but to this an objection was raised, and I had to be content with the position of guard, to give a signal if anybody took the liberty of peeping into the arcana of spiritualism. However, the refusal was turned to good account, and I daresay cost our experimenter an extra 50 francs; for after several plates had been exposed, nothing appeared on them, but on the last came a *numerous* hand! That is the only and true description of the phenomenon, and was caused by the medium thrusting his hand out from behind his curtain and moving it up and down while the plate was exposed. It was received as a hard attempt of the spirits to materialise; Thomson was, or ought to have been, in a mesmeric sleep behind his curtain, while the spirits appeared outside to allow themselves to be photographed.

As Joey called out that it was no use trying for any more

that day, for the operator's influence was fresh, and required a few sittings to harmonise it, we adjourned, and each went his own way until the next meeting. Before going up again Thomson told me that he had found it very difficult to get out of the cage, and was compelled to unwire one whole side which held the door, and fasten it up again. I told him that I felt confident they would closely examine it after the séance, to find any trace of its being tampered with, and I wouldn't be surprised if he found they had placed fresh obstacles against that mode of egress. But he answered that if they did, he had another way of escape which could not fail, and he meant to have John King out somehow.

When we arrived we found everything ready to begin, and we soon sat down for the physical, after which Thomson was again put into the wire prison. I knew full well that he was trying hard to escape, but it appeared he found it very difficult, and would take up too much time even for spiritualists, whose patience is beyond all praise at séances. "All hail, all hail!" at last roared John King.

"Hah John King; John King! how are you John?" exclaimed the circle in one voice.

"All hail, all hail!" returned he again, and he then added: "I don't understand what you say dear friends; I must ask Joey to interpret for me; I am materialised, but as I had to build up my form inside, through want of power I can't get out; Joey will now ask you to unlock the door."

Joey quickly translated John King's desire, and it was instantly agreed to let him out, and the door was soon undone, and John in a few minutes stepped forth resplendent in his glowing drapery, and gently touching me to intimate that he wanted my chair which was close to the cabinet and upon which he floated, and waving his arms about he really looked terrific.

But this colossal figure was not for long vouchsafed, and he disappeared; and after replacing the drapery Joey began explaining to the circle the spiritual philosophy of John's inability to issue from confinement, and the explanation was accepted in all good faith by his hearers.

At the photographic trial immediately afterwards several plates were exposed, and at the last being developed, there appeared on its surface the head of Napoleon III.

I had received strict injunctions from Thomson to keep a good outlook on the movements of our client and his friends, and immediately to give warning if they attempted to do any mean unworthy peeping, but apparently they had unbounded faith in the medium, and they accepted the Emperor without a murmur.

Altogether we spent a very indolent and pleasant time in the City of Brussels, never giving more than two séances for each day, which left plenty of time on our hands.

One day we received an invitation to visit the spiritualists of Liege, and as we understood that several influential believers were in the town and its vicinity, we resolved to go there before honouring Charleroi. During our stay on that part of the continent, I had to trust to the honesty and integrity of Thomson, and I don't think he deceived me much, either in translating any of the conversations or in anything else; he told me that our hospitable clients of Brussels were highly delighted, and perfectly satisfied, and that they hoped to have the pleasure of our company again very shortly. But leaving them one morning, we took our tickets, and journeyed on to the famous old town of Liege.

CHAPTER XXI.

A FULL REVELATION.

THE day after reaching Liege, we proceeded by appointment, to the rooms of the Spiritualist Association, and in the evening we had the pleasure of giving to that body a sample of our spiritualistic powers. Thomson considered it unwise for him to go into the cabinet, his chronic suspicion suggesting that the sitters might privately hatch some treasonable design against our peace. It was therefore, resolved, between ourselves, that I should, while here, be the medium for materialisation. My ignorance of the language not being specially required in that direction.

The surroundings of that séance were not inapt, the curtain, which enclosed one corner of the room for a cabinet, was a handsome blue velvet pall used at the funerals of the spiritualists.

John King, however, did not trouble much about that, for, after the test had been duly elaborated under the superintendence of the principal persons present, he gave them a slight view of his person, and gracefully bade them adieu in English, until he would again meet them.

A few days after this, when we were taking our usual stroll in the outskirts of the Ardennes, I determined to relieve my mind of a burden that had long been oppressing it.

"I have been going to ask you something for a long time, and now I think I will," I said to Thomson.

"What is it?"

"I begin to think that the whole of these spiritualistic manifestations is a huge pack of rubbish."

"You *begin* to think! It's almost time you had finished," replied Thomson; "anyhow," continued he, "you are on the right track at last?"

"That is to say, I am right?"

"Never more so in your life!"

"And you mean to say that there is not an iota of truth in your mediumship?"

"That is just what I do mean; neither in mine nor in any other medium."

"And you have actually carried on this game for all these years, and in conjunction with others too? Why, it is the fun of the age!"

"Or any other age. Now, you have been an awful long time coming to a decision. For the first four or five weeks you were with me I don't think you suspected anything, but after that, you began to look very serious, and I saw that you were too sharp to be wholly bamboozled, and at the end of a couple of months I told you, when we left London, that all mediums had to help out a little, and that seemed to satisfy you."

"Yes, it did satisfy me in some respects."

"How do mean?"

"I saw that I had done wrong in blaming the spirits for all that frivolity, and as you know I have a very retentive memory, I found they told lies, but your partial revelation I thought exonerated them altogether."

"What should you have done if I had told you everything right out at the very beginning?"

"You needn't ask. I shouldn't have had anything to do with it."

"Of course. I knew that. When I met you first I saw in a minute that you were the very man I wanted. I knew you'd never split if you found out anything. I am not at all afraid if you do now; for nobody would believe but that we had quarrelled, and you were having your revenge."

"You need have no fear on that head. I don't wish to 'expose,' and I don't believe those fellows do the least good by 'exposing,' as they call it, except to themselves."

"That's true: anybody can see there is a wide difference between a conjuror on his own platform, and a medium in a private room. And the spiritualists only laugh at their feeble attempts, even though the 'exposer' may show exactly the same trick but under other conditions; while outsiders are in numbers of cases led to investigate through the noise they make."

"I believe you are right."

"Yes; and then these Exposers are often people who would expose anything if it would pay. They'd advertise "Christianity Exposed" if they could make money by it; besides which, you very seldom meet with an Exposer who has ever attended many séances, and never with one who really does know anything from experience."

"The most wonderful part of it is, that you have been able to go on for so long a time. How did you first begin your spiritualist career?"

"It was about ten years ago, while living in America. My people took me to a séance with them, and I thought it was all humbug. And just to try these spirits, I got my head under the table and raised it up, and I made it say that I was a wonderful medium; in short I played the very mischief at all their séances. I liked it for a little while, because it made me a person of some importance. I used to go off into trances and kick up awful rows, and get lights and flash them about in the dark, and people in the streets used to say when I passed: 'There's the new medium, that's *him*, that's *him!*' but at last I got tired of it, and told my own people, but they wouldn't believe it; they said I was at that moment under the control of some evil spirit, and it must be exorcised, and a lot of nonsense about cultivating my wonderful gifts. So I thought if they would be deceived it was their own fault, and I kept on with my games, although at that time I had no money for my services, but I didn't then care about that, I was almost worshipped, which pleased me quite as well.

"Soon after that we left for England, and just then we became very poor, and hardly knew what to do for our living. One day I heard that a celebrated American medium with his wife were giving séances in London, and I visited him at his rooms. Fortunately he had a séance at home for that evening, and he fixed me in the circle next to himself, and, when the lights were put out, I released his hand and helped him in a few little things.

"After the sitting he asked me to stay and talk over old times; and when the people were all gone, he told me that he could see I was alive, and if I liked he would give me two guineas a week if I would help him twice each week; and he gave me two guineas on the spot as an earnest.

"Naturally, such an offer as this was considered a god-send, and I joyfully accepted it. I used to go to him according to agreement, and many were the pranks we played. At last it happened that he went back to America, and offered to take me with him; but I considered that I was quite capable of going out as a medium myself, and for two or three years I did exceedingly well. I was not at all dissatisfied with the result of my work in England, but I wanted a holiday, and I took a trip to Paris, thinking I might combine business with pleasure.

"Meeting with a Count de —— at a séance one day in Paris, he made me an offer of 1000 francs a month if I would hold myself entirely at his disposal. He was a very rich man and generous, and he soon increased my salary to 1250 francs, besides many bye séances which he induced his friends to have, and for which I was handsomely paid.

"When any of the mediums visited Paris, which was now my home, I often made John King tell the Count to have sittings with them. I was never jealous, but used to help them and coach them up, so that many a clairvoyant test was obtained thus and published! It was with the Count that I did that shooting at the double, which you remember made such a stir among the spiritualists; but although the Count is a generous man, he is not a fool, and it required all my wit to satisfy him. You recollect Bugot, that spirit photographer?"

"Yes," I answered, highly interested by this story. "How did he manage to do all that he did?"

"We worked it between us; of course no one knew that we were acquainted with each other, and we carried on for a long time, and made a lot of money. But he was a great fool after all. One day the police called (in disguise), and they asked if it were possible for them to obtain spirit portraits. Bugot told them he didn't know, but they could try, and he soon arranged everything for them; but just as he had got them in position, and was going to remove the cap, one of the detectives stepped forward, and said, 'Stop, M. Bugot, don't expose that plate. I am a police officer. Take it out again and come with me into the dark room. Now, please develop it. No tricks, Monsieur; that is the right bottle. Ah, just as I thought,' said the detective, as a form appeared on the plate. Bugot ought to have been prepared for all this. If I had been in his place I should have had all my bottles labelled wrong; I think that would have puzzled the policemen. But he didn't, and hence the mischief. He gave my name as an accomplice, and another who was really innocent. He was sentenced to 18 months imprisonment; I got 6 months, and the innocent man 12 months and a fine; but my friends, including the Count, believed in me just the same."

"There is a photograph of yours exhibited in the Spiritualist Society's rooms in London. How did you do that?"

"Oh, they have several pieces of my handiwork there, as you know; but as for that photograph, which shows the Count sitting on a chair and my double close beside him, it was done by Bugot and me. I was in Amsterdam at the time, and the Count, knowing nothing of our knowledge of each other, called on Bugot one day to have some portraits taken. Bugot was quite the rage at that time, everybody went to him, and on the occasion when the Count sat, not for a spirit picture, Bugot knew him and exposed a plate with a faint outline of me on it (he had several always prepared); when it was developed Bugot showed it to the

Count, and asked him if he knew what it meant. The Count knew that I was away, and he asked Bugot to say nothing about it to any one; but I was made aware of what had happened, and when the Count wrote asking me what I was doing at a certain time, I wrote back that I remembered falling asleep, and dreaming that I was with him in Paris. That quite convinced him of the genuine nature of the picture, and he had a number printed and distributed about, and that is how the London Society got one; but they have a number of casts of spirit hands, &c., which I did. Last year the Count went away for a few months, and I then came to England; but I shall try and get back to him."

The account which Thomson gave to me would of itself fill a book. Some of his adventures were very curious. I am sorry I have not space at present to relate them. It was plain to me that he had become so inured to this life that he was utterly unfitted for anything else, and he regarded himself as a thoroughly honest individual, and well worthy of the fame and money that he had made. I told him of a séance that I had once had with a noted medium, and that some strange things had then happened which I could not account for. He answered that I talked like a fool, that a person who did nothing but mediumship, in time became clever enough to deceive anybody; even conjurors themselves had publicly testified that the things they witnessed were beyond their skill. It is true that his story fully explained the mysteries which I had once regarded as incontrovertible proofs of the truth of Spiritualism, and made me resolve, also, to finish my mediumistic career. I told him, therefore, that I was completely satisfied, and did not feel inclined to proceed any further in that direction.

"What do you propose to do?" he asked.

"Anything rather than this. If you can do those things of which you have just spoken, we can make plenty of money on the stage, and what is more important, we can do it honestly. Now we may gloss this over as we will, it is nothing more nor less than a downright swindle."

"Look at other mediums."

"That is no excuse. Here is M. de Chênée, for instance, a sensible and clever man. He will do anything for us, and although he is a prominent spiritualist, he will, I am sure, give us an introduction to some of the managers of the public halls here, and we can at once begin; that we can do in perfect safety. I recognise the difficulty of getting anything to do, but at present that seems to be the only chance we have of getting out of this fearful kind of life."

"Well, it certainly is almost impossible to get any position, after once being a medium, and I think if it were not for that fact, many mediums would at once give it up. However, I am willing to give these tricks on the stage. I did once have an offer in Paris, but at that time I daren't because of the Count. However we must change our names and not say anything of Spiritualism. You see there are great numbers of good people who have always believed in me, and have stood by me through thick and thin; they'd feel bad if I came out in public, and said it was all trickery."

"I have no objection to change our names; but I wonder you never saved any money when you made so much."

"Easy come, easy go," answered he shortly.

The same afternoon we met M. de Chênée, and this gentleman at once consented to give us the desired introduction. We told him nothing of delusion or fraud, but simply said we wished for an opportunity to work in public, saying nothing for or against the cause. The manager of the Hall of Varieties agreed to have a trial with us, and if satisfactory, which he had no doubt it would be, he would offer us a lengthy and lucrative engagement.

This was so far good, and we began to prepare for our public display, and finding several things were necessary, Thomson said he would go off to Brussels to procure what was required. There was still another reason for his journey. The apparatus would cost more money than we possessed, and he thought he could procure the balance requisite from friends in that city.

I made no objection to be left alone, but I pointed out the necessity of a speedy return, otherwise I should be in an uncomfortable position, in a place, the language of which was unknown to me, not to speak of being left almost penniless, but a day or even two would not seriously incommode me.

When the time came for him to go, we drove to the station, and he asked me to meet the last train that night, by which he intended to return, and he soon after took his seat in the carriage, and with a "Be sure and meet me by the last train to-night, good-morning," and the train moving off bore away my partner; as it afterwards turned out, never to return, for I have never seen him since.

I did not feel particularly lonely that day; I roamed off to the delightful haunts of the Ardennes forest, and spent the greater part of the day there in perfect contentment. Late at night I bent my steps to the station for the last train, which duly appeared, but without the precious cargo of Thomson. I was not very much troubled by his non-arrival; we had both thought it very probable that he would be expected to give a séance in Brussels, and consoling myself with the reflection that such was the case, I went home.

Several days now passed, and no sign either by post or rail of Thomson, I began to feel very uncomfortable. I expected, too, the hotel bill every morning, which would have been an unwelcome apparition, considering my present impecuniosity, and I actually began to console myself that if the worst really did come, "mine host" would not suffer, for my wardrobe would more than liquidate every claim.

At this time I walked to the village where lived our excellent friend M. de Chênée, and fortunately he could speak German. He received me with his customary hospitality and politeness, and kindly inquired after Thomson. I informed him that he had gone to Brussels on business, but I expected that he would return shortly, a piece of faith in which my friend did not join, but he was careful to let me down as gently as possible. He told me that he had received a letter from Paris regarding us, and for my better grasping the true character of Thomson he translated it into German.

It appeared from the letter that my partner was possessed of rather an evil repute; it spoke of his extravagances and loose morals, but did not hint at anything derogatory of his mediumistic powers, on the contrary, it eulogised him in that direction, and the letter concluded by expressing sorrow that I had ever been induced to join him.

I was rather surprised at the latter part, for I imagined myself a totally unknown quantity in the gay city. Regarding the first, it confirmed a side wind report which formerly had told me that Thomson had been in many escapades, but which I thought was not borne out by my own experience of that gentleman, for respecting any charge of reckless immorality he was as steady as most men.

I was very much impressed with the graceful courtesy of M. de Chênée, who proved himself, in the widest sense of the word, a Christian and a gentleman, and a fine representation of the generous and sturdy Belgians.

Time slowly passed away, and the suspicions of M. de Chênée regarding Thomson's intention to keep away received another confirmation, besides his non-appearance.

A lady, speaking German, informed me that she had sufficient knowledge to justify her in declaring that my partner never intended to return. It was a mystery to me how she had got her news, though I was not quite so ready to credit the spirits with clairvoyance as formerly. But it appeared to me that everybody knew more of Thomson's present intentions than I did.

This lady vehemently declared that he would not come back, and excitedly advised me to break the peace of any sovereign lord or lady wherever I happened to find him, saying—

"If I were you, when I saw him again I would make him smart. I would thrash him, ah, nearly to death; that I would, the villain."

And the intense disgust she exhibited was almost comical, blended as it was with a strong desire to display her own powers of forcible persuasion upon the unlucky wight; and unlucky he would be, too, I am afraid, if ever he ventured to call at that portion of Europe again.

I certainly had not abandoned hope in the honour of Thomson, and still looked out for him by every "last train" to come and extricate me from my unpleasant dilemma. But the wearisome days dragged by and still no sail in sight. It would not have troubled me had I been able to speak the language. Often I met spiritualists in the town who knew me, but when we had shaken hands, and uttered a mutual, "Bon jour, Monsieur!" we could only look at each other, and for lack of more dictionary silently pass on our ways.

At last came the crisis which I had been long expecting. One morning I descended, and as usual inquired if there were any letters; and as if not willing I should be disappointed any longer, the landlady handed me a letter written in world-wide-known characters—The bill.

Whatever powers of speech I lacked to make her understand were fully supplied and atoned for by the irate lady before me. She flung forth into such a—well I really don't know, neither had I any particular wish for an interpreter.

But I resolved not to risk a discourteous reception by any further visits to that abode, nor subject myself to the encore of a refrain, which seemed to me as likely to offer greater charms if heard at a distance of half-a-dozen liberally measured miles, and I shook the dust off my feet and heard no more of her extraordinary eloquence.

I was now convinced beyond a doubt that Thomson had left me to get away as best I could, and after a visit to the station for that "last train," I strayed off into the solitary depths of the Ardennes forest.

Deeper and deeper I penetrated its lonesome glades, with no thought of anything in particular. I felt no anger against Thomson, or anybody else; indeed I was rather pleased than otherwise, for I was now free—and satisfied. I spent the day in —— searching for early spring flowers. At times I did try to review the past, present, and future, but my mind refused to dwell upon any single point for any length of time, and I turned again to the flowers.

When the cold and dreary day had merged into a colder

and drearier night, I bethought myself to return home, but I suddenly remembered I had nowhere to go, and found too that I had lost my bearings.

At any other time this would probably have alarmed me, but in my present predicament one place was as good as another. Fortunately I was neither assailed by fatigue nor hunger; but perhaps that is due to the fact that the means of satisfying either were beyond my power.

I wandered along through the drizzling rain which now commenced, at times stumbling over rocks and tree trunks; and the hours slowly dragged past, until I judged it must be about midnight, and then my thoughts began to take a definite shape, and I could view my position with comparative clearness.

No fretful complaints arose, for indeed I had nothing to complain about. How to extricate myself I did not for one moment consider. It appeared as though nothing short of a miracle would help me. I had neither friends to whom I could apply, nor the power possessed by those of the wealthy order of mankind. And yet the prospect did not alarm me; I was confident, if I thought of it at all, of a happy issue, even though I had empty pockets and a broken faith.

At last the night wore away and day broke, and eventually I found my way back to the town where I met M. de Chênée, who insisted upon taking me home with him.

This gentleman removed my embarrassments, and in a few days I returned to England, happier if not richer, because I was enfranchised from the horrible deception of phenomenal Spiritualism.

Turnbull & Spears, Printers, Edinburgh.

A CATALOGUE OF

NEW AND STANDARD BOOKS

IN GENERAL LITERATURE,

DEVOTIONAL AND RELIGIOUS BOOKS,

AND

Educational Books & Appliances.

PUBLISHED BY

GRIFFITH & FARRAN,

WEST CORNER OF ST. PAUL'S CHURCHYARD, LONDON.

E. P. DUTTON & CO., NEW YORK.

B

CONTENTS.

BOOKS OF TRAVEL	3
HISTORY AND BIOGRAPHY	4
STANESBY'S ILLUMINATED BOOKS	6
USEFUL KNOWLEDGE AND ENTERTAINING ANECDOTE	7
HANDBOOKS FOR THE HOUSEHOLD	8
FICTION, &c.	9
POETRY AND BELLES LETTRES	11
BIRTHDAY AND ANNIVERSARY BOOKS	13
DEVOTIONAL AND RELIGIOUS BOOKS	14
EDUCATIONAL BOOKS	18

 Darnell's Copy Books.
 Poetical Readers
 History and Geography.
 Geographical Reader.
 Grammar, &c.
 Arithmetic, Algebra and Geometry.
 Elementary French and German.
 Needlework Manuals and Appliances.

MISCELLANEOUS BOOKS	28
WORKS FOR DISTRIBUTION	30

WORKS OF TRAVEL.

Important and Interesting Book of Travels.

Unexplored Baluchistan: a Survey, with Observations Astronomical, Geographical, Botanical, &c., of a Route through **Western Baluchistan, Mekran, Bashakird, Persia, Kurdistan,** and **Turkey.** By E. A. FLOYER, F.R.G.S., F.L.S., &c. With Twelve Illustrations and a Map. Price 28s.

Mr. Floyer was the first to explore the wild district of Bashakird; he contributed a paper on that little-known country to the Plymouth Meeting of the British Association. Besides the narrative, which is full of interesting personal incident and adventure, the work will contain original illustrations, a map, vocabularies of dialects, lists of plants collected and tabulated, and observations, astronomical and meteorological.

Important Work on South Africa.

Eight Months in a Ox-Waggon. Reminiscences of Boer Life. By E. F. SANDEMAN. Demy 8vo., with a Map, cloth, 15s.

"*Mr. Sandeman was fortunate in finding more than the usual amount of adventure in the Transvaal, and sportsmen especially will derive much amusement from his hunting and shooting experiences.*"--ATHENÆUM.

Adventures in many Lands.

Travel, War, and Shipwreck. By Colonel W. PARKER GILMORE ("Ubique,") author of "The Great Thirst Land," &c, Demy 8vo. 9s.

A Visit to the United States.

The Other Side: How it Struck Us. Being Sketches of a Winter Visit to the United States and Canada. By C. B. BERRY. Cloth, price 9s.

"*A simple, straightforward, chatty narrative of his experiences; never tedious, and often instructive.*"—SCOTSMAN.

"*Mr. Berry is not only a keen observer, but has the rare talent of describing what he has seen in an entertaining style.*"—PICTORIAL WORLD.

Travels in Palestine.

"His Native Land." By the Rev. A. J. BINNIE, M.A., Curate of Kenilworth, late Vicar of St. Silas, Leeds. With Preface by the Rev. JOHN MILES MOSS, of Liverpool. With a Photograph of Jerusalem, and a Map of Palestine. Cr. 8vo., cloth, 2s. 6d.

In Ashantee Land.

Mission from Cape Coast Castle to Ashantee. With a Descriptive Account of that Kingdom. By the late T. EDWARD BOWDICH, Esq. With Preface by his daughter, Mrs. HALE. With map of the route to Coomassie. Post 8vo., cloth, 5s.

HISTORY & BIOGRAPHY.

A Bookseller of the Last Century. Being some account of the Life of JOHN NEWBERY, and of the Books he published; with a Chapter on the later Newberys. By CHARLES WELSH.

"The philanthropic publisher of St. Paul's Churchyard," as Goldsmith, in his Vicar of Wakefield, has called him, is a figure of some interest in the literary history of the eighteenth century. The first bookseller who made the issue of books for children a business of any importance, he brought before the world a number of works which have proved of incalculable benefit. But not only is he to be remembered as the publisher of "Goody Two Shoes" and kindred books; he was intimately associated with Dr. Johnson, Oliver Goldsmith, Smart, the divine, and several others; and he busied himself with many projects of a seemingly more important character than the publication of works for the young. The volume will be supplemented by an alphabetical list of books published by the Newberys from about 1730 to 1800, which the author has spent some years compiling.

Afghanistan: A Short Account of Afghanistan, its history and our dealings with it. By P. F. WALKER, Barrister-at-Law (late 75th Regiment). Cloth, 2s. 6d.

Records of York Castle, Fortress, Court House, and Prison. By A. W. TWYFORD (the present Governor) and Major ARTHUR GRIFFITHS. Crown 8vo. With Engravings and Photographs. 7s. 6d.

Historical Sketches of the Reformation. By the Rev. FREDERICK GEORGE LEE, D.C.L., Vicar of All Saints, Lambeth, &c., &c. Post 8vo., price 10s. 6d.

The Crimean Campaign with the Connaught Rangers, 1854—55—56. By Lieut.-Colonel NATHANIEL STEEVENS, late 88th (Connaught Rangers). Demy 8vo., with Map, cloth, 15s.

Memorable Battles in English History; Where Fought, Why Fought, and their Results; with the Military Lives of the Commanders. By W. H. DAVENPORT ADAMS. New and thoroughly Revised Edition, with Frontispiece and Plans of Battles. Two Volumes, crown 8vo., cloth, price 16s.

Ocean and Her Rulers; A Narrative of the Nations who have from the Earliest Ages held Dominion over the Sea, comprising a brief History of Navigation from the Remotest Periods up to the Present Time. By ALFRED ELWES. With 16 Illustrations by WALTER W. MAY. Crown 8vo., cloth, 9s.

HISTORY & BIOGRAPHY—(*continued.*)

The Modern British Plutarch ; or, Lives of Men Distinguished in the recent History of our Country for their Talents, Virtues, and Achievements. By W. C. TAYLOR, LL.D. 12mo. 4s. 6d., or gilt edges, 5s.

Politicians of To-day. A Series of Personal Sketches. By T. WEMYSS REID, Author of "Charlotte Brontë, a Monograph," "Cabinet Portraits," &c. Two Vols., Crown 8vo., cloth, 15s.

"*Mr. Reid's volumes are readable and instructive.*"—ATHENÆUM. | "*Worth reading.*"—SPECTATOR.

A Life of the Prince Imperial of France. By ELLEN BARLEE. Demy 8vo., with a Photograph of the Prince. Cloth, price 12s. 6d.

Heroes of History and Legend. Translated by JOHN LANCELOT SHADWELL from the German "Character bilder aus Geschichte und Sage," by A. W. GRÜBE. One vol. Crown 8vo., price 10s. 6d.

Pictures of the Past: Memories of Men I have Met, and Sights I have Seen. By FRANCIS H. GRUNDY, C.E. Crown 8vo., cloth, price 12s.

Contains Personal Recollections of Patrick Branwell Bronte, Leigh Hunt and his Family, George Henry Lewes, George Parker Bidder, George | *Stephenson, and many other Celebrities, and gives besides descriptions of very varied experiences in Australia.*

Six Life Studies of Famous Women. By M. BETHAM-EDWARDS, Author of "Kitty," "Dr. Jacob," "A Year in Western France," &c. With Six Portraits engraved on Steel. Cloth, price 7s. 6d.

"*Quite worthy of her reputation. . . . The book is full of information, and is to be thoroughly recommended.*" —GRAPHIC. | "*A readable and instructive collection of studies. . . . . The studies are marked by care and neatness.*"—NATURE.

Joan of Arc and the Times of Charles the Seventh. By Mrs. BRAY. 7s. 6d.

"*Readers will rise from its perusal not only with increased information,* | *but with sympathies awakened and elevated.*"—TIMES.

The Good St. Louis and His Times. By the same Author. With Portrait. 7s. 6d.

"*A valuable and interesting record of Louis' reign.*"—SPECTATOR.

HISTORY & BIOGRAPHY—(*continued*).

Tales of the Saracens. By BARBARA HUTTON. Illustrated by E. H. CORBOULD. Cloth, gilt edges, 5s.

Tales of the White Cockade. By BARBARA HUTTON. Illustrated by J. LAWSON. Cloth, 5s.; gilt edges, 5s. 6d.

Heroes of the Crusades. By BARBARA HUTTON. Illustrated by P. PRIOLO. Cloth, gilt edges, 5s.

The Fiery Cross, or the Vow of Montrose. By BARBARA HUTTON. Illustrated by J. LAWSON. Cloth, 4s. 6d.; gilt edges, 5s.

STANESBY'S ILLUMINATED GIFT BOOKS.
Every page richly printed in Gold and Colours.

The Bridal Souvenir. With a Portrait of the Princess Royal. Elegantly bound in white morocco, 21s.

The Birthday Souvenir. A Book of Thoughts on Life and Immortality. 12s. 6d. cloth; 18s. morocco.

Light for the Path of Life; from the Holy Scriptures. 12s. cloth; 15s. calf, gilt edges; 18s. mor. antique.

The Wisdom of Solomon; from the Book of Proverbs. 14s., cloth elegant; 18s. calf; 21s. mor. antique.

The Floral Gift. 14s. cloth elegant; 21s. morocco extra.

Shakespeare's Household Words. With a Photograph from the Monument at Stratford-on-Avon. New and Cheaper Edition, 6s. cloth elegant; 10s. 6d. mor. antique.

Aphorisms of the Wise and Good. With a Portrait of Milton. 6s. cloth elegant; 10s. 6d. mor. antique.

USEFUL KNOWLEDGE AND ENTERTAINING ANECDOTE.

The Commercial Products of the Sea; or, Marine Contributions to Industry and Art. By P. L. SIMMONDS, Author of "The Commercial Products of the Vegetable Kingdom." With numerous Illustrations, price 16s.

A Glossary of Biological, Anatomical, and Physiological Terms, for Teachers and Students, in Schools and Classes connected with the Science and Art Department and other Examining bodies. By THOMAS DUNMAN, Physiology Lecturer at the Birkbeck Institution and the Working Men's College. Crown 8vo., cloth, 2s. 6d.

Talks About Plants; or, Early Lessons in Botany. By Mrs. LANCASTER, Author of "Wild Flowers Worth Notice," &c. With Six Coloured Plates and Numerous Wood Engravings. Crown 8vo., cloth, gilt edges, 5s.

The Four Seasons; A Short Account of the Structure of Plants, being Four Lectures written for the Working Men's Institute, Paris. With Illustrations. Imperial 16mo., 3s. 6d.

Trees, Plants, and Flowers, their Beauties, Uses, and Influences. By Mrs. R. LEE. With Coloured Groups of Flowers from Drawings by JAMES ANDREWS. Second Thousand. 8vo., cloth, gilt edges, 10s. 6d.

Everyday Things; or, Useful Knowledge respecting the principal Animal, Vegetable, and Mineral Substances in Common Use. 18mo., cloth 1s. 6d.

Infant Amusements; or, How to Make a Nursery Happy. With practical Hints to Parents and Nurses on the Moral and Physical Training of Children. Cloth, 3s. 6d.

Female Christian Names, and their Teachings. By MARY E. BROMFIELD. Beautifully printed on Toned Paper. Imp. 32mo., Cloth, gilt edges, 1s. French Morocco 2s. Calf or Morocco, 4s.

Our Sailors; or, Anecdotes of the Engagements and Gallant Deeds of the British Navy. By W. H. G. KINGSTON With Frontispiece. Eighth Thousand. Cloth, 3s.; gilt edges, 3s. 6d.

USEFUL KNOWLEDGE & ENTERTAINING ANECDOTE—(*continued*).

Our Soldiers; or, Anecdotes of the Campaigns and Gallant Deeds of the British Army during the Reign of Her Majesty Queen Victoria. By W. H. G. KINGSTON. With Frontispiece. Eighth Thousand. Cloth, 3*s.*; gilt edges, 3*s.* 6*d.*

Anecdotes of the Habits and Instincts of Animals. By Mrs. R. LEE. Illustrated by HARRISON WEIR. Post 8vo., Cloth, 3*s.* 6*d.*, or gilt edges, 4*s.*

Anecdotes of the Habits and Instincts of Birds, Reptiles, and Fishes. By Mrs. R. LEE. Illustrated by HARRISON WEIR. Post 8vo., Cloth, 3*s.* 6*d.*, gilt edges, 4*s.*

Notabilia; or, Curious and Amusing Facts about many Things. Explained and Illustrated. By the late JOHN TIMBS, F.S.A. Post 8vo., 6*s.*
"*There is a world of wisdom in this book.*"—ART JOURNAL.

Ancestral Stories and Traditions of Great Families. Illustrative of English History. By the same Author. With Frontispiece. Cloth, 7*s.* 6*d.*
"*An interesting and well-written book.*"—LITERARY CHURCHMAN.

Strange Stories of the Animal World; a Book of Curious Contributions to Natural History. Second Edition with Illustrations by ZWECKER. By the same Author. Gilt edges, 6*s.*
"*Will be studied with profit and pleasure.*"—ATHENÆUM.

HANDBOOKS FOR THE HOUSEHOLD.

The Young Wife's Own Book. A Manual of Personal and Family Hygiene, containing everything that the young wife and mother ought to know concerning her own health at the most important periods of her life, and that of her children. By LIONEL WEATHERLY, M.D., Author of "Ambulance Lectures," "Hygiene and Home Nursing," &c. Fcap. 8vo., cloth limp, price 1*s.*

Popular Lectures on Plain and High-class Cookery. By a former Staff Teacher of the National Training School of Cookery. Cloth, 1*s.* 6*d.*

The Art of Washing; Clothes, Personal, and House. By Mrs. A. A. STRANGE BUTSON. Cloth, price 1*s.* 6*d.*

Ambulance Lectures : or, What to do in Cases of Accidents or Sudden Illness. By LIONEL A. WEATHERLY, M.D., Lecturer to the Ambulance Department, Order of St. John of Jerusalem in England. With numerous Illustrations. 9th Thousand. Cloth. thoroughly revised, price 1s.

Lectures on Domestic Hygiene and Home Nursing. By LIONEL A. WEATHERLEY, M.D., Member of the Royal College of Surgeons of England; Fellow of the Obstetrical Society of London, &c. Illustrated. Cloth, limp, 1s.

Artizan Cookery, and how to Teach it. By a Pupil of the National Training School for Cookery, South Kensington. Sewed, 6d.

FICTION, &c.

Percy Pomo ; or, The Autobiography of a South Sea Islander. A Tale of Life and Adventure (Missionary, Trading, and Slaving) in the South Pacific. Crown 8vo., cloth, price 6s.

The Story represents native character and Missionary work apart from the unrealities of the conventional Missionary Meeting, and affords correct information respecting native religion, language, manners, and customs, together with many criticisms of the weak points of our civilization; as seen from a native point of view.

The hero relates his experiences of mission life, the horrors of the kidnapping vessels, &c., &c., and demonstrates the great success of missions when carried on in a self-denying common-sense way.

Over the Seas and Far away. A Story, by CECILIA LUSHINGTON, Author of "Fifty Years in Sandbourne." Crown 8vo., cloth, price 3s. 6d.

This Story is meant to show the influence and power for good possessed by a faithful, truthful, and thankful spirit which, by following after the charity which endures and hopes all things, is upheld amidst difficulties, afflictions, and temptations.

Halek ; an Autobiographical Fragment. By JOHN H. NICHOLSON. Crown 8vo., price 7s. 6d.

Hillsland as it was Seventy Years ago. A Story in One Volume. By the Rev. F. H. MORGAN. Crown 8vo., cloth, price 5s.

The story consists of certain traditional recollections of the smuggling days in Cleveland. The names of persons and places are imaginary.

None of the former are, however, portraits, though the latter may be easily identified.

FICTION, &c.—(*continued*).

Lois Leggatt; a Memoir. By FRANCIS CARR, Author of "Left Alone," "Tried by Fire," &c. One vol., crown 8vo., price 6s., cloth.

The previous stories by this author have been exceedingly well received, and this one will, the publishers have every reason to believe, materially enhance the reputation already gained.

Worthless Laurels. A Story of the Stage. By EMILY CARRINGTON. Three vols., crown 8vo., 31s. 6d.

Louis: or, Doomed to the Cloister. A Tale of Religious Life in the time of Louis XIV. Founded on Fact. By M. J. HOPE. Dedicated by permission to Dean Stanley. Three vols., crown 8vo., 31s. 6d.

Tried by Fire. By FRANCIS CARR, Author of "Left Alone," &c. Three vols., crown 8vo., 31s. 6d.

"*The Author can sketch very well indeed.*"—CONTEMPORARY REVIEW.

Thirteen at Dinner, and what came of it. Being Arrowsmith's Christmas Annual, 1881. In attractive paper covers, price 1s. Contributions by A. B. EDWARDS, F. WEDMORE, F. E. WEATHERLY, L. A. WEATHERLY, J. A. SYMONDS, "AGRIKLER," HUGH CONWAY, &c., &c. Illustrations by G. H. EDWARDS, J. J. CURNOCK, H. WHATLEY, E. C. LAVARS. Engravings by WHYMPER.

The Vicar of Wakefield; a Tale. By OLIVER GOLDSMITH. With Eight Illustrations by JOHN ABSOLON. Beautifully printed by Whittingham, on superfine paper, 3s. 6d. cloth. 10s. 6d. Morocco Antique.

[It may not be uninteresting to state that it was from the house now occupied by Messrs. GRIFFITH & FARRAN that, under the auspices of Mr. NEWBERY, GOLDSMITH's friend, "The Vicar of Wakefield" was first issued. To the same publisher also belongs the distinction of having originally brought out GOLDSMITH's celebrated poem, "The Traveller."]

A Journey to the Centre of the Earth. From the French of JULES VERNE. With 52 Illustrations by RIOU. New Edition. Post 8vo., 6s.; or bevelled boards, gilt edges, 7s. 6d.

FICTION, &C.—(*continued*).

For a Dream's Sake. By MRS. HERBERT MARTIN, Author of "Bonnie Lesley," &c. Two vols., crown 8vo., cloth, 21s.

"*Written in the same pleasant style and graceful language as 'Bonnie Lesley.'*"—ATHENÆUM.

The Secret of the Sands; or, The Water Lily and her Crew. By HARRY COLLINGWOOD. Two vols., crown 8vo., cloth, gilt tops, 12s.

"*Brisk and exciting.*"—MORNING POST. | "*Told in a very spirited fashion.*"—SPECTATOR.

Elsie Grey; A Tale of Truth. By CECIL CLARKE. Crown 8vo., cloth, 5s.

St. Nicholas Eve and other Tales. By MARY C. ROWSELL. Crown 8vo., price 7s. 6d.

Wothorpe by Stamford. A Tale of Bygone Days. By C. HOLDICH. Five Engravings. Cloth, 3s. 6d.

POETRY AND BELLES LETTRES.

Rhymes in Council: Aphorisms Versified—185. By S. C. HALL, F.S.A. Dedicated by permission to the Grandchildren of the Queen. 4to., printed in black with red borders. Cloth elegant, 2s. 6d.

Ambition's Dream. A Poem in Two Fyttes. New Edition. Fcap. 8vo., price 2s. 6d.

The Seasons; a Poem by the Rev. O. RAYMOND, LL.B., Author of "Paradise," and other Poems. Fcap. 8vo., with Four Illustrations. Cloth, 2s. 6d.

The Golden Queen: a Tale of Love, War, and Magic. By EDWARD A. SLOANE. Cloth, gilt edges, 6s.; or plain edges, 5s.

POETRY AND BELLES LETTRES—(*continued.*)

Grandma's Attic Treasures; A Story of Old Time Memories. By MARY D. BRINE.
Illustrated with numerous Wood Engravings, executed in the best style of the art. Suitable for a Christmas Present. Small quarto, cloth, gilt edges, price

This is a pleasing and pathetic dialect poem, showing how the old furniture, which was associated in her memory with all her past joys and sorrows, was dearer to Grandma than the money offered her by the Bric-a-Brac dealers who wanted to buy it.

The story of the parting with, and recognition of, her old table (doubtless a Chippendale or a Sheraton), in the house of her rich married daughter, is as humorous as many of the other incidents of the poem are pathetic.

Indian Summer. Autumn Poems and Sketches.
By L. CLARKSON. One handsome folio Volume, with Twelve Plates, printed in colours, showing the various flowers and leaves that are found in America during that delightful warm period of the late autumn, which is called the Indian Summer. Elegantly bound in cloth, gilt edges, price One Guinea.

The poems, illustrating and describing the beauties of the Indian Summer, are entirely drawn from American sources. It is one of the most handsome and attractive books for a Christmas present that has been issued.

A Woodland Idyll. By Miss PHŒBE ALLEN.
It is dedicated to Principal Shairp, and is an attempt to represent allegorically the relative positions of Nature, Art, and Science in our World. Cloth, 2s. 6d.

The Classics for the Million; being an Epitome
in English of the Works of the Principal Greek and Latin Authors. By HENRY GREY. Second edition. Cloth, 5s.

Stories from Early English Literature,
with some Account of the Origin of Fairy Tales, Legends and Traditionary Lore. Adapted to the use of Young Students. By Miss S. J. VENABLES DODDS. Crown 8vo., price 5s.

Similitudes. Like likes Like.
16mo., cloth, bevelled boards, price 2s. 6d.

Among the numerous volumes of selections which have been offered to the public it does not appear that any one of these similes or similitudes is to be found; it is therefore hoped that the present compilation, the result of many years reading, may be acceptable.

BIRTHDAY AND ANNIVERSARY BOOKS.

The Churchman's Daily Remembrancer,
with Poetical Selections for the Christian Year, with the Kalendar and Table of Lessons of the English Church, for the use of both Clergy and Laity.

	s. d.		s. d.
Cloth extra, red edges	2 0	Morocco, bevelled	5 0
French Morocco, limp	3 0	Morocco bevelled, clasp ...	6 0
French Morocco, circuit or tuck	3 6	Russia, limp	6 0
Persian Morocco, limp	3 6	Levant Morocco, limp	6 6
Persian Morocco, circuit ...	4 6	Russia, circuit	7 6
Calf or Morocco, limp	4 6	Russia limp, in drop case ...	9 0

With Twelve Photographs, 2s. extra.

The Book of Remembrance for every Day
in the Year. Containing Choice Extracts from the best Authors, and the exact place indicated whence the Quotation is taken, with Blank Spaces for recording Birthdays, Marriages, and other Anniversaries. Beautifully printed in red and black. Imperial 32mo.

"*A charming little memorial of love and friendship, and happily executed as conceived. For a birthday or other Anniversary nothing can be prettier or more appropriate.*"—BOOKSELLER.
"*Beautifully got up.*"—LEEDS MERCURY.

May be had in the following Styles of Binding:—

	s. d.		s. d.
Cloth extra, plain edges ...	2 0	Calf or Morocco, limp, red under gold edges	5 0
Cloth Elegant, bevelled boards, gilt edges	2 6	Morocco, bevelled boards, do...	7 6
French Morocco, limp, gilt edges	3 0	Ditto, with gilt clasp	8 6
Persian Morocco, bevelled boards, red under gold edges	4 0	Russia, limp, elegant, with gilt clasp	10 0
Persian Morocco, with clasp ...	4 6		

With Twelve Beautiful Photographs.

	s. d.		s. d.
Cloth, elegant	5 0	Morocco, bevelled	12 6
French Morocco, limp, gilt edges	8 6	Russia, limp, extra	15 0
Calf or morocco, limp	10 0	Levant Morocco, elegant ...	18 0

Anniversary Text Book; a Book of Scripture
Verse and Sacred Song for Every Day in the Year. Interleaved.

May be had in the following Styles of Binding:—

	s. d.		s. d.
Cloth, bevelled boards, white edges	1 0	Imitation Ivory, rims	3 0
Cloth, gilt boards, gilt edges ...	1 6	Morocco, elegant, rims	4 6
" " " rims ...	2 0	Morocco, bevelled, and clasp ...	4 6
French Morocco, limp	2 0	Russia, limp, red under gold edges	4 6
Calf or Morocco, " ...	2 6	Ivory, rims	7 6

DEVOTIONAL AND RELIGIOUS BOOKS.

The Song of Solomon, rendered in English Verse, in accordance with the most approved translation from the Hebrew and Septuagint. By the Rev. JAMES PRATT, D.D. With 7 Illustrations. Crown 8vo., cloth, 3s. 6d.

An Epitome of Anglican Church History from the Earliest Ages to the Present Time. Compiled from various sources by ELLEN WEBLEY-PARRY. Demy 8vo., Cloth, 7s. 6d.

The Life Militant. Plain Sermons for Cottage Homes. By ELLELL. Crown 8vo., price 6s.

The Way of Prayer; a Book of Devotions, for use in Church and at Home. Compiled by Rev. H. W. MILLAR, M.A. Cloth, red edges, 1s.

Bishop Ken's Approach to the Holy Altar. With an Address to Young Communicants. New and Cheaper Edition.

	s. d.		s. d.
Limp cloth	0 8	Calf or morocco, limp	3 6
Superior cloth, red edges ...	1 0	Morocco, bevelled	4 6
French morocco, limp	1 6	Russia, limp	4 6

With Photographs, 2s. extra.

₊ Clergymen wishing to introduce this Manual can have Specimen Copy, with prices for quantities, post free for six stamps on application.

A New Inexpensive Confirmation Card. Printed in red and black, size 5 × 3½ inches. Sold in Packets of Twelve Cards for 6d.

An Illuminated Certificate of Confirmation and First Communion. Printed in gold and colours, size 6 × 4½ inches. Price 2d.

An "In Memoriam" Card. Beautifully printed in silver or gold, price 2d.

₊ *A reduction made on taking a quantity of the above Cards.*

Confirmation ; or, Called and Chosen and Faithful.

By the Author of "The Gospel in the Church's Seasons Series."
With Preface by the Very Rev. the DEAN OF CHESTER. Fcap.
8vo., cloth limp. 1s.
A Cheaper Edition for Distribution, price 9d.

Extract from DEAN HOWSON'S *Preface:—" The present volume . . . strikes me as being of the greater value because it comes to us from a woman's hand. It is written by a deaconess of the Church of England. One of the most useful duties of those who bear that title is to give help in preparing girls for Confirmation."*

Dr. Lee's Altar Services. Edited by the Rev.

Dr. F. G. LEE, D.C.L., F.S.A. Containing the complete Altar Services of the Church, beautifully printed in red and black at the Chiswick Press, enriched with Ornamental Capitals, &c., in Three Volumes ; One Volume, folio size, 15 × 10 × 1½ inches ; and two Volumes 4to., containing the Epistles and Gospels separately, each 12 × 9 × ¾ inches.

  The Set, in Turkey Morocco, plain £7 7 0
   ,, Best Levant Morocco, inlaid cross ... £10 10 0

The Folio Volume, which contains all the Services of the Altar, may be had separately—

  Turkey Morocco, plain... ... ... £3 3 0
  Best Levant Morocco, inlaid cross £4 4 0

*** The work can also be bound specially to order in cheaper or more expensive styles.

Messrs. GRIFFITH & FARRAN have a few copies remaining of this rare and valuable work, which is not only the best book for the purpose for which it is designed, but is one of the finest specimens of typographical art which the Chiswick Press has produced.

The Practical Christian's Library. A Box

containing Nine Books, bound in Satin cloth, red edges, 18s. ; or in French morocco, 25s. Size of box, 7 × 6½ × 4½, with full gilt top.

CONTENTS.

Imitation of Christ. A'KEMPIS.
St. Augustine's Confessions.
Bishop Taylor's Holy Living
 ,,   Holy Dying.
Bishop Ken's Manual of Prayer.

Bishop Wilson's Lord's Supper.
 ,,   Sacra Privata.
Sherlock's Meditations.
 ,, Self Examinations.

Any of the Volumes may be had separately, 2s. each in cloth, or 2s. 6d. each French morocco.

The Churchman's Manual of Family and

Private Devotion, compiled from the writings of English Divines, with Graces and Devotions for the Seasons, Litanies, and an entirely new selection of Hymns. [*Preparing.*

The Churchman's Text Book.

For every day in the Christian Year. Containing a Poetical Extract and an appropriate Text, with the Holy-days of the Church duly recorded. An elegantly printed and daintily bound little volume in diamond 48mo. $3\frac{3}{4}$ by $2\frac{1}{4}$ inches, cloth, limp, red edges, 6*d.* It may also be had in various leather bindings and interleaved with ruled Writing Paper, 6*d.* extra.

Seven Last Words from the Cross.

By the Rev. FREEMAN WILLS, M.A. Sewed, 6*d.*

Hints to a Clergyman's Wife,

or Female Parochial Duties Practically Illustrated. Cloth, 2*s.*

The Churchman's Altar Manual and Guide

to Holy Communion, together with the Collects, Epistles, and Gospels, and a Selection of Appropriate Hymns. Printed at the University Press, Oxford, with Borders and Rubrics in Red. Cloth, 2*s.*

May be had in various Leather Bindings—Price List on application. Also with Eight Photographs.

A CONFIRMATION CARD is presented with each copy of the Book.

On the Wings of a Dove;

or, The Life of a Soul: An Allegory. Illustrated by SISTER E.—C. S. J. B. CLEWER. Demy 16mo., with eight Illustrations. Cloth, 1*s.* 6*d.*

Emblems of Christian Life.

Illustrated by W. HARRY ROGERS, in One Hundred Original Designs, from the Writings of the Fathers, Old English Poets, &c. Printed by WHITTINGHAM, with Borders and Initials in Red. Square 8vo., price 10*s.* 6*d.* cloth elegant, gilt edges; 21*s.* Turkey morocco antique.

AMERICAN SERMONS
AND
THEOLOGICAL BOOKS.
PUBLISHED BY
E. P. DUTTON and CO., New York, U.S.A.,
AND SOLD IN ENGLAND BY
GRIFFITH AND FARRAN.

Brooks, the Rev. Phillips, D.D., Rector of Trinity Church, Boston.
    Influence of Jesus. Being the Bohlen Lecture for 1879. Eighth Thousand. Crown 8vo., cloth, price 3s. 6d.
    Sermons. Thirteenth Thousand. Crown 8vo., cloth, price 5s.

Chapman, Rev. Dr.
    Sermons upon the Ministry, Worship, and Doctrine of the Church. New Edition. Crown 8vo., price 5s.
    Clergyman's Visiting List, in morocco, with tuck for the pocket. Foolscap, price 7s. 6d.

Doane, Rt. Rev. Wm. Croswell, D.D., Bishop of Albany.
    Mosaics; or, the Harmony of Collect, Epistle, and Gospel for the Sundays of the Christian Year. Cr. 8vo., cloth, 6s.

Hallam, Rev. Robert A., D.D.
    Lectures on the Morning Prayer. 12mo., 5s.
    Lectures on Moses. 12mo., cloth, 3s. 6d.

Handbook of Church Terms.
    A Pocket Dictionary; or, Brief Explanation of Words in Common Use relating to the Order, Worship, Architecture, Vestments, Usages, and Symbolism of the Church, as employed in Christian Art. Paper, 9d.; cloth, 1s. 6d.

Hobart, Rev. John Henry, D.D., formerly Bishop of New York.
    Festivals and Fasts. A Companion for the Festivals and Fasts of the Protestant Episcopal Church, principally selected and altered from Nelson's Companion. With Forms of Devotion. Twenty-third Edition. 12mo., 5s.

Hodges, Rev. Wm., D.D.
Baptism : Tested by Scripture and History; or, the Teaching of the Holy Scriptures, and the Practice and Teaching of the Christian Church in every age succeeding the Apostolic, compared in relation to the subjects and Modes of Baptism. 6s.

Huntington, Rt. Rev. F. D., Bishop of
Central New York.

Christian Believing and Living. Sermons. Fifth Edition. 12mo., 3s. 6d.

Helps to a Holy Lent. 16mo., 208 pages, crown 8vo., 2s. 6d.

Sermons for the People. Crown 8vo., cloth, 3s. 6d.

Odenheimer, the Rt. Rev. Wm. H., D.D.,
late Bishop of New Jersey.

Sermons, with Portrait and Memoir. Edited by his Wife. Crown 8vo., 5s.

Staunton, Rev. William, D.D.
Ecclesiastical Dictionary, containing Definitions of Terms, and Explanations and Illustrations of Subjects pertaining to the History, Ritual, Discipline, Worship, Ceremonies, and Usages of the Christian Church. 8vo. 746 pp., 7s. 6d.

Vinton, Rev. Alexander H.
Sermons. Fourth Edition. 330 pages, 3s. 6d.

Vinton, Francis, S.T.D., D.C.L.
Manual Commentary on the General Canon Law of the Protestant Episcopal Church. 8vo., cloth, 5s.

Williams, Right Rev. John, D.D., Bishop
of Connecticut.

Studies on the English Reformation. 12mo., cloth, 3s. 6d.

Wilson, Rev. Wm. D., D.D.
The Church Identified. By a reference to the History of its Origin, Extension, and Perpetuation, with Special Reference to the Protestant Episcopal Church in the United States. Revised Edition, 12mo., 439 pp. 6s.

EDUCATIONAL WORKS.

GOOD HANDWRITING.

GEORGE DARNELL'S COPY-BOOKS,

After over a quarter of a century of public favour, are everywhere acknowledged as the best for simplicity and thoroughness. With these Copy-Books the pupil advances in the art of writing with ease and rapidity, while the labour of the teacher is very greatly lightened. They are used in nearly all the best schools in Great Britain and the Colonies, and are adapted to the New Educational Code.

ADVANTAGES OF THE SYSTEM.

I. It is the production of an experienced Schoolmaster.
II. It gradually advances from the Simple Stroke to a superior Small Hand.
III. The assistance given in the Primal lesson is reduced as the learner progresses, until all guidance is safely withdrawn.
IV. The number and variety of the copies secure attention, and prevent the pupils copying their own writing, as in books with single head-lines.
V. The system insures the progress of the learner, and greatly lightens the labour of the teacher.

A SHORT AND CERTAIN ROAD TO A GOOD HANDWRITING.

Darnell's Large Post Copy-Books,

16 Nos. 6d. each. The first ten of which have on every alternate line appropriate and carefully written copies in Pencil coloured Ink, to be first written over and then imitated, the remaining numbers having Black Head-lines for imitation only, THE WHOLE GRADUALLY ADVANCING FROM A SIMPLE STROKE TO A SUPERIOR SMALL HAND.

No.
1. Elementary (Strokes, &c.)
2. Single Letters.
3, 4. Large Text (Short Words).
5. Text, Large Text, and Figures.
6. Round Text, Capitals, and Figures.
7. Text, Round, and Small.

No.
8, 9, 10. Text, Round, Small, and Figures.
11, 12. Round, Small, and Figures.
13, 14. Round and Small.
15, 16. Small Hand.

A SURE GUIDE TO A GOOD HANDWRITING.

Darnell's Foolscap Copy-Books,

24 Nos., Oblong.   3d. each.

Or superior paper, marble covers, 4d. each.   On the same plan.

No.
1. Elementary (Strokes, &c.)
2. Single Letters.
3, 4. Large Text, Short Words.
5. Text, Large Text, and Figures.
6. Text, Round, and Capitals.
7. Round, Small, and Figures.
8. Text, Round, and Figures.

No.
9. Round, Small and Figures.
10, 11. Round and Small.
12, 13, 15. Round, Small, & Figures.
14. Round and Small.
16 to 20. Small Hand.
21. Ornamental Hands.
22 to 24. Ladies' Angular Writing.

Darnell's Universal Copy-Books,

16 Nos.   2d. each.   On the same plan.

N.B.—Contents same as Post Copy-Books.

"*For teaching writing I would recommend the use of Darnell's Copy Books. I have noticed a marked improvement wherever they have been used.*"—Report of Mr. Maye *(National Society's Organizer of Schools)* to the WORCESTER DIOCESAN BOARD OF EDUCATION.

"*As to the necessity of some one proposing a new way to teach writing, I do not think it is needed. Let a London Clerk inspect one of Mr. Darnell's Copy Books (I believe they are most generally in use in our schools), and I think he will say that, with a moderate amount of care on the part of the teacher, the result must be a legible, clear hand-writing.*"

—An Essex Schoolmaster; NATIONAL SOCIETY'S MONTHLY PAPER.

The Times says: "*This gentleman has conferred a great benefit, not only on the rising generation, but on those who will hereafter form the rising generation. He has composed a series of Elementary Treatises, in which the comprehension of the art or science taught is so much facilitated that children of the dullest capacities are made capable of comprehending what is required of them, whilst teachers are relieved from the difficulties of imparting knowledge in the desultory and incomprehensible manner too often practised.*"

GRIFFITH & FARRAN'S
POETICAL READERS.

The object of the compiler has been to provide the young with a repertory—full, varied, artistically arranged, and carefully graduated, of high class, and at the same time suitable, poetry.

The collection consists almost entirely of complete poems. They are arranged in four parts, the first part containing the simplest pieces, and the last the most difficult.

A few pages of explanatory matter has been appended to each part, but it has been thought desirable to make the notes as few in number and as concise as possible.

The book will thus, it is hoped, perform a double function. In the four parts it will be suitable as a series of reading books for use in elementary and other schools, while as a complete volume it will be a most suitable book for presentation.

POETRY FOR THE YOUNG.—
BOOK I., for Standards I.—IV., inclusive, crown 8vo., 120 *pp.*, cloth, price 9*d.*

POETRY FOR THE YOUNG.—
BOOK II., for Standards IV.—VI. crown 8vo., 168 *pp.*, cloth, price 1*s.*

POETRY FOR THE YOUNG.—
BOOK III., for Standard VI. and pupil teachers, crown 8vo., 176 *pp.*, cloth, price 1*s.*

POETRY FOR THE YOUNG.—
BOOK IV., for pupil teachers, training colleges, &c., crown 8vo. 128 *pp.*, cloth, price 9*d.*

Poetry for the Young. The above Collection in One Volume. Intended for use in Schools and Colleges, and graduated to suit the requirements of Public Elementary Schools. Cr. 8vo., 645 pages. Handsomely bound, cloth, price 3*s.* 6*d.*

HISTORY.

Britannia; a Collection of the Principal Passages in Latin Authors that refer to this Island, with Vocabulary and Notes. By T. S. CAYZER. Illustrated with a Map and 29 Woodcuts. Crown 8vo., cloth, 3s. 6d.

True Stories from Ancient History, chronologically arranged from the Creation of the World to the Death of Charlemagne. Twelfth Edition. 12mo., 5s. cloth.

Mrs. Trimmer's Concise History of England, Revised and brought down to the Present Time. By Mrs. MILNER. With Portraits of the Sovereigns. 5s. cloth

Rhymes of Royalty; the History of England in Verse, from the Norman Conquest to the Reign of Victoria; with a Summary of the Leading Events in each Reign. Fcap. 8vo., 2s. cloth.

GEOGRAPHY.

Pictorial Geography, for the Instruction of Children. Illustrates at a glance the Various Geographical Terms in such a manner as to at once impart clear and definite ideas respecting them. On a Sheet 30 by 22 inches, printed in colours, 1s. 6d.; Mounted on Rollers and Varnished, 3s. 6d.
"*Forms an excellent introduction to the study of maps.*"—SCHOOL BOARD CHRONICLE.

Gaultier's Familiar Geography. With a concise Treatise on the Artificial Sphere, and Two Coloured Maps, illustrative of the principal Geographical Terms. 16mo., cloth, 3s.

Butler's Outline Maps, and Key, or Geographical and Biographical Exercises: with a Set of Coloured Outline Maps, designed for the Use of Young Persons. By the late WILLIAM BUTLER. Enlarged by the Author's Son, J. O. BUTLER. Thirty-sixth edition, revised to date. 4s.

Tabular Views of the Geography and Sacred History of Palestine, and of the Travels of St. Paul. Intended for Pupil Teachers, and others engaged in Class Teaching. By A. T. WHITE. Oblong 8vo., 1s. sewed.

GRIFFITH & FARRAN'S GEOGRAPHICAL READERS

Fulfil exactly the requirements of the Education Department as explained in the Statement made by the Right Honourable A. J. MUNDELLA on the 8th August, 1881. Accepted by the School Boards for Birmingham, Derby, Leeds, Leicester, &c.

BOOK I., FOR STANDARD I.

Early Glimpses. Introductory to Glimpses of the Globe. By J. R. BLAKISTON. Fcap. 8vo., 96 pages, with Twenty-two Illustrations, cloth limp, cut flush, price 6d.

It is intended to bridge over the gap between the Object Lessons of Infant Classes and the Elementary Geography of more advanced classes, and to assist teachers in training children to habits of observation and inquiry, the first chapters being arranged with a view to implant a taste for physical, the latter for commercial, geography.

BOOK II., FOR STANDARD II.

Glimpses of the Globe. A First Geographical Reading Book. By J. R. BLAKISTON. New, enlarged, and Revised Edition. 40 Chapters. 156 pages, cloth, 1s.

"*A very commendable attempt to simplify the teaching of the elements of geography.*"—EDUCATIONAL NEWS.
"*We are strongly of opinion that Mr. Blakiston has succeeded most admirably in carrying out his intention in producing this little treatise.*"—EDUCATIONAL CHRONICLE.

BOOK III., FOR STANDARD III.

Glimpses of England. By J. R. BLAKISTON. 40 Chapters. 156 pages, cloth, 1s.

"*The language employed is well within the comprehension of Third Standard children, and the book is unquestionably written in pleasant and interesting style.*"—TEACHER.

BOOK IV., FOR STANDARD IV.

Glimpses of the British Empire. By J. R. BLAKISTON. In 66 Sections. Cloth, 1s. 6d.

"*A very good book.*"—EDUCATIONAL NEWS.
"*The whole volume contains a very fair outline of the empire on which the sun never sets.*"—SCHOOL.
"*This little volume should be specially noted by teachers in search of a good geographical reading book.*"—EDUCATIONAL TIMES.

BOOK V., FOR STANDARDS V.—VII.

Glimpses of the Earth. By J. R. BLAKISTON. 320 pages, cloth, 2s. 6d.

"*The book is admirably adapted to remind a teacher of the topics he ought to introduce in each lesson.*"—BOOKSELLER.
"*Conveys many a useful lesson.*"—DAILY TELEGRAPH.
"*Will prove real and lasting service in schools.*"—DAILY CHRONICLE.

GRAMMAR, &c.

A Compendious Grammar, and Philological Handbook of the English Language, for the Use of Schools and Candidates for the Army and Civil Service Examinations. By J. G. COLQUHOUN, Esq., Barrister-at-Law. Fcap. 8vo., cloth, 2s. 6d.

Darnell, G. Grammar made Intelligible to Children. Being a Series of short and simple Rules, with ample Explanations of Every Difficulty, and copious Exercises for Parsing; in Language adapted to the comprehension of very young Students. New and Revised Edition. Cloth, 1s.

Darnell, G. Introduction to English Grammar. Price 3d. Being the first 32 pages of "Grammar made Intelligible."

Darnell, T. Parsing Simplified; an Introduction and Companion to all Grammars; consisting of Short and Easy Rules, with Parsing Lessons to each. Cloth, 1s.

Lovechilds, Mrs. The Child's Grammar. 50th Edition. 18mo., cloth, 9d.

A Word to the Wise; or, Hints on the Current Improprieties of Expression in Writing and Speaking. By PARRY GWYNNE. Sixteenth Thousand. 18mo., sewed, 6d., or cloth, gilt edges, 1s.

The Letter H, Past, Present, and Future. Rules for the silent H, based on Contemporary Usage, and an Appeal in behalf of WH. By ALFRED LEACH. Cloth limp,

Harry Hawkins's H-Book; showing how he learned to aspirate his H's. Eighth Thousand. Sewed, 6d.

The Prince of Wales's Primer. With 340 Illustrations by J. GILBERT. New Edition, sewed, 6d.

Darnell, G. Short and Certain Road to Reading. Being a Series of EASY LESSONS in which the Alphabet is so divided as to enable the Child to read many Pages of Familiar Phrases before he has learned half the letters. Cloth, 6d.
Or in 4 parts, paper covers, 1½d. each.

Sheet Lessons. Being Extracts from the above, printed in very large bold type. Price, for the Set of Six Sheets, 6d.; or, neatly mounted on boards, 3s.

ARITHMETIC, ALGEBRA, & GEOMETRY.

Darnell, G. Arithmetic made Intelligible to Children. Being a Series of GRADUALLY ADVANCING EXERCISES, intended to employ the Reason rather than the Memory of the Pupil; with ample Explanations of every Difficulty, in Language adapted to the comprehension of very young Students. Cloth, 1s. 6d.

⁎ This work may be had in Three Parts:—Part I., price 6d. Part II., price 9d. Part III., price 6d.
A KEY to Parts II. & III., price 1s. (Part I. does not require a Key.)

Cayzer, T. S. One Thousand Arithmetical Tests, or THE EXAMINER'S ASSISTANT. Specially adapted, by a novel arrangement of the subject, for Examination Purposes, but also suited for general use in Schools. By T. S. CAYZER, Head Master in Queen Elizabeth's Hospital, Bristol. Eleventh Thousand, with a complete set of Examples and Models of Work. Cloth, 1s. 6d.

All the operations of Arithmetic are presented under Forty Heads, and on opening at any one of the Examination Papers, a complete set of examples appears, carefully graduated.

Key with Solutions of all the Examples in the One Thousand Arithmetical Tests. By THOMAS S. CAYZER. Price 4s. 6d. cloth.

THE ANSWERS only, price 1s. 6d. cloth.

One Thousand Algebraical Tests; on the same plan. Third Edition. 8vo. Cloth 2s. 6d.

ANSWERS TO THE ALGEBRAICAL TESTS, 2s. 6d. cloth.

Theory and Practice of the Metric System of Weights and Measures. By Professor LEONE LEVI, F.S.A., F.S.S. Third Edition. Sewed, 1s.

An Aid to Arithmetic. By E. DIVER, M.D. Fcap 8vo., cloth, price 6d.

The Essentials of Geometry, Plane and Solid, as taught in Germany and France. For Students preparing for Examination, Cadets in Naval and Military Schools, Technical Classes, &c. By J. R. MORELL, formerly one of Her Majesty's Inspectors of Schools. With numerous Diagrams. Cloth, 2s.

ELEMENTARY FRENCH & GERMAN WORKS.

L'Abécédaire of French Pronunciation. A Manual for Teachers and Students. By G. LEPREVOST, (of Paris), Professor of Languages. Crown 8vo. Cloth, 2s.

Its object is to teach French pronunciation systematically by simple and easy stages, each lesson being divided into two parts. The first part treats of the pronunciation of the vowels, consonants, diphthongs, nasal and liquid sounds. These are exemplified by lists of from fifteen to twenty words each, with the English meaning, containing no other sound than those previously explained. The second part, called "French as it is Read and Spoken," treats of the connection of words, of the elision of the "E" mute (including as many as nine E's in succession), a very important subject, without a complete knowledge of which it is impossible to speak French correctly: of the divisions of words into syllables, and of accents and emphasis.

Le Babillard: an Amusing Introduction to the French Language. By a FRENCH LADY. Ninth Edition. 16 Plates. Cloth, 2s.

Les Jeunes Narrateurs, ou Petits Contes Moraux. With a Key to the Difficult Words and Phrases. Third Edition. 18mo. Cloth, 2s.
"*Written in pure and easy French.*"—MORNING POST.

The Pictorial French Grammar. For the Use of Children. Forming a most pleasant and easy introduction to the Language. By MARIN DE LA VOYE. With 80 illustrations. Fcap. 8vo. Cloth, 1s. 6d.

Rowbotham's New and Easy Method of Learning the French Genders. New Edition, sewed, 6d.

Bellenger's French Word and Phrase Book; containing a Select Vocabulary and Dialogues. New Edition. Cloth limp, 1s.

Der Schwätzer; or, The Prattler. An Amusing Introduction to the German Language. Sixteen Illustrations. Cloth, 2s.

GRIFFITH & FARRAN'S NEEDLEWORK MANUALS AND APPLIANCES.

RECOMMENDED BY THE EDUCATION DEPARTMENT.

They contain full instructions as to PIN DRILL, POSITION DRILL, and NEEDLE DRILL, as required by the New Code.

Mundella's Code, Education Department, Needlework Schedule, 1881. Girls' and Infants' Department, Boys and Girls below Standard I. "Needle Drill," "Position Drill," "Knitting Pin Drill," to which is added, "Thimble Drill." By Mrs. A. FLOYER, Principal of the London Institute for the Advancement of Plain Needlework, late Senior Examiner of Needlework to the London School Board, &c., &c. Price 3*d*.

The Invariable Stocking Scale will suit any size or any Wool. Designed by Miss J. HEATH, Senior Examiner of Needlework to the School Board for London. On a wall sheet 30 inches by 22 inches, price 9*d*. plain, or mounted on roller and varnished, price 2*s*. 6*d*. UNIFORM WITH THE SERIES OF

Needlework Demonstration Sheets (18 in number). Exhibiting by Diagrams and Descriptions, the formation of the Stitches in Elementary Needlework. By Mrs. A. FLOYER. 30 by 22 inches, price 9*d*. each; or, mounted on rollers and varnished, 2*s*. 6*d*.

Plain Needlework, arranged in Six Standards, with Hints for the Management of Class and Appendix on Simultaneous Teaching. By Mrs. A. FLOYER. Twenty-first Thousand. Sewed, 6*d*.

Plain Knitting and Mending, arranged in Six Standards, with Diagrams. By the same Author. Fourteenth Thousand. Sewed, 6*d*.

Plain Cutting out for Standards IV., V., and VI., as now required by the Government Educational Department. Adapted to the Principles of Elementary Geometry. Sixth Thousand. By the same Author. Sewed, 1*s*.

A Set of Diagrams referred to in the Book may be had separately, printed on stout paper and enclosed in an envelope. Price 1*s*.

NEEDLEWORK, &C., *continued.*

Plain Hints for those who have to Examine Needlework, whether for Government Grants, Prize Associations, or local Managers ; to which is added Skeleton Demonstration Lessons to be used with the Demonstration Frames, and a Glossary of Terms used in the Needlework required from the Scholars in Public Elementary Schools. By Mrs. A. FLOYER, Author of " Plain Needlework." Price 2s.

The Demonstration Frame, for Class Teaching, on which the formation of almost any Stitch may be exhibited, is used in the best German Schools. It may be had complete with Special Needle and Cord. Price 7s. 6d.

Needlework, Schedule III., exemplified and Illustrated. By Mrs. E. A. CURTIS. Fifth Thousand. Cloth limp, with 30 illustrations, 1s.

Directions for Knitting Jerseys and Vests, with scale for various sizes. By M. C. G. Work especially suitable for elderly Ladies or Invalids. Dedicated by kind permission to Her Grace the Duchess of Marlborough. Sewed, 6d.

Crewel Work. Fifteen Designs in Bold and Conventional character, capable of being quickly and easily worked. With complete instructions. By ZETA, Author of "Ladies' Work, and How to Sell it," and including Patterns for Counterpanes, Bed Hangings, Curtains, Furniture Covers, Chimneypiece Borders, Piano Backs, Table Cloths, Table Covers, &c., &c. Demy, 2s. 6d.

Designs for Church Embroidery and Crewel Work from Old Examples. Eighteen Sheets, containing a Set of upwards of Sixty Patterns, with descriptive letterpress, collected and arranged by Miss E. S. HARTSHORNE. In a handsome cloth case, 5s.

" *Well and clearly drawn.* . . . *Strongly to be recommended.*"— VANITY FAIR.

" *The designs are well chosen and effective.*"—MANCHESTER EXAMINER.

Preparation for Science Teaching : a Manual of Suggestions to Teachers. By JOHN SPANTON, Translator of Chevreul's Book on "Colour," &c. Small crown 8vo., price 1s. 6d.

MISCELLANEOUS BOOKS.

The Confessions of a Medium. Crown 8vo., illustrated, price 3s. 6d.

Ophidiana; or, Snakes as they are. By Miss CATHERINE C. HOPLEY, Author of "Aunt Jenny's American Pets." Profusely ilustrated by A. T. ELWES.

In this work the authoress presents the results of widely collected and carefully sifted evidence concerning the many still disputed questions connected with snakes. Popular errors and prejudices are traced to their sources, and the serpent is presented to the reader in a zoological point of view, divested of prejudice and superstition. Original matter from personal observation enters largely into the work, and the great utility of zoological gardens and museums will be seen. Many of the illustrations are original and from nature, and the numerous quotations from Owen, Huxley, Günter, Dumeril, Fayrer, &c., &c., will invite the confidence of the reader as to the more scientific character of the work.

The Care and Treatment of the Insane in Private Dwellings. By LIONEL A. WEATHERLY, M.D., C.M., Member of the Royal College of Surgeons of England; Member of the Medico-Psychological Associations of Great Britain; Fellow of the Obstetric Society of London. Fcap. 8vo., cloth, price 1s. 6d.

Everyday Life in our Public Schools. Sketched by Head Scholars of Eton, Winchester, Westminster, Shrewsbury, Harrow, Rugby, Charterhouse. To which is added a brief notice of St. Paul's and Merchant Taylors' Schools, and Christ's Hospital. With a Glossary of some words in common use in those Schools. Edited by CHARLES EYRE PASCOE. With numerous Illustrations. Crown 8vo., cloth, new and cheaper edition, price **6s.**

The Day Dreams of a Sleepless Man; being a series of Papers contributed to the *Standard*, by FRANK IVES SCUDAMORE, Esq., C.B. Post 8vo., cloth, 3s. 6d.

A Complete GUIDE TO THE GAME OF CHESS, from the alphabet to the solution and construction of Problems. Containing also some Historical Notes. By H. F. L. MEYER, Chess Contributor to "The Boy's Own Paper," formerly Chess Editor of "Hannoversche Anzeigen," "The Gentleman's Journal," and "Echo Americano." Demy 8vo., cloth, price 7s. 6d.

Miscellaneous Books.

Queen Mab; or, Gems from Shakespeare. Arranged and Edited by C. W. A dainty bijou volume, uniform in size with The Churchman's Text Book, with illustrated title. Price 6*d.*

Caxton's Fifteen O's, and other Prayers. Printed by command of the Princess Elizabeth, Queen of England and France, and also of the Princess Margaret, mother of our Sovereign Lord the King. By WM. CAXTON. Reproduced in Photo-lithography by S. AYLING. Quarto, bound in parchment. New and cheaper edition, 6*s.*

Masterpieces of Antique Art. From the celebrated collections in the Vatican, the Louvre, and the British Museum. By STEPHEN THOMPSON, Author of "Old English Homes." Twenty-five Examples in Permanent Photography. Super-Royal Quarto. Elegantly bound, cloth gilt, Two Guineas.

The Bicycle Road Book: compiled for the Use of Bicyclists and Pedestrians, being a Complete Guide to the Roads and Cross Roads of England, Scotland, and Wales, with a list of the best Hotels and notable places, &c., with map. By CHARLES SPENCER. Paper, 1*s.*; cloth, 1*s.* 6*d.*

Patranas; or, Spanish Stories, Legendary and Traditional. With Illustrations by EDWARD H. CORBOULD. 5*s.*; gilt edges, 5*s.* 6*d.*

Sagas from the Far East; or, Kalmouk and Mongolian Tales. With Historical Preface and Explanatory Notes. By the same Author. 9*s.*

Household Stories from the Land of Hofer; or, Popular Myths of Tirol, including the Rose Garden of King Laryn. By the same Author. With Illustrations by T. GREEN. Cloth, 5*s.*; or gilt edges, 5*s.* 6*d.*

Tales and Legends of Saxony and Lusatia. By W. WESTALL. Illus. by H. W. PETHERICK. 4*s.* 6*d.*; gilt edges, 5*s.*

Basque Legends. Collected chiefly in the Labourd. By the Rev. WENTWORTH WEBSTER, M.A. Oxon, with an Essay on the Basque Language by M. JULES VINSON, of the Revue de Linguistique, Paris. Demy 8vo., gilt edges, cloth, 7*s.* 6*d.*

WORKS FOR DISTRIBUTION.

A Woman's Secret; or, How to make Home Happy. Thirty-third Thousand. 18mo., sewed, 6*d.*

By the same Author, uniform in size and price.

Woman's Work; or, How she can Help the Sick. 19th Thousand.

A Chapter of Accidents; or, the Mother's Assistant in Cases of Burns, Scalds, Cuts, &c. Tenth Thousand.

Pay to-day, Trust to-morrow; illustrating the Evils of the Tally System. Seventh Thousand.

Nursery Work; or, Hannah Baker's First Place. Fifth Thousand.

The Cook and the Doctor; Cheap Recipes and Useful Remedies. Sewed, 2*d.*

Home Difficulties. A Few Words on the Servant Question. Sewed, 4*d.*

Family Prayers for Cottage Homes, with Passages from the Scriptures. Sewed, 2*d.*

Taking Tales for Cottage Homes. Edited by W. H. G. KINGSTON. 4 Vols., cr. 8vo., each containing three Tales, cl. extra, 1*s.* 6*d.* each. 2 Vols., cr. 8vo., each containing six Tales, cl. extra, bev. bds., 3*s.* 6*d.* each. Each Tale separately in paper covers, 4*d.*; or cloth, with Chromo, 6*d.*

LIST OF SUBJECTS.

1. The Miller of Hillbrook; a Rural Tale.
2. Tom Trueman, a Sailor in a Merchantman.
3. Michael Hale and his Family in Canada.
4. John Armstrong, the Soldier.
5. Joseph Rudge, the Australian Shepherd.
6. Life Underground; or, Dick, the Colliery Boy.
7. Life on the Coast; or, The Little Fisher Girl.
8. Adventures of Two Orphans in London.
9. Early Days on Board a Man-of-War.
10. Walter the Foundling; a Tale of Olden Times.
11. The Tenants of Sunnyside Farm.
12. Holmwood; or, The New Zealand Settler.

Taking Tales for Cottage Homes. Second Series. They are each complete in one part, containing 64 pp., in clear, large type, and attractive Engravings. Price 6*d.* each in cloth cover.

THE FOLLOWING WORKS ARE IN PREPARATION:

A Bit of Fun and what it cost. By A. LYSTER.
Helpful Sam. By Mrs. M. A. BARLOW.
Sweethearts. By Miss GERTRUDE SELLON.
Others will shortly be announced.

IMPORTANT ANNOUNCEMENT.

Messrs. GRIFFITH & FARRAN beg to announce that they have in active preparation, and will shortly publish,

A New Series of School Reading Books,
TO BE ENTITLED

The "STANDARD AUTHORS" READERS,
BY
THE EDITOR OF "POETRY FOR THE YOUNG."

THE Books have been planned throughout to meet exactly the requirements of the New Mundella Code. They will be well printed from clear type, on good paper, bound in a strong and serviceable manner, and will have *interesting and useful Illustrations from beginning to end.*

In the Infants' Books of the Series, very careful graduation in the introduction of sounds and words will be combined with that great desideratum in Infants' Readers—an interesting *connected narrative form.*

The distinctive features of the Series in the Higher Books will be that the passages selected (both Prose and Poetry) will be taken from the *Works of Standard Authors,* thus complying with the requirements of the New Code, and that they will be of such a nature as to awaken, sustain, and cultivate the interest of youthful readers.

The Explanatory Matter will be placed at the end of each Book, so that children may, at the discretion of the Teacher, be debarred access to it, and will take the form of three Appendices:—

(*a*) Explanatory Notes.
(*b*) Biographical Notes.
(*c*) A Glossary of Rare or Difficult Words.

The compilation has been made with the utmost care, with the assistance and advice of gentlemen long conversant with the requirements of Public Elementary Schools; and the Publishers feel that the literary, artistic, and mechanical excellences of the Books will be such that the Series will be pronounced

The "Ne Plus Ultra" of School Reading Books.

The Books for Standards V., VI., and VII. will be ready shortly; and Specimen Pages and full Prospectuses, with Tables of Contents of the various Books, are preparing for distribution to all Teachers applying for them.

GRIFFITH & FARRAN,
WEST CORNER OF ST. PAUL'S CHURCHYARD, LONDON.

Made in the USA